MUSIC IN AMERICAN LIFE

Books in the series:

Only a Miner: Studies in Recorded Coal-Mining Songs
ARCHIE GREEN

Great Day Coming: Folk Music and the American Left
R. SERGE DENISOFF

John Philip Sousa: A Descriptive Catalog of His Works
PAUL E. BIERLEY

The Hell-Bound Train: A Cowboy Songbook
GLENN OHRLIN

Oh, Didn't He Ramble: The Life Story of Lee Collins as Told to Mary Collins
FRANK J. GILLIS AND JOHN W. MINER, EDITORS

American Labor Songs of the Nineteenth Century
PHILIP S. FONER

Stars of Country Music: Uncle Dave Macon to Johnny Rodriguez
BILL C. MALONE AND JUDITH MC CULLOH, EDITORS

Git Along, Little Dogies: Songs and Songmakers of the American West
JOHN I. WHITE

A Texas-Mexican Cancionero: Folksongs of the Lower Border
AMÉRICO PAREDES

San Antonio Rose: The Life and Music of Bob Wills
CHARLES R. TOWNSEND

Early Downhome Blues: A Musical and Cultural Analysis
JEFF TODD TITON

An Ives Celebration: Papers and Panels of the Charles Ives Centennial Festival-Conference
H. WILEY HITCHCOCK AND VIVIAN PERLIS, EDITORS

An Ives Celebration

CHARLES IVES
Photo by Clara Sipprell

An Ives Celebration

PAPERS AND PANELS OF THE CHARLES IVES
CENTENNIAL FESTIVAL-CONFERENCE

Edited by

H. Wiley Hitchcock

Vivian Perlis

UNIVERSITY OF ILLINOIS PRESS
Urbana Chicago London

*Publication of this book was supported by a grant
from the Martha Baird Rockefeller Fund for Music.*

Material in the appendixes was previously published as the program of the Charles Ives
Centennial Festival-Conference, 17–21 October 1974. © 1974 by H. Wiley Hitchcock.

LIBRARY OF CONGRESS CATALOGING IN PUBLICATION DATA

Charles Ives Centennial Festival-Conference, New York,
   New Haven, 1974.
   An Ives celebration.

   "The Ives Festival-Conference was sponsored by the
Institute for Studies in American Music at Brooklyn
College of the City University of New York and the School
of Music of Yale University."
   Includes index.
   1.   Ives, Charles Edward, 1874–1954—Congresses.
I.   Hitchcock, Hugh Wiley, 1923–   II.   Perlis, Vivian.
III.   Brooklyn College. Institute for Studies in
American Music.   IV.   Yale University. School of Music.
V.   Title.
ML410.I94C4   1974b   780'.92'4   77-7987
ISBN 0-252-00619-4

Contents

CONTENTS

Preface

Charles Ives was born on 20 October 1874 in Danbury, Connecticut. The greatest influence on his life, his thought, and his music was that of his father, George Ives, Danbury's principal musician, a versatile instrumentalist, conductor, and musical arranger who had a passionately inquiring and open mind about musical possibilities and experimented constantly with unconventional tone systems, instruments, and sounds ("musical" and otherwise). George Ives gave his son Charles a thorough foundation in traditional (and nontraditional) musical theory and a lasting love and respect for all kinds of music, including the American vernacular music of hymns, popular and traditional songs and dances, ragtime, brass bands, and theater orchestras.

Ives attended Yale University from 1894 to 1898, studying there with Horatio Parker, eminent figure among the German-trained "Second New England School" of American composers. After graduation, although his vocation was clearly to musical composition and he was a church organist from 1889 to 1902, Ives discovered that his music—eclectic in the best sense, individualistic, often radical—found almost no sympathetic performers or listeners, and he decided to give up a career as a professional musician for one in the insurance business. This he pursued with great success from 1898 until his retirement in 1930. Meanwhile, he went on composing—furiously, at white heat—during evenings, weekends, and vacations. However, the onset of World War I, a severe heart attack and illness in 1918, profound disillusionment with the results of the American elections of November 1920, and—perhaps most fundamentally—the strain of his double life and the rejection by others of his music virtually broke his creative impulse: few new works postdate 1921 (which saw a final burst of songs), although Ives was to live on until 19 May 1954.

Ives's private printings, between 1919 and 1922, of his *Second Piano Sonata* ("Concord, Mass., 1840–1860"), a book entitled *Essays Before a Sonata,* and a volume of *114 Songs* were the first steps in the diffusion of his music beyond a small circle of family and close friends. But not for many years thereafter was his music to be heard on any significant scale, let alone accepted or prized; and, essentially, the current view of Ives as America's first great composer (some would say its greatest) dates only since World War II. Reflecting that view was the convening of the Charles Ives Centennial Festival-Conference in New York and New Haven on 17–21 October 1974—the first international congress ever to be dedicated to an American composer.

The Ives Festival-Conference was sponsored by the Institute for Studies in American Music at Brooklyn College of the City University of New York and the School of Music of Yale University. The editors of this book were its directors. Its support came from foundations (the Rockefeller Foundation, the Martha Baird Rockefeller Fund for Music, the CBS Foundation), publishers of Ives's music (G. Schirmer, Inc./Associated Music Publishers, Peer-Southern Organization, C. F. Peters Corporation, Theodore Presser Company), corporate organizations (Broadcast Music, Inc., Mutual Insurance Company of New York), the National Institute of Arts and Letters, and of course the sponsoring institutions.

The present book is an outgrowth of the Ives Festival-Conference. It embodies the papers read at the conference and its panel discussions, as well as some of the commentary from the floor following them. It omits, necessarily, the experience of the seven concerts (virtually all of them "all-Ives" concerts) that emphasized the "festival" aspect of the congress, and it can hardly hint at the informal but treasurable discussion and arguments (to borrow two movement titles from Ives) which marked five days of inquiry into, and celebration of, the mind and music of Charles Ives for the many Festival-Conference participants, registrants, and auditors.

The Festival-Conference was initially organized around four basic themes: Ives and American Culture; Performance Problems in Ives's Music; Editorial Problems of Ives's Music; and Ives and Present-Day Musical Thought. As it turned out, these were not adhered to strictly in planning the sequence of conference sessions; however, in the interest of producing a coherent publication in book form, we have reverted to these four themes in organizing the present volume. The papers read at the conference have been edited for publication by their authors. We have similarly edited the panel discussions and commentary among participants and discussants (who are identified by name in the text), as well as questions from the floor, which were transcribed from tape recordings. We are grateful to the speakers for trusting us to edit these materials without misrepresentation, and of course we assume all responsibility for any errors or lacunae.

We wish to acknowledge with great appreciation the help we have had, from many, in fashioning this book out of a great mass of "proceedings," especially Caitriona Bolster, Susan Marchant, Kathleen Mason, Rita H. Mead, and Frances Solomon. We are particularly grateful to Roger Reynolds for his ingenuity and perseverance in the preparation for publication of the materials from the panel "Five Composers' Views." We acknowledge with appreciation permission from W. W. Norton and Company to quote from Charles Ives, *Essays Before a Sonata, The Majority, and Other Writings,* edited by Howard Boatwright; from Oxford University Press to quote from Henry Cowell and Sidney Cowell, *Charles Ives and His Music;* and from the American Academy and Institute of Arts and Letters to quote from Charles E. Ives, *Memos* (W. W. Norton and Company), edited by John Kirkpatrick. Our thanks go also to the John Herrick Jackson Music Library at Yale University for permission to reproduce materials in the Ives Collection. Finally, we wish to record with gratitude the fact that the Martha Baird Rockefeller Fund for Music has lent support to the publication of this volume, as it did to the Ives Festival-Conference itself.

H.W.H./V.P.

I

Ives and American Culture

Gilbert Chase's introduction to the opening session of the Festival-Conference says so well what the editors of this volume would wish to say that it is here reproduced, with Professor Chase's permission.

I'm glad to announce that Charles Ives has really arrived. I have the evidence before me in the form of a clipping from the current issue of the *New Yorker* magazine [19 October 1974]. It's a cartoon by William Hamilton, the chap who draws cartoons of very sophisticated New Yorkers. There are four pictured at a cocktail party, and three of them are looking very impressed as the fourth says, "And you know who else was heavy? Charles Ives! Charles Ives was very, very heavy." I'm sure he was inspired by a look at the program of the Festival-Conference.

The key to Ives in American culture, I believe, is found in William Brooks's manuscript on Billings, Ives, and Cage [being prepared for publication], where he writes, "There is no reason to believe that American music lies mysteriously outside American culture as a whole." Charles Ives's case is paradigmatic for demonstrating the inherent and necessary relationship between a creative artist and his culture. With Ives, this relationship is so striking, the evidence for it so impressive, that he has become a catalyst for the fusion of musical analysis and cultural history. This is the first time, to the best of my knowledge, that cultural historians have been given a major role in interpreting the life and work of a composer in the context of a predominantly musical conference. We now have American music being accepted as an integral part of American studies, and the impact of Charles Ives on cultural historians has been largely responsible for this development. Robert Crunden and Frank Rossiter are professionally trained historians who have chosen American culture as their special field of history. However, I doubt if either Dr. Crunden or Dr. Rossiter would have become so excited, so involved in American music, without Charles Ives. Neely Bruce, as a conductor and pianist, was similarly led by Ives to a broad consideration of American music, especially certain music now very unfashionable and relatively little known but most important in understanding Ives's background in American musical culture.

Ives started a lot of things that now seem important to us for putting American music and American culture together. We can thus be grateful to that remarkable man from Danbury.

3

Charles Ives's Place in American Culture

ROBERT M. CRUNDEN

A cultural historian who comes to the literature about Charles Ives familiar with other areas of American culture cannot help being struck by the perplexity Ives apparently causes in both musicologists and biographers. Here we have a man who seems to be, with little question, one of the most important native American composers; yet the articles and dissertations imply, even when they do not flatly assert, that Ives does not really fit into the history of American music and that he himself found his place within American culture psychologically very hard to tolerate.

The musicological version of this assessment can be found, for example, in the generally admiring article that Leo Schrade, then professor of the history of music at Yale, wrote shortly after Ives died. Schrade found that Ives's contributions to modernism were fully developed between 1900 and 1906, a time so early that no European composer, not even Arnold Schoenberg, had done anything so radical. Not until the 1920s did Schoenberg, Stravinsky, and Hindemith shock European audiences with comparable innovative techniques. Schrade also noted that America seemed to offer Ives no context within which he could develop: he seemed to have no real predecessors, no friends of stature who developed along similar lines, and for a long time no successors who showed signs of continuing an Ives tradition of influence. Schrade also noted that the old and the new, musicologically speaking, seemed to exist side by side in Ives, without any obvious temporal or historical development. He seemed especially puzzled that some of Ives's most innovative compositions were composed before some of his more traditional ones. The implication of the article seems to be that Ives somehow emerged into the world fully formed, unlike anyone around him, and unable to interact with the culture of his time.[1]

On the other hand, Frank Rossiter, Ives's most thorough biographer, has insisted that in fact Ives was submerged in his culture. In his recent Princeton dissertation, Rossiter stressed that he was writing about Ives as a musician

---

1. Leo Schrade, "Charles E. Ives: 1874–1954," *Yale Review,* 44 (1955): 535–45.

4

in a social context. Within this frame of reference, Ives appears not so much as an autonomous artist working out his solitary concerns, but rather as "a prisoner of his culture; his attachment to certain American values and institutions was so complete and so literal as to narrow and stifle his career as a creative artist." Not only American culture but Ives himself rejected his role as an artist, and he was thus a man hopelessly divided against himself. He was divided between the demands of his business and the demands of his craft. He was divided between his desire to be masculine and vernacular in his own music and his admiration for the whole European tradition of cultivated musical forms, which seemed to have effeminate connotations in the minds of many Americans. He was so divided, in fact, that Rossiter can write about "the underlying paranoia about masculinity and femininity, in his writings about music."[2]

Taken together, these two positions about Ives add up to the rather basic assumption that Ives was some kind of freak, however original, gifted, or talented he might have been as a man or as a composer. A great deal could be said in support of this view and the various refinements that have been made on it in the work of other commentators on Ives, and what I have to say will not, I hope, leave the impression that I have anything but the highest respect for much Ives musicology, and for the enormous amounts of labor and intelligence that have been spent on learning the details of Ives's life. However, to someone with my peculiar interests in cultural history, both assessments miss the mark in several important ways in their analysis of Ives and his place in American history. For me, Ives had many precursors in America, and there were many individuals whose creative careers paralleled his; they simply were not chiefly engaged in music, and they remain little known to musicologists. Likewise, Ives was not nearly so maladjusted or unhappy, in my analysis, as he sometimes seems; his problems were, at least until his medical difficulties ended his active career, often quite typical of innovative individuals in other areas of American life.

In short, what I would like to argue is that Charles Ives was a creatively functioning artist resembling other innovating pioneers of his own time in many ways. Since this period, from let us say the early 1890s until the end of World War I, is usually known as the Progressive Era, I suggest that we should think of Ives as a "progressive" American, who seems strange and out of place to us only because other progressives did their innovating in other disciplines, like educational psychology, politics, or business administration. Compared to Edward MacDowell or Horatio Parker, Ives may well seem rather strange; compared to John Dewey or Woodrow Wilson, he seems

2. Frank R. Rossiter, "Charles Ives and American Culture: The Process of Development, 1874–1921" (Ph.D. diss., Princeton University, 1970), pp. 3–4, 58, 63. Also available as part of *Charles Ives and His America* (New York: Liveright, 1975).

strange only in the sense that men of great creativity always have their idiosyncracies, and always stand out from the crowd around them.

Defining a climate of opinion like "progressivism" is never easy, but if we study this period as a whole, certain generalizations emerge. Progressivism was, above all else, an outgrowth of the whole tradition of nineteenth-century Protestantism in America, and individual progressive leaders usually took this Christian world view for granted, even when they themselves had lost their overt faith and severed any connection with organized religion. Developed during the crusades against slavery, liquor, cruel prison conditions, and many other social wrongs in the years before the Civil War, this religious heritage formed the childhood milieu of the vast majority of young progressives, and thus they seemed to assume, almost unquestioningly, that a divine vision of a Kingdom of God on earth should motivate all kinds of reform activity. In such a frame of reference, political reforms of the most mundane variety, from Theodore Roosevelt's pursuit of boodling policemen in New York to Jane Addams's persistent efforts to clean the garbage out of her Chicago ward, took on the character of participation in a divine plan. A political economist like Richard Ely could teach, at Johns Hopkins and Wisconsin, that Christianity had to be practical and applied, and that a democracy that functioned honestly and properly could be presumed to have divine approval. His students could then go into reform and make very practical attempts to Christianize democracy, as Frederic C. Howe did during several reform administrations in Cleveland, or as President Woodrow Wilson did in his attempts to reform first America and ultimately the entire world.

Within this progressive relationship between religious values and democracy, certain specific tendencies are obvious. This frame of mind was clearly idealistic, always measuring current reality against some abstract standard. It was optimistic, believing that progress was so inevitable and apparent that it hardly needed to be discussed. It tended to be personal, stressing the individual soul and its righteousness, and quite often confused the ability of an individual to be righteous with the possibility of living in an entire society of equivalent righteousness; in short, it had a tendency to see social problems as personal problems writ large. This frame of mind likewise preferred a classless society, assuming without question that just as all men were equal before God, they should have an equal voice at the polls and an equal opportunity to succeed. It assumed, further, that small-town values, like compassion and neighborliness, were all the more vital in a newly urbanized society and ought to be encouraged by law if possible, and by social agencies where necessary. It also assumed, rather smugly, that its values and conception of human nature were universal, as true for immigrants and citizens of other countries as they were for Protestant Americans. At the same time, it rather prided itself on its pragmatism, its willingness to solve problems and fix errors. This adaptability, this willingness to solve problems in an ethical way, could lead both to an undue emphasis on action for its own sake and to a philosophy that made such a response the substance of ethics. Thus we have, on the one hand, the remark of Henry Adams that his friend Theodore Roosevelt "showed the singular primitive quality that belongs to ultimate matter—the quality that medieval theology assigned to God—he was pure act," and, on the other, the whole philosophy of instrumentalism, the philosophy of ethical action that John Dewey used with such stunning effect to remake both the schools and American philosophy.[3]

To someone immersed in the literature of progressivism, certain elements in Ives's life and writing seem immediately familiar. The very tone of his rhetoric, for example, is quite familiar. The stress on masculinity and nonconformity, which has distressed some writers, seems mild indeed when placed next to the words of Theodore Roosevelt and his friends when they exhorted the country to go to war or to preserve national parks. Ives's contempt for "mollycoddle ways with music easy on the ears" sounds much like what William James called the moral equivalent of war in a more musical context. The same can be said about Ives's outburst at the concert where Carl Ruggles's *Men and Mountains* received an unenthusiastic reception: "Stop being such a God-damned sissy!" he exploded at one listener. "Why can't you stand up before fine strong music like this and use your ears like a man!"[4] It seems to me hardly an exaggeration to hear echoes here of Roosevelt in the Dakota badlands, or on his famous, muscle-stiffening hikes, while he was President, to demonstrate to effete bureaucrats the virtues of the strenuous life.

Similarly, to touch on several subjects I will not examine in any detail, Ives found much to appreciate in Woodrow Wilson, and he especially approved Wilson's basic approach to World War I and his great yearning for some sort of world government that would enable nations to work together in peace. Ives's wife, Harmony Twichell Ives, to whom he was entirely devoted, became personally involved in one of the most basic of all Progressive Era reform movements, when she worked, in the years before her marriage to Ives, in the Visiting Nurses' Association in Chicago, doing some of the most exhausting kind of slum settlement work, and at the famous

3. The best interpretive synthesis of the progressive frame of mind, although only one of many that have helped me form these paragraphs, is Clyde Griffen, "The Progressive Ethos," in *The Development of an American Culture,* ed. Stanley Coben and Lorman Ratner (Englewood Cliffs, N.J.: Prentice-Hall, 1970), pp. 120–49. For Adams on Roosevelt, see *The Education of Henry Adams* (New York: Modern Library, 1918), p. 417.

4. Henry and Sidney Cowell, *Charles Ives and His Music* (New York: Oxford University Press, 1955), pp. 124, 106.

Henry Street Settlement in New York. We also have what may well seem surprising at first glance, Ives's antipathy to musical modernism. Just like Theodore Roosevelt viewing with indignation the modernist paintings at the Armory Show, Ives was too deeply religious and moralistic to appreciate aesthetics divorced from real life. He could thus snort that Debussy's "content would have been worthier his manner if he had hoed corn or sold newspapers for a living, for in this way he might have gained a deeper vitality and a truer theme to sing at night and of a Sunday." Likewise, he could dismiss Stravinsky's *Firebird* as "morbid and monotonous" and find the work of Ravel "weak, morbid, and monotonous."[5] No matter how innovative Ives might have been, he was a part of pre-war America to his very bones, and he was proud of it.

While these qualities of Ives's life and thought are striking, they are hardly central to his place within progressivism. To get at the really basic aspects of Ives's progressivism, we must first examine his religious orientation. No one who has heard much of Ives's music or read his writings can doubt for a moment that Ives was deeply influenced by the evangelistic, revivalistic religious currents that had been so important in Connecticut until well into his own lifetime. His music and writings are both full of religious references, and the context is most often respectful and reverent, so long as one does not take automatic offense when a hymn is subjected to variations that might not appeal to the average parishioner. In addition, we know that Ives was a church organist for at least three different Protestant denominations, that Harmony Ives was the daughter of a well-known minister, and that the Iveses apparently attended church conventionally during their mature lives.[6]

Yet despite this outward connection with the institutional church, Ives very much shared the progressive feeling that institutions could fetter a man and so conventionalize his responses as to get in the way when a man wished to commune with God, nature, or even the divinity within his own soul. Ives's terminology is not always precise, and his sense of irony can make his literal meaning hazy, but I think that in at least one place, when discussing Emerson, he comes through clearly. "But every thinking man knows that the church part of the church always has been dead," he writes. Religion could be an idea or a state of mind, and Ives's religion was definitely Christian, but he had no illusions about the stuffiness of churches on many occa-

5. For the Wilson material, see particularly Charles Ives, *Essays Before a Sonata, The Majority, and Other Writings,* ed. Howard Boatwright (New York: W. W. Norton, 1962), esp. pp. 136–38, 228–31; for Harmony Ives, see *Charles E. Ives: Memos,* ed. John Kirkpatrick (New York: W. W. Norton, 1972), pp. 276–77; for Debussy, see *Essays,* p. 82; for Stravinsky and Ravel, see *Memos,* p. 138.

6. Both Rossiter and the Cowells have many details. For example, see Rossiter, *Ives and His America,* p. 169, and Cowell and Cowell, *Ives and His Music,* pp. 6, 43.

sions. "Many of the sincerest followers of Christ never heard of Him," he continues, clearly assuming that the essence of Christianity has to do with the way a man thinks and acts, not with any institutional affiliation or creed. Ives insists that being true to ourselves "*is* God, that the faintest thought of immortality *is* God, and that God *is* 'miracle.'" Ever since the days of Emerson and Theodore Parker, New Englanders had been translating such ideas into reform activities, and in Ives's own day countless progressives, from Jane Addams to Frederic C. Howe, retold the story of how their moral and religious ideas developed into settlement houses and reformed tax laws. Ives, while sharing these imperatives, nevertheless worked chiefly in music, and so the fruits of his concern were compositions. Thus he could write: "The last movement of the *Fourth Symphony* and the last movement of the *Second Orchestral Set* are built essentially on religious subject matter," and then instead of proceeding with what one would normally expect in a musical reminiscence—a musicological or thematic analysis—write "that religious services have a tendency . . . to make a man conservative—that they restrict, in a certain way, freedom of thought and action. I feel differently, because it seems to me most of the forward movements of life in general and of pioneers in most of the great activities, have been [the work of] essentially religious-minded men."[7] In other words, what is significant is to be a religious man without worrying about orthodoxy; and, in the progressive context, to regard Ives's compositions as being essentially similar to the "compositions" of other progressives, like Hull House or the Clayton Anti-Trust Act.

Like most progressives, Ives took this religious vision with him when he analyzed human nature, and he found it essentially good and even wise. Ives speaks in his essays of "the great transcendental doctrine of 'innate goodness' in human nature" and translates this doctrine into what he calls "the great primal truths: that there is more good than evil, that God is on the side of the majority (the people), that he is not enthusiastic about the minority (the non-people), that he has made men greater than man, that he has made the universal mind and the over-soul greater and a part of the individual mind and soul, that he has made the Divine a part of all." To the minds of people like ourselves, who have experienced the impact of Reinhold Niebuhr, original sin, and existentialism, nothing seems more striking about the progressives than this blandly liberal assumption that people are basically good, that they seem to be even better when they gather together, and that God, whatever or whoever he is, blesses the political and social results of their deliberations. Ives even carried the idea forcefully into music. Despite the inability of almost everyone to understand and appreciate his music, and despite the popular success of music he detested,

7. *Essays,* p. 19; *Memos,* p. 129.

he still could believe that some day everyman would be a composer. The common man "while digging his potatoes will breathe his own epics, his own symphonies (operas, if he likes it)" and will sit in the evenings "in his backyard and shirt sleeves smoking his pipe and watching his brave children in *their* fun of building *their* themes for *their* sonatas of *their* life."[8]

Given his idealistic habit of thinking in natural and universal laws, Ives had only a short step to take to the assertion that "the law of averages has a divine source," and the application of this assumption directly to political concerns. Many progressives wished to level down the great fortunes of the rich and redistribute this income in some way to the poor, most obviously by the income tax that was reenacted during the Wilson administration. Ives explicitly favored the limiting of the personal property a man could acquire, by means determined by a clear majority vote. He insisted that this leveling of wealth would "not be a millennium but a practical and possible application of uncommon common sense," an assumption that many progressives would have accepted without a murmur. In addition, he shared with them the assumption that there were no really important differences between capital and labor, as of course there could not be if all men were equal and basically good and God was benevolently guiding the progress of society toward perfection. He also had a progressive insistence on the value of direct voter participation in the maximum number of important legislative decisions. Although most progressives thought this could be obtained through the institution of the initiative, the referendum, and the recall, Ives sincerely wished to extend and broaden the process. "The initiative and referendum," he said, are at best "remedial or corrective rather than constructive," and what he wanted went beyond them in the direction of what seemed to be a gigantic town meeting of the whole, called to the polls regularly to express the will of the country. Given such a procedure, even what looked like an incorrect decision was really correct, because the majority was right by definition according to the laws of nature. "It must be assumed, in the final analysis and consideration of all social phenomena," Ives insisted flatly, "that the Majority, right or wrong, are always right."[9]

Ives moved effortlessly with these ideas into his own career as a life insurance businessman. Along with their tendency to moralize everything they did, the progressives also wished to rationalize and make scientific the business and political procedures that had developed so chaotically during the industrial expansion of the Gilded Age. For Ives, the symbolic core of his business career was the actuarial department of the Mutual Life Insurance Company. In an actuarial department, a life insurance company uses mathematical formulas to determine how many claims will probably be

8. *Essays*, pp. 59, 29, 128–29; see also p. 144.
9. *Ibid.*, pp. 33, 62, 145, 162–63, 166.

made, and for how much money, over the life of a given policy and a given period of time of company operation. This may seem hopelessly prosaic to modern ears, but to Ives it meant that somewhere in the actuarial department could lie the secret of the divine average man, and thus of the whole concept of the majority. To him, the word *science,* which he used frequently, seemed to mean some sort of congruence with natural law, and in this I think he was very typical of progressives. The influence of science, he said in his writings on life insurance, "will continue to help mankind realize more fully, the greater moral and spiritual values," and thus life insurance was one key to the democratic utopia that so often occupied his mind. Note, for example, in this quotation, the combination of Rooseveltian rhetoric, progressive politics, and majoritarianism: "The great majority of men today, in this country at least, know, perhaps only subconsciously, that a life insurance policy is one of the definite ways of society for toughening its moral muscles, for equalizing its misfortunes, and hence—the old problem—of supplying a fundamental instinctive want. Because this is now appreciated, no matter in what degree, the normal mind today knows that to carry life insurance is a duty. . . ."[10]

Given this material I have sketched in so briefly, I cannot help concluding that Ives's thought, whether applied to religion, human nature, politics, or business, is all of a piece, that it is reasonably consistent, and that it is quite typical of the age in which he lived. Ives was a progressive leader fully as much as Woodrow Wilson, Theodore Roosevelt, or Jane Addams.

At first glance, the connection of this material to Ives's music may seem obscure, but I do not think that it is. Literary critics and musicologists, in my experience, seem to share an aversion to the idea that a work of art can be "about" anything. Readers or viewers or listeners are supposed to experience the creative work as a whole, and ignore the time, or the place, or the biography that might lie behind its creation. Ives explicitly denied this, and I think any listener or critic who wishes to understand him and his music must agree with him. ". . . Is not all music program music?" he asked. "Is not pure music, so called, representative in its essence?"[11] I do not want even to raise this question for any other composer, but I do think that for Ives we have to say yes, all his music is program music, and it is "about" ideas like those I have been discussing here.

Two words will sum up my key points in this context: *process* and *form.* Ives came of age in what, for intellectual historians, was the age of Darwin, and no literate individual of the time could escape the pervasive influence

10. *Ibid.,* pp. 235–39; see also Cowell and Cowell, *Ives and His Music,* pp. 38, 61–62.
11. *Essays,* p. 4.

of the idea of evolution; Ives's writings show its influence everywhere. In 1890, William James, in his extremely influential textbook *The Principles of Psychology,* applied the evolutionary frame of mind to the subject of consciousness and insisted that ideas did not come, as previous writers had implied, in "chains" or "trains" or other discrete particles, but rather in streams. Ideas flowed, one into another, into an entity resembling a moving body of water. "In talking of it hereafter, let us call it the stream of thought, of consciousness, or of subjective life." John Dewey read the book immediately, it had an enormous impact on him, and within a matter of only a few years he had worked out his own version of an evolutionary pragmatism and was applying it successfully in his experimental school in Chicago. Now, the connections between Dewey and Ives may not seem readily apparent, but I think they are actually rather clear and obvious. Dewey used ideas of evolution and the flow of life and consciousness to develop a philosophy which stressed the organic development of the child and the child's growth through the solving of successive problems. He, too, had a democratic, reform bias and a faith in the will of a properly informed majority that developed out of a religious New England background.

Ives used similar ideas to make music that is very often about a process. The sense of formlessness that so distresses some listeners to his music is misleading. The form is there, but it depends on extramusical stimuli, on ideas and memories and desires and yearnings rather than on formal, finished thematic material. George Ives had once told his son, "Everything in life is relative," and, like so many of his memories, the memory of this early statement of pragmatism always stayed with Charles Ives when he composed. Ives's rejection of conventional notions of form very much resembled the pragmatists' rejection of conventional notions of the absolute, and his experiments with various elements of chance composition, and much of his experimentalism, seem to me clearly in the spirit of Dewey and his faith and trust in the natural, organic process.[12]

This emphasis on the program, and on the process, often led Ives to what sound like musical dead ends, or what a pragmatist would admit were experiments that did not work. Ives might argue, as he does in one place, that "vagueness is at times an indication of nearness to . . . truth," but on at least some occasions it was possible to get so near to an object that you

12. William James, *Principles of Psychology* (New York: H. Holt & Co., 1890), 1:239; for Dewey, see esp. Jane M. Dewey, "Biography of John Dewey," in *The Philosophy of John Dewey,* ed. Paul Arthur Schilpp (Evanston & Chicago: Northwestern University Press, 1939), pp. 3–45, and the recent biography by George Dykhuizen, *The Life and Mind of John Dewey* (Carbondale: Southern Illinois University Press, 1973); Cowell and Cowell, *Ives and His Music,* pp. 6, 18, 106, 169; *Essays,* pp. 71–73; the whole subject receives extended attention in Rosalie Sandra Perry, "Charles Ives and American Culture" (Ph.D. diss., University of Texas, 1971), ch. 6, also available as *Charles Ives and the American Mind* (Kent, Ohio: Kent State University Press, 1974).

could not see it at all, and the impact of the work became lost in its private incommunicability. Ives realized this, although he noted that "what is unified form to the author or composer may of necessity be formless to his audience." To critics, such talk is something of a contradiction in terms, since form is presumably universal and reducible to rules that can always be perceived by the acute. But to be fair to Ives, we have at the very least to try to understand what he thought he was doing; and he seems to me very clear in trying to express process and in trying to create a form dependent on process. The recently published *Memos* give many examples of this; I have chosen one paragraph, on a little-known work, that ties these themes together and is extremely suggestive for any analysis of other works. The piece was called *A Yale-Princeton Game* and now exists only in part.

> It is "Two Minutes in Sounds for Two Halfs within Bounds." It was short, only four or five pages for full orchestra. The last two pages are quite clear and fully scored—the first part [I] have only in sketch. But to try to reflect a football game in sounds would cause anybody to try many combinations etc.—for instance, picturing the old wedge play (close formation)—what is more natural than starting with all hugging together in the whole chromatic scale, and gradually pushing together down to one note at the end. The suspense and excitement of spectators —strings going up and down, off and on open-string tremolos. Cheers ("Brek e Koax" etc.)—running plays (trumpets going all over, dodging, etc. etc.)—natural and fun to do and listen to—hard to play. But doing things like this (half horsing) would suggest and get one used to technical processes that could be developed in something more serious later, and quite naturally.[13]

There we have, I like to think, a progressive mind, both at work and at play. It is healthy and strenuous enough for a Theodore Roosevelt, and as full of nature, the natural, and process as even John Dewey could have wished. The form clearly expresses the content—even, as it were, when it is not clear. Ives and his work do indeed have their places in American culture, however odd they may appear when considered solely as a part of this history of music, and no matter what conflicts Ives might have felt with the life he chose to lead.

AARON COPLAND: There was one sentence in this interesting talk that I don't understand. Mr. Crunden said, "But to be fair to Ives, we have at the very least to try to understand what he thought he was doing, and he seems to me very clear in trying to express process and in trying to create a

13. *Essays,* pp. 22–23; *Memos,* p. 61.

form dependent on process." I don't quite understand how you're using the word *process*.

ROBERT CRUNDEN: The "how things happen" rather than the "what"—in other words, the way something is done and enacted, rather than the final result of that act.

COPLAND: That seems to lessen the importance of the end result.

CRUNDEN: Oh, very much so, because the end result is merely a step in another process that will develop as soon as the given thing is over. It is always ongoing and is never completed.

GILBERT CHASE: There is an interesting connection there. An analysis of Ives's *Fourth Symphony* by William Brooks also makes *process* the key word, if I'm correct.

QUESTIONER: What I missed in the speaker's fine talk was some sense that progressivism as a movement in American culture underwent a number of changes in the very years that the speaker was using to reflect on Ives. There were considerable developments in progressivism in that period, and considerable shocks to its development, and in the end one might be able to talk about its failure. It strikes me that Ives was of a younger generation than Teddy Roosevelt or Woodrow Wilson and that he was very disappointed in Woodrow Wilson. I think there's a premature cutoff in this paper at about 1917: if one followed the situation further, one would see how very much Ives was upset and even devastated by the failure of progressive aims in others like Wilson, particularly over the American entrance into World War I. On the other hand, he was of a slightly older generation than young critics like Randolph Bourne and Van Wyck Brooks and Henry Mencken, who were able to be more critical of progressive aims than I think Ives ever was. I really do miss a time sense in the exposition that was given.

CRUNDEN: There's a similar truncation in the careers of Woodrow Wilson and Charles Ives, and almost all progressives with whose careers I am familiar felt the very thing that you have stated. It was a very progressive frame of mind to be disillusioned and upset after the failure of the Treaty of Versailles in World War I. What you've said simply reinforces my argument rather than weakening it.

WILLIAM AUSTIN: To put Ives in a context with the thinkers and the doers of his time is valuable, but, like the questioner from the floor, I felt disturbed by your static picture of a "frame of mind." The things that Ives shared with other people certainly changed. Some of them extended to earlier periods, as you yourself pointed out; some extended to later periods; and many were not shared universally—they are not typical of the entire population in the period that's commonly labeled that of progressivism. You spoke of the progressive innovators, but your frequent sentences using "frame of mind" as a subject—possible for acting, feeling, and so on—disturbed me.

CRUNDEN: Let me just say that frames of mind can evolve without leaving a concept. In other words, a frame can change. I do think there's a reasonably consistent complex of values. The basic values do not change so much as become articulated as new problems arise—new elections, for instance, new attempts to enact laws, new works of art having impact on succeeding works of art. We may need to define *frame of reference* or *frame of mind* more precisely, but I don't think it invalidates the concept to admit quite freely that it can change.

Charles Ives: Good American and Isolated Artist

FRANK R. ROSSITER

Charles Ives's extraordinary isolation is, I think, a factor that explains a great deal about the man, both as a composer and as a figure in American culture. There has been much debate about the effect on his compositions of his lack of an audience and of contact with other musicians during the twenty years or so of his mature work. Some have contended that this very isolation encouraged the remarkable innovations in his music; others have pointed to the communicative weaknesses of presentation and scoring in many works, blaming them on his lack of that self-criticism which comes from the reaction of an audience. But I am concerned here with the effect of isolation on the man himself. His musical writings and the margins of his music manuscripts are filled with shrill outbursts and abusive diatribes that suggest a man deeply troubled in his isolation, a man very lonely and somewhat musically misanthropic. We often hear of the traditional isolation of the creative artist in America, but nearly all such artists have had at least a small circle of friends who sustained them artistically and intellectually. Ives had nothing of the kind during his creative years; he was about as close to complete isolation as it is possible for a creative artist to be.

There is a widespread belief that Ives's musical isolation during his active years as a composer was necessary and unavoidable since his musical imagination was so far in advance of that of anyone else in the United States at the time. While not denying that this explanation has some importance, I should like to suggest that his isolation had another—and equally important—source. Ives was isolated not only because he was a musically autonomous man, pursuing his lonely path with integrity and independence; he was isolated also, I think, because he succumbed to enormous pressures that his society and culture brought to bear upon him, pressures that insisted he be a "good American" in his attitude toward music.

We all know that when Charles Ives was growing up in Danbury, Connecticut, during the 1880s and early 1890s, he absorbed from his father an abiding love of music and a decided taste for musical experimentation. I believe that he also accepted from his Danbury environment two other powerful attitudes toward music, both of them connected with his father's life as a professional musician in the town. The first was the notion, widely held by families of the "better classes" like the Iveses, that music was a fine and ennobling thing, to be cultivated and patronized, but that no self-respecting gentleman would become a professional musician. For most composers of Ives's generation, the first task was the very difficult one of courageously overcoming this attitude and taking up a musical career. Ives, however, was never able to take that step. Undoubtedly he was powerfully dissuaded by the example of his father's career as a professional musician in Danbury. Overshadowed and somewhat patronized by his more successful relatives who were in business and the respectable professions, never taken quite seriously by the town, forced to eke out a living by musical and non-musical odd jobs, and finally compelled to give up his musical career for a full-time job in the savings bank in order to support his family, George Ives was the *déclassé* member of the eminent Ives family.

His son, in contrast, went to Yale and became a highly successful insurance executive in New York. It is often said that upon graduating from college, Charles Ives rejected a musical career because (by his own testimony) he desired the wider human contacts that business allowed and wished to keep his music free from commercial pressures, but this idea of a conscious decision seems to me a product of hindsight. I doubt that Ives ever seriously considered becoming a professional musician. His parents, after all, sent him not to a conservatory but to Yale, a liberal arts college and a widely recognized entrance into the business and professional world. It is significant that after graduation he did not return to Danbury, but took the tested path of opportunity to New York City, where money and success were to be had. By spending his adult life in business, Ives wasted his enormous talents on trivialities and circumscribed his cultural experiences by the narrow limits of respectability and gentility.

However, if Ives kept music an avocation and conformed outwardly to his peers' notion of the proper work for a gentleman, he was inwardly seething with revolt against the whole complex of views about music held by his social class. This revolt had begun very early in his life, and its source was the other powerful attitude toward music that had been impressed upon him in Danbury. It was a notion that a boy would naturally absorb while growing up among other boys, namely, that classical music was for sissies and women while popular music was the only *real* music. In later years Ives became very articulate about the way in which the ladies who had controlled Danbury's art music had musically emasculated both his father and him. He recalled how his father had once prepared and rehearsed an orchestral concert for Miss Hollister, one of the town's music teachers, and how

Miss Hollister had gotten all the credit for conducting, "as this was a ladies' society concert!" He remembered how ashamed he had been to have to stay inside and practice his classical pieces while the other boys had been engaged in outdoor activities. Ives maintained his masculinity as a boy by playing baseball and football and by giving his heart to popular music, a democratic and down-to-earth music that excluded genteel ladies and therefore allowed him and his father to be real men. For the average businessman of Ives's class, the adult form of such a boyish revolt against cultivation would simply have been the willingness to patronize the New York Philharmonic (for one's wife's sake) while feeling that one only *really* enjoyed music when singing Yale songs with the boys. But for Ives, who cared so much more deeply about music, the revolt led to a glorification of popular music by building quartets, sonatas, and symphonies around popular tunes and the elements of vernacular music-making.

Drawing on his father's musical experiments, the boy Charles Ives also championed dissonant music—which was masculine and would shock "the ladies"—against effeminate, "nice," "easy-on-the-ears" music. In fact, I believe that both the dissonance and the vernacular elements in his earlier works were used primarily because of the sexual connotations of masculinity that they had for Ives. Only later in life did he justify those features of his music by developing an aesthetic and moral philosophy based on the distinction between "substance" and "manner."

As a mature composer, Ives continued to assert his masculinity in his compositions and his writings. He condemned his own social class (especially the "old ladies" of both sexes in it) for its conventional musical taste and for its patronage of the leading concert artists, whom he despised. He denounced those artists not simply as sissies who practiced a highfalutin, artificial art removed from the people; he also saw in them what was apparently just the opposite fault. Drawing from nineteenth-century romanticism the ideal of a pure, transcendent art, Ives accused prominent composers and performers like Rachmaninoff of lowering and commercializing their music, of pandering to the desire of audiences for cheap effect, and of selling themselves as exotic personalities. Thus Ives wanted music to be high, noble, and idealized, but also down-to-earth and democratic—and full of challenging innovation to boot! This extraordinary hodgepodge of apparently contradictory musical standards was probably held together in Ives's mind by his favorite philosophy of transcendentalism, with its faith in the unseen unity of all things.

It must be remembered that Ives's musical revolt, for all the vociferousness of his views, was a one-man revolt carried on in strict privacy. The outward conventionality and respectability of his own life prevented him from making contact with others who might have shared his musical values. It may be objected that there was no one else in America who could have understood Ives during his active years as a composer, but this contention is, I think, not strictly true. There were in New York City during the decade of the 1910s, when Ives was living there and was at the height of his creative powers, a small number of musicians who appreciated the significance of Schoenberg, Stravinsky, and other modernists who had begun to appear in Europe. Two of these musicians—the critics Hiram K. Moderwell and Paul Rosenfeld—would, I think, have been more than slightly interested in what Ives was doing and might very well have given him needed encouragement. In their articles in the *New Republic* and *Seven Arts,* these two men expressed not only their enthusiasm for the latest European musical developments but also their desire for an American classical music based on vernacular sources; Moderwell's hope for such a music based on ragtime sounds very much like a call for Ives's *First Piano Sonata.* But Ives's mode of life cut him off completely from the organs and movements of cultural rebellion that might have brought him into contact with these two men, even though this cultural rebellion of the 1910s was taking place literally around the corner from him. Instead, Ives showed his compositions to thoroughly conventional and second-rate musicians who were closer to his world and were personally acceptable to him. Naturally, they rejected his work.

The contention that Ives's isolation was partly self-imposed is strengthened by the evidence from the next decade, the 1920s, during which Ives gave up composition. In the early twenties, an organized and well-publicized musical avant-garde, centered in the International Composers' Guild and the League of Composers, appeared in New York, but Ives could not bring himself to make even the most tentative contact with either of these groups. The concept of a self-consciously separate avant-garde, alienated from the mass of Americans, undoubtedly seemed undemocratic and snobbish to him. I suspect a more important reason for his remaining aloof was simply his unwillingness to expose his values and style of life to the threatening atmosphere of bohemianism. His musical revolt remained largely private, then, until he eventually met two men connected with the modern-music movement who were personally acceptable to him: first the pianist E. Robert Schmitz and then, of far greater importance, the composer Henry Cowell. They became Ives's mediators, channeling his compositions to the avant-garde while carefully shielding him from direct contact with its members. Ives loved to rail against the conventional musical world represented by Carnegie Hall and the Metropolitan Opera, but I doubt that he ever really understood the spirit or the underlying assumptions of the modern-music movement.

I have been arguing that Ives's musical isolation arose not only from his following an experimental and independent path in composition but also from his succumbing to certain powerful cultural demands that he be a good American in his attitudes toward music. Many will probably feel that I have not proved my case—that, indeed, I cannot prove it and that I am multiplying hypotheses unnecessarily. They will maintain that a consideration of Ives's extremely advanced musical thought in the midst of a backward American musical culture gives us a wholly satisfactory explanation of his isolation, particularly during his active years as a composer. I should like, therefore, to draw an analogy between Ives's musical activity and another aspect of his life during these same years—an area in which he was not far in advance of everyone else, yet one in which he displayed the same pattern of isolation and a purely private revolt. I am referring to Ives's relationship to the leading artistic, cultural, intellectual, and political movements in America during the first two decades of this century.

In a sense, the only creative artists with whom it is logical to compare Ives are the other outstanding American innovators of his generation: Frank Lloyd Wright in architecture, John Marin in painting, Alfred Stieglitz in photography, Isadora Duncan in the dance, Theodore Dreiser and Sherwood Anderson in fiction, and Carl Sandburg and Vachel Lindsay in poetry. In spite of all his thinking about art, however, Ives's conventional life as a businessman cut him off from any contact with these bohemians, and, aside from Lindsay's poem on General Booth, Ives was unaware of the work that they were doing contemporaneously with his own. Nor do his writings show an acquaintance with the significant ideas in philosophy and social thought that were appearing among American intellectuals in these same years; the pragmatism and relativism of much of this work, such as that of James and Dewey, would very probably have been anathema to his transcendentalist mind.

For a creative artist, Ives showed an unusual interest in political and social questions. It is all the more remarkable, then, that he had so little connection with the great progressive reform movement of the 1900s and 1910s and that his interest in and knowledge of some of its most important aspects were so minimal. Ives was very generous in his private charity, but he avoided any direct involvement in political and social movements or even in organized church and charitable work. There were in Ives's generation a considerable number of social reformers, social critics, and progressive writers with whom he would have had much in common—men and women who retained their gentility much as he did but who also broadened their earlier experiences through contact with new political, social, intellectual, and artistic movements. Amos Pinchot, who had been a friend of Ives at Yale, was such a reformer. Nevertheless, Ives's own views were severely circumscribed by the experience and interests of a businessman.

Ives has been praised for the wide reading and learning that are manifested in his *Essays Before a Sonata,* but nearly all his references are to either nineteenth-century works or works written from a nineteenth-century viewpoint. His writings show little acquaintance with the significant literature of his own time, the first two decades of the twentieth century. He also tended to quote an author for his own purposes without attempting to enter into that author's point of view or grasp his thesis. Moreover, like many other businessmen with only a haphazard knowledge of the currents of their age, Ives relied for many of his ideas on the daily newspapers.

The narrowness of Ives's cultural experiences can be traced back to the influences of his formative years. Probably he arrived at Yale not far removed from the usual cultural Philistinism of the time, but it was Yale which molded him, limited him, and determined the pattern of the rest of his life. Compared with today's notions of what the college experience should be, his Yale environment in the 1890s was total in its demands upon the student. As Santayana said, "Everything is arranged to produce a certain type of man." Ives yielded to those demands, satisfied them, and attained a considerable college success, which was perhaps his greatest curse.

Yale trained for leadership in society. There was much talk of democracy, but the college system was actually a highly competitive one that weighed heavily on the life of every student; it resulted in the creation of an elite clique, made up by and large of members of the three senior secret societies, who ran college life and dominated the student body. The Yale system did not reward intellectual and artistic excellence. The students who made the senior societies were the "big men" who could show solid organizational achievements in the college's managerial, athletic, religious, journalistic, and musical activities. Ives was not a big man, but the big men were able to bring certain of their friends into their societies with them, and Ives, who was personable and well liked, fell into this category. His close friends at Yale were not the scholars, the poets, the lovers of fine music, the alienated. His friends were the big men, and it was these friends from both prep school and college who secured for him an honored position among Yale's elite. His music that he shared with his friends at Yale was mainly popular music, and in spite of his later diatribes against commercialism he was not above composing potboilers in order to increase good fellowship. His more serious music he seems to have kept largely to himself.

There was always a saintly streak in Ives's personality, and I doubt that he lent himself to the cruelties of Yale's competitive system. In fact, he was admired for a certain independence and for never getting a swelled head from the social success gained in his early Yale years. At college, however, Ives was very different from the cantankerous heretic that he later became. He met the demands of the system so well that he was even mentioned for Skull and Bones, the most prestigious of the senior societies. However, he was actually elected to Wolf's Head, a lesser and much narrower group.

Then, after graduation, he was off to New York to enter the business world and to room with a number of ambitious law and medical students from his "crowd." These were carefree years of bachelorhood, but Ives's friends and associates (particularly among the alumni from Wolf's Head) were not the kind of people who were likely to broaden his horizons. In 1908, as if to cap his career as a successful Yale man, he married the daughter of a prominent minister who was a member of the Yale Corporation.

The circumstances of the first thirty-four years of Ives's life explain much about the genteel conventionality of his opinions. He often fell into a rigid moralism, as when he judged great composers like Wagner and Franck on the basis of their devotion to their wives and families. Ives revealed something of his attitude toward art in a memo that he wrote to himself in 1914 after talking on the train with Dan Beard, an older artist who had done the illustrations for Mark Twain's *Connecticut Yankee in King Arthur's Court.* (Ives's father-in-law had been close to Mark Twain, and it was probably through this connection that Ives knew Beard.) Far from being a bohemian, Dan Beard was actually a leading figure in the Boy Scouts of America, but when he told Ives about having had male art students paint from naked female models, Ives was deeply distressed: "His idea of manliness is *not* very wholesome. He cultivates the 'rough and ready man style,' but he is an artist (damn him—he can't get away from that)." Then there was this astounding statement: "The human anatomy can never be and has never been the inspiration for a great work of art. It's a medium to be used in God's service and not stared at by God's servants." Ives seemed to be actually afraid of physicalness and the bodily senses. Contrary to what is generally believed, he did *not* respond favorably to the earthy poetry of Whitman. It is also significant that the theme of romantic love is conspicuously absent from his mature works.

Yet, in spite of the apparently placid conventionality of his life, Ives was seething inwardly with political and social rebellion, just as he was with musical revolt. His rebellion consisted largely of ceremonial gestures and rhetoric that were kept safely private; nevertheless, his was a very genuine discontent, and it had immense importance for his life and work. Ives's rebellion seems to have arisen during the years just after 1906. It apparently received its greatest impetus from his marriage in 1908, an event which changed the pattern of his life. Even before their marriage, Harmony Twichell told him that she hoped they would not become trapped in New York social life but would instead devote their time together to self-cultivation. Ives apparently fell in with this plan enthusiastically, for the young couple went out little and Ives refused to take up the "Yale man's burden" —the round of civic and social responsibilities that most of his college and business friends assumed as a matter of course. Within a few years he had cut himself off from nearly all his Yale friends. His withdrawal from the world is often said to have begun with his heart attack during World War I, but it might better be dated ten years earlier.

During these same years, Ives began to think seriously for the first time about artistic, political, and social questions and to want to express his strong opinions about them. There was clearly a change in his personality. By 1912 the former college boy, who had blended shyness with unpredictable humor, had given way to the cantankerous and excitable fighter, whose shyness alternated with explosive outbursts. Any issue that he felt strongly about could set him off, but for long periods of time his wife was probably his only audience.

The source of Ives's revolt is evident in the political ideas that he developed during the 1910s. Of the whole range of questions raised by the progressive movement, Ives was little interested in plans to alleviate poverty or improve the condition of the working class. What monopolized his attention was the legislative process. He proposed a scheme for converting the American national government from a representative to a direct democracy, a scheme so extreme that it would have abolished Congress and the presidency as we know them today. He also devoted an inordinate amount of time to a scheme for imposing limits on individual income and property. Neither of these plans was close to the central concerns of progressivism, but the plans were close to *Ives's* concerns, for it is obvious that what he wanted to do was to destroy leadership in society and the power that goes with leadership. The hatred of leadership and elitism is the central theme in his political writings. Leaders must be pulled down and denied their power, the money that enabled them to lead must be severely restricted, and all power must be returned to the people. Even his scheme for world peace was an attack on leadership, for his denial of national sovereignty was a denial that certain nations should take the leadership in world organization.

In calling for the abolition of leadership, Ives was rebelling against the very essence of the Yale system, whose whole tradition centered around training for leadership. Sometime during the first decade of the century he had come to see the Yale life and its aftermath no longer as innocent but as stained with evil. He had come to feel that leadership—the practice of taking responsibility for others and making decisions for them and exercising authority over them—was corrupting to both leaders and led. He apparently believed that his own individuality (including his artistic independence) had been stifled by the Yale system of leadership but that he had saved himself before it was too late. He was very specifically rebelling against the Yale type of man—including his college friends, his business associates, his own relatives, and his wife's relatives—who had assumed leadership positions in government and business.

It was almost as if Ives had made a bargain with himself. After all the commitments he had made up to this point in his life, he could not bring himself to break away from the conventional pattern and become some sort of bohemian. He would work hard and make a success of his business, but he would rebel by retreating *within* the conventional system. He would confine himself to office and home and would refuse all leadership positions and their trappings; he would not take any responsibility for the system.

Ives's peculiar solution to his problem, a solution of revolt through isolation and private retreat, explains much about the naïve and autistic quality of his thinking. His world consisted of hardheaded businessmen whose philosophy of strong leadership and power must have seemed all-pervasive to him. His rebellion became a long and lonely one-man guerrilla war against the leaders of the conservative business and professional community, carried on from within that community without outside allies. Having contact only with mediocrities, he had little knowledge of other criticism that was being directed against these same leaders. His ideas, worked out on his own, were too often simply the opposite of the opinions that he encountered daily among his peers. He would not or could not submit these ideas to a dialogue with outside reformers and thinkers and artists, a dialogue that might have refined them and given them a more fruitful application. In 1919 and 1920, for example, when he defended President Wilson and the League of Nations, he was apparently unaware that many liberals and reformers were critical of the president for having made an unjust peace and then having embodied it in the league.

Although Ives used democratic majoritarianism to attack leadership, he was perhaps spiritually closer to a different American tradition of opposition to leadership in church, state, and society. I refer to the long New England come-outer tradition, the tradition of removing oneself from an institution which violates one's conscience. Ives expressed admiration for the abolitionists Henry David Thoreau and William Lloyd Garrison, who had certainly been come-outers, and he spoke fondly of the old New England independent tradition of standing up in town meeting or church and speaking out one's mind and conscience, without respect for the consequences. By the same token, Ives's intense individualism certainly precluded the desire for community that motivated many progressives. The sweeping mechanical changes that he proposed in government and society became ends in themselves; he did not advocate them as the means of fulfilling a larger vision—of bringing about a more organic society, a Kingdom of God on earth.

In the years following 1908, Ives's wife and his business partner willingly served as his foils so that he might play two different rebellious roles; each role was connected with certain of the masterpieces in the larger forms that

24

he composed in these years. One role, which he had long been accustomed to, was that of the prankish, outlandish boy, but now his wife encouraged this role by herself playing the proper woman shocked by his shenanigans and yet indulging him because he was a mere boy. The compositions that deal with the innocence of boyhood experience—"Decoration Day," "The Fourth of July," "Putnam's Camp"—arose from this role. The other role, which was new to him, was that of the transcendental and crotchety old man on his mountaintop, a Bronson Alcott philosophizing while his wife took care of the practical details of life. Both Ives's wife and his partner took a protective attitude toward him in this role of visionary, and his partner assumed the leadership responsibilities in the business so that Ives could remain a saintly, aloof scholar, writing insurance material in his office. The compositions that dealt with transcendental exaltation—the *"Concord" Sonata,* the *Fourth Symphony*—arose from this second role. It might even be said that Ives passed from boy to old man within the space of a very few years after 1908. Such a swift passage allowed him to escape just what he wanted to escape: adult manhood, the time of responsibility and leadership, and the guilt of authority. Both the boy and the old man were innocent; they were not responsible for the system of things.

Ives's extraordinary solution to his problems as a mature man and artist sustained him through a number of years of musical productivity until World War I, but the terrible strain of his self-contradictions took its inevitable toll. After the breakdown of his health in 1918 his creativity was brought to an early end.

I believe that in both his musical life and his larger cultural life Charles Ives succumbed to enormous social pressures that committed him inexorably to a life of narrow conventionality—a life spent in business, with music kept as an avocation and with a careful avoidance of anything bohemian. On both these levels, however, Ives experienced a private revolt against conventionality, the musical revolt coming many years before the more general one because of his father's experimentation and his own need to defend his boyish masculinity against effeminate classical music. Both revolts involved Ives's redefining for himself what it meant to be a good American, his attacking conventionality by asserting against it the American values of democracy, masculinity, and even transcendentalism. But the more he shouted about democracy and the majority, the more he was forced toward the isolated position of being a majority of one. American culture was too much for Ives. In order to define himself as primarily an artist—a definition which the European artist would have assumed as a matter of course—the American of Ives's day had first to accept his inevitable alienation from his society. Ives's tragedy was that he could not accept that alienation. Even in extreme isolation, Charles Ives remained to the end a good American.

AARON COPLAND: What amazes me is how this cranky man you have depicted, so full of kinks and peculiarities, could have created this *music!* This is the important thing about Ives. The fact that he was conventional, that he was very private, that he didn't fulfill the usual picture of the genius in music in many ways—all this makes the music in my mind even that *more* remarkable. It's the most unusual and most individual creation, coming out of such a background and environment, and that mystery I don't think is going to be solved very soon.

GILBERT CHASE: Long live the mystery!

QUESTIONER: Is it not true that Ives's father sent him to Yale in part to study with Horatio Parker—that somehow, in the beginning, there may have been a chance that he was going to be a professional musician?

FRANK ROSSITER: I don't think so. There is a letter that he wrote to his father a few months before he entered Yale mentioning that it might be possible for him to take some music courses. But I think the whole context of the letter indicates that he wasn't going for that explicit purpose at all. And I know of no other indication that his father might have wanted him to study with Parker.

QUESTIONER: Ives lived after his heart attack from 1918 to 1954. Could any of the panel comment on his attitude toward politics and the world scene in America? We went through some of the most critical times in world history and American history in that period. Are there any indications of Ives's attitude toward the holocaust, toward National Socialism as a political ideal, toward World War II, toward other events after 1920?

ROSSITER: Well, as I said, he did not become disillusioned with Woodrow Wilson and with the results of World War I as so many Americans did. But after his spurt of writing both songs and the essays on government in 1919, 1920, and 1921, he cut down on his political interests. He seemed to become much less disturbed by things. However, he did support Al Smith in 1928 and was, of course, very much opposed to the rise of Hitler in the thirties. On the other hand, he did not like Franklin Roosevelt, for the very good reason that Roosevelt didn't seem at all to fit his notions of more direct democracy. He did not like the bureaucracy in Washington in the 1930s, and he had enough knowledge of what was happening in the thirties and forties so that, when he resurrected some of his political ideas in response to the rise of Nazism and fascism, he tended to temper them by what he knew was popular with Americans. In the late thirties, he got up a proposal for a direct vote on whether a nation should go to war, and he didn't mention anything about international organization because he knew that was very unpopular. But then, a few years later, after we'd gotten into World War II, he turned back to the international organization idea. He apparently followed World War II to some extent, because in the Ives Collection at Yale there are a lot of newspapers in which he had underlined things in editorials. But I would say that after World War II he had very little further interest in politics.

JOHN KIRKPATRICK: The more I listened to Professor Rossiter's paper, the more it seemed to me that it was a whole amalgam of peripheral things, that he missed out on what was the most central fact of Ives's life—that is, its being centered in a spiritual faith, a faith in the power of the spiritual core of a human individual or a human race to transcend everything of a material nature. In that way it seemed to me a paper written by a thoroughly convinced materialist. Now, in my book, as in Ives's, a materialist is not a realist. In his marginalia in the *Universe Symphony* he said, "The only hope of humanity is the unseen Spirit."

ROSSITER: I think my paper does de-emphasize the spiritual qualities in Ives, but I'm not unaware of them, and as a matter of fact I would put a good deal of emphasis on them. I think where Mr. Crunden and I might disagree is on the religious influences on Ives, He, I think, feels that some of these religious influences came from Ives's wife and her family. I would tend to see more of a revolt against the people he was associated with: his own relatives, his business associates, his wife's relatives. As I say, I think his wife to some extent was a foil which he operated against. On the other hand, I think there was a spiritual tradition in New England that he did look back to, and it was partly in his own family. It is interesting that his great-great-great-grandfather, who was the Reverend Ebenezer White, minister of the established Congregational Church in Danbury in the 1760s, was a New England come-outer and led most of his flock out of the church when they could not agree with the larger presbyterial system in Connecticut.

I also think that perhaps the best comparison with Ives's music would be the political and social ideas of William Lloyd Garrison and Henry David Thoreau, both of whom were immensely spiritual men and drew their own very interesting ideas of asserting conscience against the State from a spiritual heritage going back to Puritanism. Ives admired both those men. Of course, he couldn't understand their intellectual arguments for civil disobedience or nonresistance, but he admired them, and I think he felt a certain connection with their very spiritual tradition. It was also a tradition of political revolt, and the reason I feel that their work might be comparable to Ives's is that, just as his music seemed to be composed without a great deal of reference to the European musical heritage, so Garrison's and Thoreau's political ideas were formed without reference to either the conservative or radical European political heritage. Also, although they too were not much recognized in their own day for their political ideas, those ideas were taken up later in other parts of the world—by Gandhi and Tolstoy, for example— just as Ives's music was taken up in the 1960s in Europe. So I think I'm not unaware of that spiritual background, even if perhaps I de-emphasized it in this paper.

WILLIAM AUSTIN: I'd like to ask Mr. Rossiter if I misunderstood what seemed to me a spiritual, ethical point toward the end of his paper. It seemed to me that he condemned Ives for evading responsibility and suggested that this was a peculiar solution to the problem in his own time. I read between the lines that it's perhaps less peculiar nowadays—but that Mr. Rossiter would warn us all. Was I reading too much between the lines?

ROSSITER: Well, in part, Ives's evading responsibility was a moral position, I think, because the only responsibility that he would have been able to take within the context of his life would have been within the political and business world in which he moved. So, in a sense, it's rather admirable that he did refuse to take up that responsibility, although his cultural experiences were too limited for him to seek alternatives to refusing responsibility —alternatives based more, I think, upon conscience than upon one's being true to one's own integrity.

Ives and Nineteenth-Century American Music

NEELY BRUCE

Charles Ives frequently acknowledged his debt to the musical past. His fondest memories of musical performances in his childhood, to judge from his enthusiastic account of them, were of the music of the people: the music was masculine and utilitarian, and he embraced it and identified with it. Ives was proud to have made it a part of his compositional equipment and told anecdotes of his experiences with this music with great zest. When the music of Ives began to attract critical attention in the late 1920s and 1930s, his identification with this music of the American people was widely re-marked and commented upon.

Ives also paid homage to the great men of the European tradition of art music, especially the three big B's of music: Bach, Beethoven, and Brahms. He also seems to have admired the music of César Franck, and to have had a few grudging words of praise for Debussy and even Wagner. The music of Beethoven seems to have been uniquely meaningful in Ives's life, in particu-lar because of the loftiness of Beethoven's vision and his unabashed attempts to deal with the sublime in music. Ives surely realized that he was one of the few composers since Beethoven to attempt a genuinely sublime statement, and he was proud to acknowledge his spiritual predecessor.

There is a third type of music in Ives's past, however, which is not the music of the people in any sense, and which is emphatically not the music of the European masters. He does not acknowledge any debt to this music, so far as I can determine, but he mentions it from time to time. I am referring to the music of other American composers, particularly composers of the mid- and late nineteenth century, composers of serious ambition who had, for the most part, studied in Europe and were seriously concerned with raising the standards of American taste. These were the composers of church music (as opposed to hymns), the composers of music for amateur use (as opposed to parlor music), and the composers of symphonies (as opposed to marches and variations on well-known tunes).

Of course the distinction just stated is a rough one, and it will not account for many of the composers whom I am grouping together. Many of them were trained in this country; many of them wrote music of unabashed popular appeal; some were pretentious merely by being commercial. Nonetheless, this group of American composers, only roughly definable, can be identified rather precisely by Ives's reaction to them.

In his childhood, when concerts of such music were presented in church in Danbury, Ives felt compelled to liven things up in a kind of boyish protest. Throughout his adult life, he frequently felt moved to attack the composers and performers of such music and to deny it. It was effeminate, sentimental, and dated. It stood in sharp contrast to the excitement of the music of the people and the ambitious statement of the music of the great masters. It was, in fact, worthless, and the progress of the art of music would, he felt, be well served by eliminating it altogether from the musical life of mankind.

Considering the strength of Ives's convictions on the matter, it is surprising, if not startling, to realize the quantity of music that he wrote which is directly modeled on the music of these American predecessors. Ives not only wrote such music; he published it at his own expense. Eight of the songs in *114 Songs* are specifically labeled as being of "little or no musical value." Indeed, considering the songs which he labels thus, he could have included quite a few more of the 114 in this list. He justified their insertion in a volume that he clearly wanted to represent his work at its best "principally because in the writer's opinion they are good illustrations of types of songs, the fewer of which are composed, published, sold or sung, the better it is for the progress of music generally." The lack of quality to which Ives refers is clearly the sentimentality, and the dependence on low-intentioned European models, of the songs in question.

Ives presents us with the paradox of a major composer who denounced a kind of music which he himself composed in considerable quantity and even published and distributed at his own expense. Before attempting to deal directly with this paradox, I would like to examine briefly some aspects of nineteenth-century American music, in particular the solo vocal music of the middle of the century, and suggest ways in which this music is related to that of Ives. A convenient starting place for this inquiry is the music of the only American composer for whom Ives had unqualified enthusiasm, Stephen Foster.

Ives recalls that his father taught the music of the best composers to the children of Danbury, in particular that of Bach and Stephen Foster. The *Second Symphony,* according to a letter from Harmony Ives to Elliott Carter, was conceived as a tribute to the spirit and music of Stephen Foster. The *Second Orchestral Set* begins with a slow movement originally entitled "An

Elegy for Stephen Foster," and several Foster tunes are frequently quoted throughout the body of Ives's work.

It seems clear that Ives in some way identified himself with Foster and his music, an identification which seems on the surface a strange one. Foster's career was spent in the company of people of whom Ives would not have approved. Foster's wife and child left him because he could not support them, and Ives had few kind words for artists who could not or would not support their families. In his last years, Foster was what we would call today an alcoholic, and he died a virtual failure under strange conditions. What would a successful insurance executive from Yale find in common with such a man?

Ives makes it clear in many phrases scattered through the *Memos* that he considered Foster's music part of the music of the people. Ives was certainly aware, however, that Foster was a professional composer, and in fact a composer of some artistic pretensions. The fact that another American composer had written music that had become accepted, on a large scale, as the music of the people was perhaps a source of hope to Ives, who felt that he was writing a music of the people. Both Ives and Foster experienced failure as artists in their lifetimes, although Foster's failure was the more bitter for his having been at one time a success. But posterity has vindicated each man and has confirmed that each was in some sense composing a truly populist music.[1]

More fundamentally, each man experienced tremendous conflict as an artist. Foster, as is well known, agonized over his success as a composer of Ethiopian songs and felt that his talent should be turned to writing a more elevated kind of music. He lived his entire creative life with one foot in the music hall and one foot in the parlor. He was a tremendous success in both genres, as *Oh! Susanna* and *Beautiful Dreamer* eloquently testify. Ives lived out the same kind of conflict, although in his case it took the form of a conflict between the music he wanted to write and the music other people wanted him to write. What he wanted to write was a populist music, experimental, not easy on the ear; what his friends and the few professional musicians with whom he associated wanted him to write was an elitist music, easy on the ear, indebted to all that he considered worst in his background. Like Foster, he could have had great success in writing this kind of music, although ironically he seemed to have the same sort of guilt feelings about producing it as Foster had had about writing his more popular pieces.

1. It is difficult in contemporary English to find an adjective which means "of the people," or "not elitist," without necessarily meaning "popular." I am using "populist" in this general sense, although I am aware that Ives was not a Populist. The political connotations of the word, however, do not seem inappropriate in discussing Ives or even, in a remote way, in discussing Foster.

In 1896, Morrison Foster, Stephen's brother, published in Pittsburgh a book entitled *Biography, Songs and Musical Compositions of Stephen C. Foster, Author of "The Old Folks at Home."* This volume was essentially a reprint of the original editions of Foster's songs plus his hymns, three of his six piano pieces, and an excerpt from *The Social Orchestra.* If one compares the Morrison Foster songbook with *114 Songs,* a number of significant similarities emerge between Ives's musical thinking and that of Foster.

The critical literature on Foster, as far as I have been able to determine, has concentrated almost exclusively on his work as a melodist. Melody was, of course, a great gift of Foster's, and as a great melodist his music is unlike that of Ives. However, if one looks at the piano accompaniments which Foster wrote for his songs, accompaniments which unfortunately have been rearranged or totally rewritten in most editions of Foster's songs published since his death, a very different picture of his art emerges.

The typical European art song of the nineteenth century establishes a figuration in the piano part which in some sense sums up the poem or reflects some central image in it. Most of the songs of Schubert, Schumann, and Brahms, and to a lesser extent those of Wolf, proceed in this manner. The second song in Schubert's cycle *Die Schöne Müllerin,* entitled "Wohin?" is a perfect example of this type of song. The rippling accompaniment figure is suggestive of the brook which the young miller is interrogating, and the constant presence of this figure informs us of the significance of the brook, which is the central idea of this particular song, in the cycle.

Although Foster wrote a few songs that establish a central image through a consistent accompaniment pattern, the great majority of his songs proceed in a radically different manner. All of Foster's lines are standard four-bar phrases, grouped into larger patterns of multiples of two. His accompaniments, however, are constantly shifting their figuration—inverting patterns, adding or subtracting voices, changing Alberti-bass-type figures to solid chords, changing the rhythmic patterns of the bass line, and the like. Although the total repertory of Foster's accompaniment figurations is far more limited than that of Schubert, his use of different and contrasting accompaniment figures within individual songs is in most cases far greater. Within a limited vocabulary of patterns, Foster constructs elegant forms of figurations, sometimes supporting the general progress of the melodic line but more often creating a gentle counterpoint to the form of the tune. These subforms of accompaniment patterns become in some songs unusually subtle and expressive, as in *Oh! Susanna, Hard Times Come Again No More,* and *Mr. and Mrs. Brown.*

Many of Ives's songs proceed in the same manner, although, like Foster's, a number of them conform to the normal European procedure of establishing a single figuration which reflects some central idea of the poem. Subforms of accompaniment patterns are found, for example, in *Luck and Work*, the three songs which concern months of the year [*August, September, December*], *Where the Eagle*, and, more extreme, in *The Swimmers, Majority*, and *Charlie Rutlage*.

According to traditional descriptions of standard European practice, vocal melodies are assumed to proceed basically by conjunct motion, disjunct motion being reserved for special effects. Melodies which proceed basically by skip are atypical and rather rare. However, over half the songs of Foster contain a sizable majority of disjunct intervals rather than conjunct ones. The proportion of songs by Ives which have more skips than steps is not so great as of those by Foster, but many songs by Ives, such as *Walt Whitman, Resolution*, and *Incantation*, have basically disjunct melodic lines. Moreover, these lines are usually disjunct; they are based on arpeggios of chords which are the underlying harmonic ideas of the pieces.

If one examines the songs of Foster from the point of view of their conformity to the prescribed rules of partwriting supposedly governing European art music, one discovers virtually a catalog of "errors": parallel octaves and fifths, parallel fifths and octaves by contrary motion, incorrect use of six-four chords, vocal basses that cross instrumental basses, chords with no thirds, doubled sevenths and leading tones (in the bass line, no less), unresolved dissonances, and progressions not generally allowed. Some of these violations occur so systematically and so repeatedly that they must be considered stylistically significant. In particular, Foster's use of parallel fifths is remarkably consistent, as is his use of chords which have no third, both as open fourths and open fifths. One also discovers a miscellany of other irregularities, not exactly errors but peculiarities such as crossed voices (with the alto frequently above the soprano melody), unusual spacing of voices, arbitrary addition and subtraction of voices, false relations, four-measure phrases which utilize only one chord, voices which move in and out of parallel motion (so that one is not sure whether or not they are doublings), sudden changes of register, and various unusual dissonances, including several which clearly imply the superposition of two different triads.

The same sorts of irregularities can be found in Ives, of course, although Ives's use of them is much more extreme, so this is a quantitative difference, not a qualitative one. Perhaps it is easier to understand the sense in which Ives differs from Foster quantitatively from the following particular case. In a vivid anecdote, Ives relates how his father stood in a thunderstorm, listening to bell sounds, and went back and forth from the rain to the piano inside, attempting to imitate the sounds precisely. Shortly thereafter he built his apparatus for producing microtonal chords. William Brooks, in a forthcoming book on American music which concentrates on the music of Billings, Ives, and Cage, demonstrates in great detail how many of Ives's most characteristic sonorities are based on bell sounds and their distortions. *114 Songs* contains several pieces which imitate bell sounds—for example, *Serenity, Thoreau, Walking,* and of course *Those Evening Bells.* Foster's song *Ellen Bayne* also contains bell imitations, and, incidentally, other songs of Foster have imitations of drums, banjos, lutes, and birds.

In the solo vocal and solo piano literature of the nineteenth century, bell imitations abound, sometimes to the point of seeming obsessive. American and European composers alike indulged in this popular form of program music, *La Campanella* and the end of *Papillons* being only two of the most famous examples out of hundreds, perhaps thousands. Ives's bell imitations, and sonorities based on them, are not fundamentally different in effect or intent from *Les cloches du monastère;* they are simply more realistic.

One of the attributes of Ives's music most often cited is his frequent use of quotation, usually quotation of tunes from the body of American popular music. There is at least one Foster song which uses quotation, a little-known piece with the singularly Ivesian title *The Song of All Songs.* This is a pastiche of phrases from different songs, and the words are likewise a pastiche of song titles of the day, with a wonderfully nonsensical effect, as in the following couplet:

> "Mother, is the battle over?" "What are the men about?"
> "How are you, Horace Greeley?" "Does your mother know you're out?"

A particular form of quotation is self-quotation, another attribute of Ives's style often noted. Some dramatic examples in *114 Songs* are the wholesale similarities between *Lincoln, the Great Commoner* and *Nov. 2, 1920* and the notorious *A Song—for Anything,* which in successive stanzas is by turns a love song, a Yale song, and a religious song and can be performed as one piece or as three different ones. In the Morrison Foster songbook, *Dolcy Jones* and *Ring, Ring de Banjo* have virtually identical melodic lines, and *Uncle Ned,* a very sad Ethiopian ballad about death, was reworked slightly by Foster and reappeared in a later edition as *There's a Land of Bliss,* suitable for more genteel circumstances. Individual phrases recur with great frequency, of course, in the work of both men.

Parenthetically, on the general subject of quotation, let me say that the use of borrowed material is quite commonplace in nineteenth-century American music; by itself it could be the subject of an entire investigation. Two outstanding examples of mid-nineteenth-century songs which include quotations are *The Village Blacksmith,* by David Warden, which quotes "Angels Ever Bright and Fair" of Handel (incidentally sung by the village choir referred to in Longfellow's poem, whose members conveniently put in an appearance to sing about two-thirds of the way through Warden's solo song), and *My Trundle Bed,* by J. C. Baker, which quotes the hymn tune

"Nettleton" (commonly sung to the text "Come thou fount of every bless-ing") in the same place in the song, and with the same effect, as in Ives's *The Innate*.

Several of the songs in *114 Songs*, most notably *He Is There!*, *Old Home Day*, and *A Son of a Gambolier*, have parts for extra instrumentalists, usually flute or violin. There are no such parts in the Foster songs because they are assumed to be there if one wishes to add them. In fact, in providing these obbligati, Ives is not being an innovator or expanding the resources of song at all but is reverting to a common practice of the late eighteenth and early nineteenth centuries.

Comparisons of individual songs and technical procedures show many details shared by Ives and Foster as composers, and, viewed from a broader perspective, the two books of songs share several striking general character-istics. First, one can be overwhelmed with the sentimentality and the ideali-zation of social concerns of both Foster and Ives. Both men write frankly sentimental love songs, though perhaps fewer of these than one would have expected. The idealization is vividly reflected in the songs that Foster wrote about the Civil War and Ives's songs of World War I. It is also in the often-noticed idealization of black people in Foster and the rarely noted but equally sentimental portrait of Indians in Ives's songs. Ives, of course, is famous for his majoritarian songs, and for the utopian vision of *Nov. 2, 1920*, but I find it not so very different from the basic idea of Foster's *There's a Good Time Coming*.

A related concern of both composers, indeed an obsession of virtually every major American artist, is a constant involvement with the past. Re-membered people and places are the subject matter of a large percentage of songs by both men, and the memories we are constantly presented with are invariably pleasant or idealized. Both books contain a number of hymn settings and other religious pieces. The religious perspective tends to be a sentimental one, especially in the Foster songbook. Both songbooks contain a variety of humorous songs, particularly ones that are nonsensical. Some of these songs are indeed outrageous and seem unimaginable in the song collec-tions of the run-of-the-mill art music composer, notably the more extreme Ethiopian songs of Foster and *Romanzo di Central Park* and the kazoo chorus of *A Son of a Gambolier* by Ives.

Ives and Foster show a remarkably similar attitude in their choice of texts. There are relatively few songs by either composer that use the words of great poets, although Ives has some songs by English romantic poets and Foster has an ambitious duet with words adapted from Shakespeare. Both composers often take their texts from sources very different from the major poets of the language. Ives takes sentences from sermons and lectures; Foster uses moralistic poetry by little-known poets. Both men got several song texts from newspapers. Both men set familiar hymn texts to music. Both men frequently set to music the poems of their friends and relatives. Significant, too, is the fact that both Ives and Foster wrote their own texts for a large number of their songs. The quality of their texts, considered as literature, is highly variable.

With respect to what may be called orchestration, the two songbooks are profoundly similar. Both contain pieces for chorus, occasionally in four parts. Ives writes out the obbligati which are implied in Foster. It is even possible that Ives had in mind performances of his songs as instrumental solos, a practice common in Foster's day which Ives's father is known to have kept alive in Danbury in Ives's youth. In nineteenth-century European art song collections, of course, the standardized format of voice and piano is used almost exclusively, and the introduction of unison choruses, duets, four-part choruses, and instrumental parts, to say nothing of piano solos and kazoo choruses, is unusual if not unthinkable.

Finally, and perhaps most important, both books contain within their covers extremes of quality which are without parallel in the works of most composers of art songs. That the same composer wrote both *Jeanie with the Light Brown Hair* and *I'd Be a Fairy* is straining credulity; that the same composer wrote both *From Paracelsus* and *The World's Wanderers* is equally preposterous. Perhaps the key to understanding the range of quality in both songbooks is realizing that it functions precisely as do all other aspects of the two books; that is, within the limits of the style of each composer, maximum variety is achieved. There are, in both books, very good songs, very bad songs, and all kinds of songs in between. There are very good texts and very bad texts. There are very small, unambitious songs and very large, ambitious ones. There are various instrumental and choral possibilities that make the books more colorful. Indeed, the variety of both books is so astonishing that one is tempted to say that they are not songbooks at all, but microcosms giving us an image of the world and its possibilities as heard through the ears of Charles Ives, in the one, and the ears of Stephen Foster, in the other. Of course Ives said as much when he admitted, quite accurately, that he had not written a book of songs at all, he had "merely cleaned house." Likewise, Foster literally never wrote a book of songs; his brother cleaned house for him, long after his death.

In concentrating on a comparison between the Ives and Foster songbooks in this paper, I do not wish to imply that this is the extent of the relationship between Ives and nineteenth-century American music. Many other similar comparisons could be made. First, there are at least two other collections of nineteenth-century American music which invite comparison with *114 Songs*—the collected songs of Henry Clay Work, which were posthumously published by his nephew in the 1880s, and Anthony Philip Heinrich's extravagant Opus 1, *The Dawning of Music in Kentucky,* published in 1820. Second, the irregularities which I have discussed in the songs of Foster are by no means unique; any number of American songs of the mid-nineteenth century display a similar method of composition.

Outside the repertory of solo vocal music, several areas of American music in the nineteenth century also suggest comparison with Ives. The choral music of Dudley Buck is known to have influenced Ives, since Ives refers in one of his lists of compositions to "about 20–25 Anthems, responses, and hymn-anthems (alla Harry Rowe Shelley and Dudley Buck)." (All, unfortunately, have been lost.) In his excellent dissertation, "The Life and Church Music of Dudley Buck," William Gallo gives examples of Buck's choral writing which to me seem very much like some passages in Ives's choral music. Gallo describes Buck's choral style as follows: "Probably the most distinctive feature of Buck's style was his use of texture which, like the harmonic and melodic aspects of his style, was text oriented. As the moods of the text changed, Buck varied the texture along with the tempo, dynamics, and so forth to musically emphasize nuances of expression in the text. Through its textural fluidity, Buck's music attained a degree of flexibility and expressiveness previously unknown in American church music."[2] This paragraph could easily serve as a description of Ives's *Psalm 90,* among other choral works. Perhaps Ives learned a great deal indeed from Buck's sacred music. Ives's relationship to his slightly older contemporary, Harry Rowe Shelley, remains to be investigated.

There is a vast literature of late nineteenth-century and early twentieth-century American music for voice and for piano solo which I feel can appropriately be termed "Rollo-music." Rollo-music is generally written for amateur pianists and singers of very high pretensions, who, however, do not aspire, either because of technical limitations or because of lack of spiritual awareness, to the performance of works by the great masters. The quintessential composer of Rollo-music, perhaps, is Ethelbert Nevin, although the number of the composers of this genre is legion. Surprisingly, many of Ives's pieces borrow specific progressions and textures from the Rollo-music repertory.

Most of Ives's pieces for piano solo are programmatic, and there is a vast repertory of nineteenth-century American descriptive piano music which invites comparison with them on many counts. The history of organ music in this country is also filled with a number of Ivesian details. Howard Bakken, in his D.M.A. thesis, "The Development of Organ Playing in New York and Boston, 1700–1900," quotes several descriptions of mid-nineteenth-

2. William Gallo, "The Life and Church Music of Dudley Buck (1839–1909)" (Ph.D. diss., Catholic University of America, 1968), p. 216.

century organists which suggest the young Charles Ives in his role as church organist:

> . . . we hear . . . voluntaries, made up of a mixture of parts of songs, marches, waltzes, &c. . . .

> . . . upon the glorious organ, that sublime achievement of genius . . . have been performed arias from "Robert le Diable," marches from military bands, and waltzes from the ballroom. These were interspersed with chromatic improvisations, and complicated fantasias, and voluntary variations on popular airs, and perhaps, here and there, a Kyrie from a Mass or a fugue from an opera.

> These endless, aimless wanderings among solo stops, the *potpourris* of operas, popular airs, bits of secular and bits of sacred, strung together upon idle fancies of the moment . . . fatigue and dissipate the mind just when it seeks to be edified. . . .[3]

There are even pieces of chamber music by nineteenth-century American composers that invite comparison with Ives. For example, there is a violin and piano sonata by Ernst Richard Kroeger, born and trained in St. Louis, with an academic, rather straight-laced first movement, a second movement which vividly suggests Latin American popular music, and a finale which is a perpetual motion piece in the style of turn-of-the-century gypsy fiddle imitations.

The music of Ives owes much to the music of his older contemporaries, the so-called Second New England School, in particular the music of Horatio Parker and George Chadwick. As is well known, Ives was a student of Parker at Yale. He was personally acquainted with Chadwick, who even had words of praise for some of his music. The programs of the New Haven Symphony for the years when Ives was at Yale suggest that Ives heard several works of these composers, and there are scattered references to Parker and Chadwick in the *Memos* which suggest that Ives took the music of both men quite seriously.

Finally, there is growing critical recognition that certain major figures of nineteenth-century American music can rightly be regarded as precursors of Ives. Several persons have noted many similarities between Anthony Philip Heinrich and Ives; David Hall refers to Gottschalk's piano piece *Columbia* as "proto-Ivesian";[4] and Richard Jackson, in his review of the American Music Group's revival of George Bristow's opera *Rip Van Winkle,* describes the style of the work as "a natural extension of the parlor ballad, the patriotic

3. Howard Bakken, "The Development of Organ Playing in New York and Boston, 1700–1900" (D.M.A. thesis, University of Illinois, 1974), pp. 21, 24, 27, 28. The first two quotations are from newspaper accounts, the third is from John Sullivan Dwight.

4. *Stereo Review,* 32, no. 6 (June 1974): 120.

song, and the Protestant hymn," containing "evocations of revolutionary era marches and dances"[5]—a description which could fit a number of pieces by Ives.

Indeed, the more one examines nineteenth-century music in this country, the more "Ivesian" it becomes. Perhaps this is only to be expected, since, as several critics have pointed out, Ives was in many basic respects a nineteenth-century American man, and if that is true, then he should be, in some fundamental sense, a nineteenth-century American composer. Indeed, as I have suggested in discussing the songs of Ives and Foster, the differences between Ives and his nineteenth-century predecessors in this country are quantitative rather than qualitative; that is, he does more frequently or more extremely that which many others before him had done rarely or timidly.

When one realizes the extent to which the music of Ives grows out of and is indebted to the music of America in the nineteenth century, one begins to see both older American music and the music of Ives in a very different light. One becomes increasingly aware of a multitude of strange details in older American music and learns to take them in stride, even to take a great delight in them. One is no longer surprised by pieces like Edward Hoffman's piano fantasy on *Listen to the Mockingbird,* which ends with a set of variations on *Auld Lang Syne,* or J. Albert Snow's variations on *The Old Oaken Bucket,* which not only refers to *Auld Lang Syne* on the last page but ends with an "Amen" cadence. Conversely, many of the most problematical aspects of Ives's music become clear, even commonplace. The extraordinary internal variety of his accompaniments, the instrumental obbligati to the songs and the mysterious appearance of the flute in the *"Concord" Sonata,* the seemingly endless quotations—all of these techniques seem part and parcel of the American composer's normal stock-in-trade. Even the most elusive aspect of Ives's music, his notion of musical form, becomes much more transparent.

Ives's grasp of musical form has been resoundingly criticized by many writers since the *"Concord" Sonata* appeared. In one of his rare statements about such matters, in "Some 'Quarter-tone' Impressions," Ives mentions "the drag of repetition in many phases of art." Clearly, Ives was interested in exploring various nonrepetitive musical structures. It seems equally clear to me that he got the idea for his nonrepetitive structures from various forms in common use in the nineteenth century in America.

These forms are found, for example, in short dramatic cantatas such as *Sailor Boy's Dream* by F. H. Pease. This piece describes the slumber of a sailor boy, asleep in his hammock, who dreams of his home, his family, and

---

5. *Music Library Association Newsletter,* no. 16 (March-April 1974): 3.

his beloved; while he dreams, a tempest arises, his ship is wrecked, and the sailor perishes beneath the waves. The unity of the piece is achieved purely by the narrative; there are no large-scale repetitions of musical ideas, or even of key areas, to create the kind of unity one normally expects in music. Another nonrepetitive piece, already referred to, is *The Village Blacksmith* by David Warden, which takes its form entirely from the Longfellow poem and lets the unity of the music be a natural consequence of the unity of the narrative. Another type of piece which routinely achieves this kind of unity is the descriptive piano piece—for example the battle piece, which flourished in this country long after it had ceased to be fashionable in Europe.

Ives's forms are precisely this kind of narrative music, usually without the narrative, of course, though generally with some hint of it such as a programmatic title. From the narrative songs of the nineteenth century and the descriptive instrumental narratives, Ives conceived the notion of a narrative music without the narrative, and then, having written instrumental pieces of this type, began writing songs of the same type, that is, songs based on instrumental narratives which are in turn based on narrative songs of the past. However implausible this line of thinking may appear, it seems a very precise description of the actual process by which many of Ives's songs were written, since we know that many of them are based on instrumental pieces with programmatic titles and free forms.

It should also be pointed out that the notion of this type of narrative music is commonplace in the works of Heinrich and can be found occasionally in the instrumental compositions of other nineteenth-century American composers—for example in the *Santa Claus Symphony* of William Henry Fry, which, without the program, would be an excellent example of narrative music.

In conclusion, I would like to suggest that the paradox referred to earlier—that of Ives as a composer who denounced a kind of music which he himself wrote and published—is not really a paradox at all. Ives could rejoice in his identification with the music of the people and could take pride in his appreciation of the music of the great masters. He could not rejoice or take pride in his debt to the music of most of his immediate predecessors, since he considered it, as most people still do, music of doubtful quality. Still, he had used it, he had learned from it, and, as he knew full well, it was a part of him, just as the music which he considered to be better music was a part of him. Ives refused to renounce his past, or himself; in fact, he was careful to affirm his past and clearly state his acceptance of it in every aspect of his life. As a result, he wrote songs and much other music which reflect even those aspects of his past which he thought to be questionable, for the same reason that John Cage wrote *Imaginary Landscapes #4* for twelve radios: to come to grips with them. Ives published and distributed the music to demonstrate that he was not denying this aspect of himself, but he was able to state categorically that he didn't think that the music was very good because he was an honest man. There is something characteristically American, it seems to me, about the notion of accepting all of one's heritage, good and bad, and living with and affirming all that one is and has been, rather than adopting a particular stance as an artist and presenting only that stance to the public. Ives has often been compared to Whitman, and this quality of accepting and affirming himself and his heritage, with no regrets, seems eminently Whitmanesque. The motivation for Ives's doing this seems to have been that he genuinely loved his past, whatever he may have thought its faults might have been. As he genuinely loved his father, he also genuinely loved "the things our fathers loved."

WILLIAM AUSTIN: A question about the possibility of Ives's knowledge of Foster's songs: You carefully hedged, but I think that some people might not be aware that you were not implying anything very definite about that.

NEELY BRUCE: Yes, I did very carefully avoid saying that any particular piece had anything directly to do with Ives. Even if we knew that Ives heard *Ellen Bayne,* even if we know for certain that he heard, say, *Oh! Susanna* or *Camptown Races,* we don't know that he knew the original publications of them.

AUSTIN: One wonders, in particular, whether Ives ever looked at the biography of Stephen Foster published by Morrison Foster in 1896.

BRUCE: He could have. If it had come out just a few years earlier, it could have been around the home when Ives was growing up, but of course it was while he was at Yale that it appeared.

AUSTIN: As far as John Kirkpatrick knows, there is no trace of the Morrison Foster book having been in Ives's possession at any time.

QUESTIONER: I was surprised you didn't mention Chadwick or Hadley. Could you explain that omission to us?

BRUCE: Well, I deliberately didn't, because Ives was a younger contemporary of Parker and such people and I tried to avoid dealing with contemporaneous nineteenth-century composers in dealing with Ives. I tried to get farther back than that in the paper. However, you're quite right to suggest that such an investigation should be undertaken, and I understand that, particularly in the works of Chadwick, there might be quite a number of examples of the type that I gave in connection with earlier composers.

PAUL ECHOLS: I have a question about Foster in relationship to Ives. You mentioned several categories of composers and music at the beginning of your paper and there was one category of composers, by which I assume you mean the Second New England School, that represented composers and works of doubtful value that Ives didn't care for, even though he recognized they were part of his heritage. You never quite placed Stephen Foster. Is Stephen Foster part of that or is he part of the proletarian aspect?

BRUCE: In terms of my original categories I don't think Stephen Foster fits in too well. I think if Ives had known, for example, *Ellen Bayne,* which is a song that we discussed, he would have considered that one of the sentimental, undesirable type of songs. In that case, maybe Foster would fit in that category, but he has a foot in two worlds.

ECHOLS: Yes, there are really two kinds of Foster songs: the kind of songs that have turned into really popular music like *Oh! Susanna* and *Camptown Races,* things that are part of the American musical heritage in a popular sense, and then a whole other category of parlor songs. I would be curious, for example, about whether Ives knew any of Foster's strictly parlor songs, as opposed to those that became popular.

BRUCE: That, I am afraid, I have no way of knowing, but, as Mr. Austin said, it would be wonderful if we could find out.

ECHOLS: What information do you have on what Ives thought about Foster as a composer?

BRUCE: It seems that he treated Foster as he treated other popular things. In the *Memos* he mentions a whole bunch of things, including revival hymns and Stephen Foster, in the same breath, and he says, "Now, the old ladies say that isn't nice"—or words to that effect. In other words, he's clearly identifying Foster with the popular side of American music in the nineteenth century.

ECHOLS: I wonder if he even thought of Stephen Foster as a composer at all, but instead really thought only of some of Stephen Foster's songs.

BRUCE: I'm assuming that he did think of Foster as a composer, at least to a minimal degree.

ECHOLS: One of the big problems of Ives research is that most of our documentation comes from after the period when he was composing. We are in the unenviable position of taking things out of the *Memos,* written in the 1930s, or out of other things written in the 1920s or even later, and applying them to the music that Ives wrote in the 1900s or the 1910s. I wish we had more in the way of letters and things from the time when Ives was writing these songs. Who knows that he wasn't already involved in creating his own myth in the 1920s and '30s?

BRUCE: Well, that could be, but we know for sure certain things in Ives's past. For example, he played, I believe, the *Variations on the Star-Spangled Banner* by Dudley Buck. Well, that is an extremely Ivesian little piece. Buck does quite a fresh and interesting thing with the tune. I think there are other examples like this, but they are few and far between and fragmentary.

Ives and Nineteenth-Century American Music

GILBERT CHASE: What is very interesting here is that perhaps for the first time in the history of American music we are seeing a composer many-dimensionally. Now, we're never going to get at an absolutely definitive portrait of Ives, any more than we're going to get at the absolutely definitive interpretation of any of his compositions. What we're going to get, though, is this many-sided view. The miracle of the thing is that Ives has been able to engage the passionate interest of so many individuals with different back-grounds—materialism, idealism, spiritualism, or anything—and they all find something to identify with in the person of Ives.

II

Ives Viewed from Abroad

*Recognition of Ives in his own country as a major composer has been fol-
lowed closely by similar recognition abroad: all-Ives concerts and radio
broadcast series are by no means unknown; an Ives Society was organized in
Amsterdam in the 1960s; books on Ives have been published in Italy, Holland, and England; the University of Keele has organized an "Ives Choir";
the first documentary films on Ives were produced in Germany. In sum, Ives
has joined a handful of other American composers—one could name few
besides Gershwin, Copland, Foster, and Cage—as a well-recognized presence
on the international musical scene. This was reflected in the Festival-Conference by the participation of a number of composers, performers, critics, and
scholars from outside the United States. Some fifteen foreign participants
were invited to prepare statements concerning their experience and views
of Ives's music, or those of their compatriots. These statements were printed
in the Festival-Conference program book and constituted a point of departure
for the panel discussion that follows here. (They are reproduced below as
Appendix I.) Chairing the panel were Earle Brown and Vivian Perlis.*

EARLE BROWN: I have spent quite a lot of time in Europe, and I know
many of the panelists very well, although some of them I know only slightly.
With some, like Hans Helms and Betsy Jolas, I've had long conversations
about American music, about Ives, about European music, about everything
—wide-ranging, exciting kinds of conversations. I've observed a great increase
in interest in American music and in Ives, especially, in the times that I
have spent in Europe. Europe is said not to be very much interested in
American music, but to a large extent Europeans *are* really interested. But
they're interested in the kind of music that is indigenously American, if
there is such a thing. They're not particularly interested in music like that
they already have. Ives is a sparkling example of a point of view and of
techniques that are not typical of Europe.

We might start by asking about your first experience of Ives—whether
it was by ear or by scores or both, or whatever it was—and how it struck you.
What was your first reaction to hearing Ives, and what was Ives's reputation,
if any, in your country at that time?

GUIDO BAGGIANI: What I felt was that Ives was a real composer. I felt that perhaps in his major works he didn't exactly know what he was doing; but I think this in itself is a very important starting point for a composer—not to be worried about the result at the moment he writes, just face some problems and try to resolve them. Never mind what happens. That's being a creator, I think. That's exactly the opposite concept of the nineteenth-century idea of a creator who always has to know exactly what the final work will be like.

MARTINE CADIEU: I learned of Ives in Venice for the first time. It was *Three Places in New England.* I discovered suddenly that strong immediateness in the music of Ives. You can recognize a whole country and a whole world—an entire universe.

ANDREJ RIJAVEC: It was in the late 1950s that I heard Ives for the first time. It was *The Unanswered Question.* I thought immediately it was a great piece, and I said, "Oh, yes, here is a composer." Then I began to think about our music histories. They are usually histories of music in Western Europe, and nowhere will you find American music. Ives appears to be an outsider. But then I thought something is really wrong with our history, and, as a music historian, I realized that history can't be written only as the history of one, two, or three nations. A sort of polycentricity should be applied: many things, many important things, have gone on in different places, at different times. I also realized that no one will ever write about all the composers in a foreign country. Each nation has to write its own history.

VIVIAN PERLIS: Yes, there are some composers who are as well known in their own countries as Ives is becoming in this country, and we don't really know them; we don't even know their names. Your mentioning *The Unanswered Question* reminded me that Betsy Jolas published an article on that work, and that made me wonder whether there are only certain pieces of Ives's music that are known outside of this country.

BETSY JOLAS: I happen to be in mid-stream or mid-ocean, having roots in both France and the United States, but I live in Paris and I did react as a European when I heard my first Ives piece, which was indeed *The Unanswered Question.* That was in 1958.

BROWN: Hans Helms's interest in Ives has been deep for a very long time; he's even done film documentaries on Ives. Hans, how did you first hear this music to which you've devoted so much time?

HANS HELMS: It was some twenty-five years ago, in 1950, in Stockholm, when I accidentally found a recording of the *"Concord" Sonata* by Mr. Kirkpatrick. That was the very first recording that was available in Europe, I think. I understood immediately that this was a music that came out of a mind that was very much interested in the continuity of society, the continuous societal process. That was what fascinated me, and that, I think, is

Ives Viewed from Abroad

what Ives is all about and what I have been writing about since I first started writing on Ives in the 1950s.

PERLIS: Hans Helms's films were the first to be done on Ives. Although shot here, they were produced outside the United States, and, curiously, the first Ives society was also established abroad. It was five or six years ago that we first heard from the Charles Ives Society in Amsterdam. They were filled with enthusiasm and with the desire to communicate about Ives. They were mainly young composers, like Louis Andriessen.

LOUIS ANDRIESSEN: The first time I heard Charles Ives was when I was a pupil at the conservatory in The Hague, around 1959. I had a very intelligent teacher, Kees van Baaren, and he had the class listen to *Three Places in New England*. We were all very impressed by the daring music, but it really didn't mean anything, it didn't have a function, it didn't influence us at that time in Holland. The influence of Charles Ives started to be felt only later: it was not until 1968 that the Charles Ives Society was founded. The gap related, I think, to a social question. The growing importance of Ives's music in Holland had directly to do with the democratic movement there, with its development after the revolution in Paris in 1968 and with the democratic movement at the universities and the conservatories. Not until this very lively period in Europe—I would say a revolutionary period—did we recognize the revolutionary aspects of Charles Ives's music.

YANNIS IOANNIDIS: I am a Venezuelan composer and conductor of Greek origin. I was born in Athens, studied in Athens and Vienna, and I first heard about Ives in Vienna. I heard *about* Ives; I didn't hear music by Ives. As far as I remember, I heard music by Ives for the first time in Athens, when Daryl Dayton was cultural attaché of the American Embassy and was presenting American music, and there I heard for the first time recordings of various works by Ives.

Our problem in Europe was that we heard too much about the myth of Ives—this tremendous character, this isolated personality, and all these things—and very little about the music. When we heard the music of Ives, I remember very clearly one thing. Nobody was indifferent; either they liked it or they didn't like it at all. You may ask how it is possible they didn't like the music of Ives. It is because, in Europe, there exists a kind of dogmatism. I mean that either you are with Stockhausen or you are with Ligeti or you are with Xenakis or you are with Kagel, and so on. Ives is with no one of these, because Ives is Ives, and this was an obstacle which prevented many people from getting nearer to his music. But I think that this is changing, little by little, because it's not difficult to discover the beauty in the works of Ives. What I would like to point out is that we need works—essays and analyses—by specialists. These are missing at the moment, and I believe they are something urgent to be done.

49

I use Ives as an example for my composition pupils: they analyze many works of well-known composers, like those I mentioned before, and then they come and say, "And now, what do I do?" I very often answer, "Do it like Ives. He didn't ask anyone. He did what he felt it was right to do. He did it in the most normal way." I mentioned dogmatism as a European problem. I find in the work and the spirit of Ives the opposite—an anti-dogmatism—as one of his most precious characteristics.

PETER DICKINSON: I have had a rather special experience because, after graduating from Cambridge, I studied at the Juilliard School for about a year and it was there that I met Ives's music. It was probably *The Un-answered Question* first. From then onward, as a composer and as one interested in new music and in American music, I became very involved in the ideas of Ives. When I wrote in 1964 for *The Musical Times* [105/1455, pp. 347–49] about the ninetieth anniversary of Ives, like most people I concentrated on his pioneering aspects. I liked the dissonant pieces, and I kept the schmaltzy early pieces out of the way of my friends in case they should laugh about them, because we weren't yet ready to understand Ives's whole output, including all of the sentimental works. But things gradually changed. For example, there's been an important underground for Ives since the days of World War II. Boulez took up Ives in 1970 and conducted *Three Places in New England* for BBC television, and many American performers have come to England to perform Ives at different times. So, by the time I wrote in 1974 for *The Musical Times* for the Ives centenary [115/1580, pp. 836–38], I was able to try to take him as a whole. I think that is what we who are not Americans must be able to do: we must take the whole Ives and, when we do, I think it will lead us toward a much larger experience in American music. We'll find music that we haven't otherwise come across.

The success story of Ives goes on. There's a one-hour documentary on BBC television today [20 October 1974]; there've been five concerts in central London; and the whole day today on Radio 3, our serious network, is devoted to American culture. Some skeptical Americans have said to me, "Really, have we got that much culture?" That's kind of a sick joke, which I find monstrous. With the tradition of New England culture and arts, it's incomprehensible that somebody should even say that as a joke. In this connection, I'd refer you to a book by Stephen Spender called *Love-Hate Relations*. It's about the British and the Americans in their literary culture, and it shows how very much more important American developments are becoming as we, in Europe, become somehow more Americanized.

What I would personally protest about is the attempt to use Ives as anything but a composer—in other words, to ally him to certain kinds of movements. He is rather a symbol to allow us to contain different kinds of experience. This is our struggle: to have the homespun and personal as well as the experimental, we must see our world whole. Ives's music acts as a symbol when we're desperately trying to reconcile opposites and different kinds of cultural crosscurrents, in Oriental music, in jazz and pop and rock, and in God knows what. All of this coming together is an aspect of our time. This is all happening at the moment, and Ives does in a way teach us that, but let's not make it explicitly political in any way.

BROWN: That's the most impressive thing about Ives to most people—that incredible breadth of relevance and the number of sources from which he draws.

KARL AAGE RASMUSSEN: I cannot claim to be one of the pioneers for Ives, even in Denmark, but I remember that in the beginning of the 1960s we had something called "The New Simplicity." That was a kind of collage music made by some composers probably not known in the States. I was working along the same line. I suddenly heard some music of Ives, and it sounded better than most of the Danish music in the style of "Pluralism," as it was also called.

BROWN: Did Ives sound "national," in the sense of American national music?

RASMUSSEN: We didn't think about that at the time.

ILHAN USMANBAS: I think my first contact with Ives's music was around 1948, in the last of my student years at the Ankara conservatory. Perhaps it was through USIS or perhaps on the radio that I found the *Second* or *First String Quartet* (I don't remember which, now), and it struck me very much. At the time I was rather more concerned with Bartók's music, and Ives was forgotten, but it's not always the first impression that is important. In 1957–58, while I was here on a Rockefeller Foundation grant, I heard more Ives and I was able to see some scores. Even so, it was through Elliott Carter's or perhaps even more Henry Brant's music that Ives's influence came to me—indirectly. Later, I found recordings of such works as *Tone Roads* and *Over the Pavements,* and I tried to see what was in them and to analyze them in my courses on modern music at the conservatory in Ankara.

I would say that Ives's overall impression on me is that he is rather special—a peculiar example, not an accomplished composer but one who shows us some possibilities in music. Even in his great works, for instance the *"Concord" Sonata* or the *Third* and *Fourth* symphonies, I always have the impression that Ives is and will go on being a special, marginal example in music history.

AUSTIN CLARKSON: I was involved with Ives for the first time in Salzburg, strangely enough, where I was studying at the Mozarteum one summer in the late 1950s. A friend of mine, an American student, had brought along *114 Songs*. I spent quite a bit of time, in addition to preparing scores for classes, looking at those songs with my friend, and I was simply astonished at what I saw. Although Ives didn't have an immediate effect on my musical studies, I felt that some day or other I would have to deal with him seriously.

It was perhaps the premiere of the *Fourth Symphony* [26 April 1965] that really made people choose sides about Ives: there were the professional composers, who saw him as wanting in various dimensions, and a large majority of the public, who had a tremendous response to him. It's quite obvious from this Festival-Conference that Ives remains a distinct threat. I think he's a threat to our professionalism. This is one matter that we have not dealt with at all, and all the discussions which try to explain the Ives "problems" miss the fact that we do not accept him as the citizen-composer that he, I think, wanted to be considered as.

One thing that occurred earlier in the Festival-Conference is symbolic of how I, at least, feel about Ives at this point. It was at the first concert, when John Kirkpatrick was coming to the conclusion of his encore, *The Seen and Unseen*, and the audience applauded before the final chord, which is a chord that requires that overtones be heard. So he silenced us peremptorily, I'm glad to say, and insisted on playing that chord again. I felt at that point, and feel now, that there are a lot of other tones about Ives that we still need to hear.

Paradoxically, this reminds me of an opposite problem in Ives, the problem of what to do with the unheard. The professional conductor, of course, feels obliged to make everything, the least note, heard. But then what happens is that, at the moment when that overtone, as I would prefer to think of it (even an unheard one), is being performed by a single *piccolista*, one cranes around to see if, indeed, it is happening, not hearing what everyone else is singing and playing and also missing the whole point of the passage—which is that, in fact, you don't hear it. Here again, we're faced with the fact that we have music that requires us to be in a transcendent frame of consciousness (or at least seeks to lead us there), and we do our best to prevent it from doing so! Whether it's in the political sense or in the ethical, aesthetic, in whatever dimension Ives is being appreciated, our categories find some ways of damping that effect, it seems to me, and I feel that the importance of Ives is to challenge all those dimensions.

DICKINSON: Hear, hear! Let's see Ives as a Thoreau, rather than a Dewey or a Wilson or a politician. In other words, as a person with a soul. Can I slip something in as a composer? If Ives is a threat to our professionalism, then there is something wrong with our professionalism and we have to reconsider it. I can recall Morton Feldman saying to me once, "Everything we use to make music kills it." Well, without necessarily going as far as that, I'm worried about Ives being a threat to any professionalism. That's surely what this Festival-Conference is about: the exploring of what is within Ives, the finding out how to chronicle it, maybe catalog it, and discover and investigate it—in other words, to find a new professionalism out of his imagination.

ALFRED HOFFMAN: A very graphic illustration of the progress in Romanian artistic life toward an acquaintance with the works of this great figure of contemporary music is that these very days, when we are here paying tribute to Charles Ives, the American Library in Bucharest is playing host to a very comprehensive American Music Week, including two substantial programs devoted to Ives's chamber music, songs, and choral pieces, interpreted by some of the most outstanding Romanian musicians.

Since you are interested in foreign performances of the music of Ives, I should like to mention the first Romanian performance of the *Second Symphony* by the Symphony Orchestra of the Romanian Radio-Television on 16 November 1967, which was conducted by Iosif Conta in Bucharest. Then *The Unanswered Question* was performed in a program of music by the composer Anatol Vieru, in April 1970. The *Piano Trio* is also very well known in Romania, since two important chamber music groups, the Musica Nova, led by Hilda Jerea, and the trio of the Gheorghiu brothers, play this piece and have toured the United States with it.

PERLIS: A number of times today *The Unanswered Question* has been mentioned. Why this particular piece? Might it be perhaps because it is less regional, less "American" in character, in that it doesn't quote recognizably American material?

HOFFMAN: Perhaps it appeals the most to the sensitivity of listeners.

BROWN: It's also not as difficult to perform as much of his other music is.

DICKINSON: I think that one of the reasons for its international importance is indeed the fact that it doesn't have quotations, but another point is that it's the Ives experience, the quintessential Ives experience, at its most simple and elementary, and it comes across to you in a very powerful way. One other point, which I've developed in a review in *The Musical Times* [115/1581, pp. 947–48] and which I haven't seen anybody else mention, is that the piece, with its different layers and levels, relates to some of the classical music that Ives played, in particular the first Mendelssohn organ sonata, which has several different levels of rapt, soft music and then loud music at the same time. I think that listeners find that *The Unanswered Question* gives them a bridge between Ives and other music of the past, whereas the unself-conscious, popular tunes in other pieces, like "The Fourth of July," may upset them. But that's only the beginning; it's only part of Ives. Ives, as we know, is big enough to be several different kinds of composers; it's the incorporation of all the kinds of composers he was, in the big pieces, which is so exhilarating and such a discovery to us all.

BROWN: That leads us almost to the even broader area of cross-influences between literature, music, painting, and sculpture. Mr. Bernlef might have something to say about that.

J. BERNLEF: Well, I'm a poet, and I came across Ives by way of written words. It was in an article by the other founder of the Charles Ives Society in Holland, Reinbert de Leeuw, about our first performance of *Three Places in New England*—in The Hague, I think it was. It was around 1966–67. When he described, for instance, the "Putnam's Camp" movement in *Three Places,* it came as a shock of recognition for me, because I was very much involved at that time with American poetry, and especially with the poetry of Marianne Moore (which I translated into Dutch) and her use of all kinds of strange materials to put into her poems and make a whole or not a whole of it. *Paterson,* the long poem by William Carlos Williams, also came to mind when I read this article of de Leeuw. I thought they all had very similar ways of working. I immediately went to a record shop. They were amazed, because they had never heard of Charles Ives. They tried to sell me a record of Burl Ives, but I said I didn't want that. So I had to wait for six weeks until the record—it was *Three Places in New England*—came from the United States.

After that, I bought the *Second Symphony* and "The Fourth of July," which is a very explosive piece. There was a little explanatory record with those, made by Leonard Bernstein. What he was saying was completely counter to my first experience: I didn't experience Ives as an especially American composer, not at all. It was just wildly exciting music; it had nothing to do with exclusively national American feelings. I was completely against the interpretation of Mr. Bernstein. I still feel that this kind of interpretation is lingering around, and I think it should be broken down so that we can see Ives as he is, just as one of the outstanding modern composers. In this putting-down of all the nationalistic feelings about Ives, I should like to quote John Cage's dedication in his book *A Year from Monday,* in which he hopes that the United States will become "just another part of the world." I think that makes very good sense.

JOHN BECKWITH: One detail of the Canadian experience of Ives that I did not mention in the little piece that I wrote for the program book of the Festival-Conference occurred to me only later. In the 1940s, Harry Somers, one of our leading Canadian composers, studied piano in San Francisco with E. Robert Schmitz. Schmitz, of course, knew Ives and played some of the piano music as early as the 1920s. He seems to have passed on firsthand impressions rather vividly to his students, and I recollect Somers talking especially of the multilevel arrangements of Ives's scores and attributing to Ives some of the effects and structures that he worked into his own music around that time. An example might be Somers's *First Symphony,* composed around 1951. I mention this because it probably antedates traces of Ives's influence in the music of other Canadians such as Udo Kasemets and Murray Schafer and Pierre Mercure.

Another small Canadian contribution which I offer for what it's worth is in the form of a literary composition. It illuminates, for me anyway, Ives's thinking in a way that Ives's thinking seems to need illuminating—by analogy. It is a poem called *The Table of Dishes* by James Raney, one of the best-known contemporary poets in English-speaking Canada. It consists mostly of a detailed description of plain items of china and cutlery used in daily meals for several generations, by both ordinary and extraordinary human beings. The cups and spoons and plates are depicted as participating in a kind of performance which reaches its apogee or climax—or perhaps one should say, in Ivesian terms, its transcendence—through an imaginary, ideal use in a ceremony resembling the Eucharist. The point is not a sectarian one, but the last lines of the poem suggest that ordinary objects, through repeated, fond use in everyday human life, can evolve into something like a state of holiness. That, to me, is certainly part of the Ives message.

PERLIS: I wonder if we might pursue this matter of quotation a bit. I think it is particularly interesting to have people from places other than the United States talk about how the Americanisms in Ives are handled by audiences.

HELMS: I don't think that they handicap the performance, no matter what the country. I rather think that these materials can be understood quite easily—the way, for example, an American musician can understand the folklore material that appears in the music of Gustav Mahler, who worked to a certain extent in a way comparable to Ives at the same time. (I think that was one of the reasons why Mahler became very much interested in the *Third Symphony* of Ives when he saw the score, by accident, in 1910 and wanted to perform it in Vienna.)

The fact is that now, in Germany, the catalogs of our radio stations list some 200 recordings of Ives works. I think there are seventy different works that are available on radio tapes, and you find Ives's music on all the symphonic programs nowadays in Germany. He is not regarded as an exotic being; he is regarded as the composer that he was, one of the great composers of the century and of musical history.

BROWN: I disagree with you that Ives's handling of indigenous or folk materials is similar to Mahler's. I think it's completely different.

HELMS: I didn't say "same." I said, "to a certain extent comparable." That's not quite the same.

RASMUSSEN: Of course, in Denmark we cannot recognize a lot of the melodies that were sung in America fifty or seventy years ago. But I don't think that's a problem, because I think that the point of this music lies in the stylistic field. I think that Ives used quotations as keys to certain styles which you can refer to. I cannot resist pointing out some resemblance between Mahler and Ives. Earle Brown said that he didn't agree about such a resemblance, but I think there is one, because I think that, in both Ives and Mahler, for the first time in musical history, we have to distinguish between what a music seems to be and what it is. Take for instance the third movement of Mahler's *First Symphony* with the famous quotation of "Frère Jacques." This melody cannot just be heard as itself. Mahler *does* something to this melody by placing it in quite another context, and that is the same in Ives. I think the main thing to understand about quotation as a whole is that it's not a matter just of recognizing something, it's a matter of hearing in which context things appear.

JOLAS: The so-called European avant-garde was first interested in what I would call the "far-out" aspect of Ives—the experimental aspect, such as twelve-tone rows and polymetric and polyrhythmic things. They were interested in the fact that these were being written before anything like them had been done in Europe. They also had to cope with the other aspect, that is to say the hymn tunes and the rags and the Foster songs, and the rest; and that troubled them and still troubles them, because they can't relate it to anything in their music. They've tried to relate it to what they thought were similar experiments by, shall we say, Ravel (the jazz elements) and the popular themes in Bartók and Berg (in *Wozzeck*), but I think that there is a great difference in the way those elements are presented. When European composers use these nonserious elements (that's what they are), they feel they have to make them undergo transformations to make them fit into their serious musical thought. It's a bit like servants being admitted to the master's living room in Sunday clothes on New Year's Eve. Ives didn't feel he had to do that at all, and these elements are brought in "democratically," in a very American way. They don't have to undergo any transformation: they come in just the way they are normally dressed; they don't have to wear nice clothes. And that's something which Europeans don't really understand, but which I can because I have American ties. I remember when Earle Brown and I were listening to a rehearsal of *Three Places in New England* in Strasbourg, and I said, "We are hearing more than the French are in this music, but you hear more than I do because you live in the United States." I think Europeans have to understand that Ives can be listened to as Oriental people listen to their theater: they know the story, they know exactly what's happening, and they are taking pleasure in hearing these things which they know.

BAGGIANI: I find it extremely dangerous to continue to speak about Americanisms in Ives, even though, of course, they are a great part of his music. There's a Chinese saying that when a wise man points the direction, silly people look at the finger. I'm afraid in the next ten years we shall have a lot of music which has to deal with, for instance, American tunes or other popular tunes, but I don't think this is the message of Charles Ives.

RIJAVEC: Speaking of Americanisms, I agree with Mr. Helms. They're not a problem, because art can be understood in many ways. You can understand Ives without knowing anything about these citations. Of course, then you can go deeper and deeper, and you'll understand him in another way.

Another thing: I don't think that the problem of European audiences is to understand the serious Ives. It's much more difficult to understand the *un*serious Ives. Here, I think, Europe can really learn a lesson. In Europe, art—written with a capital *A* and perhaps a capital *R* and a capital *T*—is a sacrosanct thing: it mustn't be touched, and whenever it appears one must fall on one's knees and worship it. Europe can't understand, or hasn't understood yet, that art can be also funny. It can be fun.

BECKWITH: I wonder if anyone has suggested a comparison, in looking at the matter of quotation, between Ives and Joyce.

BROWN: Mr. Dickinson has pointed that out in his essay for the Festival-Conference program book.

DICKINSON: It's not original, as I found after I'd finished it: Lou Harrison suggested it first, apparently, in an article in *Modern Music* [23 (Summer 1946): 167–68]. I develop the comparison at greater length in my *Musical Times* article [115/1580, pp. 836–38]. Obviously there was no direct contact or connection between Joyce and Ives in the sense of meeting, or anything like that. I used the comparison in England intentionally to emphasize the stature of Ives. I make no bones about it: I regard Ives as a great composer, alongside Schoenberg and Stravinsky, but you can't say that and get away with it in Europe yet. However, the times are changing. The Joyce-Ives question could be discussed at length, of course, especially the way in which they transmute ordinary materials into art. It doesn't matter whether we use expressions like "fine art" or "people's art"—it is all these things at once, I think. In that sense, the two men are real counterparts.

LOU HARRISON: There seems to be a problem about the transition between "fine art" and "people's art"—or maybe between "courtly" composition and "citizen" composition. Which one of you used that marvelous phrase, the "citizen-composer"? The conferring of status and sufficient money for a composer to live on used to lie in courts. Of course, when Europe became more democratic, then the courtly repertoire—Mozart and Haydn and so on—turned into a concert life, which is the term we still use. Mr. Ives, though, even avoided that aspect of it and did not join in the concert life of his time, which means that he avoided the remains of the courtly life. He presented all at once the image of the citizen-composer who, in fact, supports himself and has little to do with the power compounds of concert-giving or publication or any public performances or any public stature at all of that sort. It was some of us later who caused his work or helped his work, as it were, to enter into the stream of public consciousness. I like the phrase "citizen-composer." It seems to me to stand very well for what Mr. Ives was up to. I suggest that those of the composing fraternity who might have some trouble with Mr. Ives as a professional may be in transition between court status and citizen status.

I would like to pose a different question. Where are our Asians? Certainly Japan must play Ives.

ROGER REYNOLDS: The performance of Ives's music was extremely rare in Japan until quite recently. I had a part in organizing some concerts in the late 1960s at which we did first performances of about five or six Ives works. They were very fondly received, and large numbers of records were immediately ordered. I think that many of the leading musicians now know his music well and play it. However, that was a rather late development.

ALAN MANDEL: My wife and I have had the pleasure of playing in most of the countries that our visitors have come from. We've also discussed Ives with many people from other countries. One underlying theme in Ives which seems to attract people from other countries is that of freedom: in this day of bureaucracy and limits on personal freedom, one finds in Ives an emphasis on musical freedom, theoretical freedom, human freedom, and social freedom.

QUESTIONER: Mr. Mandel has mentioned freedom in general. I understood Mr. Andriessen to be talking, we might say symbolically, about the kind of freedom of 1968. Now, there are freedoms and freedoms. I would very much like to hear what the members of the panel (perhaps particularly Mr. Helms) have to say about this.

HELMS: Well, I think the answer can be found in the work of Ives himself, for example, the piece called *An Election*, which was written apropos of the 1920 presidential elections in the United States. This piece is about corruption; it is about Watergate and the C.I.A., so to speak—I mean, in the forms that U.S. imperialism took at that time. Ives also made a very positive contribution with his *Suggestion for a 20th Amendment* to the Constitution of the United States, in which he suggested that the President should be elected not by electors but by direct vote. This, I think, lies very close to European ideas developed about the same time which are called in Russia "Soviet Democracy" or in Germany *Realdemocratie* and which are based, of course, on Marx's and Engels's thinking, whereas Ives's ideas derived from the more individualist, anarchistic point of view that was developed in the United States by the Concord Transcendentalists, especially by Thoreau. I think this political connection that is ever-present in Ives's work has much to do with the strong influence that his music is exerting upon the minds of music-minded Europeans at the present day.

ANDRIESSEN: I have the strong feeling that this audience does not really have the habit of speaking about music in relation to politics, so I think we have to give a sort of elementary example about the production of music. The Ives Society in Amsterdam was founded during the time, as I said earlier, of the democratic movement not only in the universities but also in the musical world, the world of symphony orchestras and of young musicians. In fact, more or less at the same time we organized a very big anti–Vietnam War demonstration, which was called Musicians for Vietnam. All kinds of musicians gathered together to perform all kinds of music—from, let's say, Schubert on to pop music and avant-garde music. There was a lot of Ives performed, too. We called these occasions "inclusive concerts," which meant that they were free and that all genres of music were considered authentic—avant-garde, pop groups, performances of Charles Ives, a medieval music group, and so on. The whole atmosphere of these concerts was one of inclusivity of musical material. That had a very important influence on musical thinking, on composing, and on the organization of musical production. I think Ives would have been very happy with those concerts, because the whole thing was very nonconformist.

JOLAS: This is really getting away from the mythical Ives, but I've been trying to get Ives scores, and I came here in the hope that I would bring back a lot of them. My reason for wanting scores is that I'm very anxious to bring Ives into the official conservatory in Paris, for instance, where I think they're ready to know him. They don't know him yet—there still are two sides expressed even in that school: some people think he's a genius and that's that; some others think he's not serious and that he's only an amateur and Sunday musician. I think this is stupid: we have to get over that kind of talk and accept the fact that Ives is a great musician, quite great enough to enter that very old institution.

BROWN: It would be interesting to hear some discussion of innovation in Ives.

JOLAS: Concerning Ives's innovation, some of it may have come from the fact that he had grown terribly isolated from the professional milieu of composers, and he felt that he could just go as far as he wanted and sometimes went further than he could actually realize. I have found this absolutely fascinating. In *The Unanswered Question,* for instance, he says in the preface, about the wind parts that go faster and faster, that they should not play absolutely together, but he writes them rhythmically together. There seems to be a sort of contradiction between what he wanted and what he actually did. There is a related problem, especially for Europeans, now that there is a recording that has appeared of Ives playing his own music. It is going to make things very complicated, to look at the score and then find he's not playing exactly what's in it. What are we going to do?

59

PERLIS: John Kirkpatrick and other performers of Ives's music have told us many times that they don't see the necessity of performing Ives's music the same way each time, since Ives himself did not really seem to want it to be done that way.

JOLAS: That's something that's very hard for Europeans to understand.

PERLIS: That kind of freedom for the performer?

JOLAS: Yes, when it isn't actually indicated in the score. I mean, the score looks like a closed, written form. That's the trouble.

CADIEU: I once read a sentence by Ives that is perhaps an answer to Betsy. "Vagueness," says Ives, "is at times an indication of nearness to perfect truth."

BECKWITH: Listening to Ives's orchestral pieces, one catches this sort of heaving continuity of the piano that runs all through them; it's characteristic, and you don't find the same thing treated this way in any other music. Orchestration teachers have said that's just his lack of knowledge of the orchestra: it is bad orchestration. I was interested, in reading the general article on orchestration by Henry Brant in the new Dutton *Dictionary of Contemporary Music,* to see that some of the examples are taken from Ives. I think that illustrates how, in twenty-five years, attitudes have changed. Also, in reading just the other day the note that Ives wrote for the second movement of the *Fourth Symphony,* I realized that it could almost have been written by Brant, because it has to do with the sort of planar distinctions in the music that Brant would make.

HELMS: I would like to put on the record a very strange historical coincidence. There was a double first performance in Germany in 1956 by the West German Radio Symphony Orchestra, with Michael Gielen conducting *The Unanswered Question* and *Central Park in the Dark,* which, as you know, are both for separated orchestral groups. At the same time, Karlheinz Stockhausen was writing a big orchestral piece—actually it was the very first one he ever wrote—for a very large orchestra of over a hundred players. At that point, it was to be a piece for one big orchestra, although the lines of the individual players were very independent. Then this Ives concert came along and all of a sudden, a few months later, out came *Gruppen für Drei Orchester,* the very famous piece by Stockhausen. I once tried to get him involved in discussing this coincidence. I saw him at the Gielen concert, so he must have heard those pieces, and I don't think he is one of those people who sleeps on his ears, but he never admitted that Ives ever influenced him in the tiniest bit. Actually, it's only a superficial influence, but the idea of not only diversifying the orchestra into individual lines, but also diversifying it spatially, can without any doubt, I think, be traced back from Stockhausen to Ives.

DICKINSON: Can we look at some John Cage examples? The piece that immediately comes to mind in extending some of the ideas of Ives with many different levels is, of course, Cage's *Music Circus,* where many pieces, many concerts happen: you just put them under the same roof and let them take place. This seems to me to be an Ivesian idea. Cage doesn't, of course, write a single note down. He develops something of a procedure, but that puts him in a way in a direct line with some of Ives's ideas (as opposed to some composers who may only imitate Ives's sound).

HOFFMAN: We must clearly acknowledge the debt to certain aspects of Ives's music and aesthetic thinking owed by some Romanian composers. The most typical example, I think, is Anatol Vieru, who introduced *The Unanswered Question* as part of a concert which otherwise included only his own works. He has insisted on pointing out the seminal effect which his knowledge of the American maestro's creation has had on molding his own personality. I should especially like to mention in Vieru's music a type of construction, determined by a certain philosophical and musical vision, inspired by Ives. On a sound track with a uniform and continuous pulsation—a sort of symbol of the abstract flow of time, which we could call the "master tape"—other musical events are superimposed, each of them having its own course and time. Vieru calls such events "ephemerides"—fragments which may range from folk riddles, nursery songs, and carols to more abstract formulas, each of them belonging to a different emotional world. This type of organization appears in *Clepsydra 1,* for orchestra, and in *Clepsydra 2,* which, however, utilizes a choir, together with panpipes and dulcimer, for the ephemerides. The same thing, though employing different means, is found in Vieru's *The Land of Stone*, where there is a continuous electronic background upon which ostentatiously concrete ephemerides are superimposed.

CADIEU: I might mention a French composer named Luc Ferrari, who is often played in Germany and who uses the kind of collage or *rapportage* that we sometimes find in Ives. Ives is very powerful because he has a great love of man and he can put in his music the noises, the sounds, and the cries of people working, enjoying, loving, and everything: that is part of his music —the part of *rapportage*.

BROWN: A recent comment about Ives by Pierre Boulez really stimulated me: "The origin of his music, of his invention, is to be found in the surroundings of his life, and from this point of view it is impossible to establish Ives's evolution." I have a tremendous respect for Boulez, but I do think this indicates the European attitude toward musical evolution: life surroundings are not to be considered as related to evolution; evolution should be traceable through previous music, in the sense of technique and technical matters. I think that Ives and other American composers feel that their evolution includes more than the counterpoint, fugue, and so on that they studied.

BAGGIANI: I wonder if Ives wouldn't agree with Boulez in a certain way. I mean, I wonder if he didn't have a certain guilty conscience. On the one side was the fantastic musician that we know; on the other side, he was strangely fond of fugue. Perhaps this is the worst side of Ives; I think his fugues are boring, frankly.

BROWN: Boring? The fugues are boring?

BAGGIANI: The fugue of the *Fourth Symphony* I can't understand. What does it mean, this fugue in the *Fourth Symphony?*

QUESTIONER: It's a pure assumption, because I don't think that Ives has commented on it literally, but I think that his putting the fugue there has the meaning of a critique of music. I think that, in this, Ives is a very modern artist, because his art is not just music, it's also a critique on music, on what has happened before, on the musical definitions and behavior of the past. I think this all played through Ives's mind when he put the fugue in the *Fourth Symphony.*

JOLAS: I think fugues, ever since Bach, have been boring as fugues, and they appear in music all through those centuries—except for Beethoven, perhaps—as though the composer were saying, "I'm a serious musician and I know how to write." I mean, they have to do that. I think Ives did that too, to a certain extent.

BAGGIANI: I think so, too.

DICKINSON: I don't agree with you. I think that in the *Fourth Symphony* and the *Second Quartet* the fugues destroy the idea that the composer must sound the same all through the piece—that sort of stylistic homogeneity of the European tradition. Here you've got a composer who's big enough to write different kinds of music in the same piece, and it's *his piece.* That's what's marvelous. Joyce could do this, too. This is a lesson to Europeans. I might go so far as to say that this is one of the greatest breaks with tradition, one of the greatest expansions, since the birth of polyphony. Because, instead of having more than one part at once, you now have more than one kind of music. This is something which Ives virtually invented and which Cage's *Music Circus* also embodies. This is why it's so shattering to us and why it's such an incredibly new experience. Composers will find we've got something to explore for a hell of a long time into the future, offering an enormous amount of new material.

RASMUSSEN: I think that Ives incidentally commented on that fugue, in relation to the whole symphony's being about the eternal question "Why?" in life. The second movement is some ·sort of an answer, and the third movement, the fugue, is another sort of answer—the one Rollos would give to the "Why?"

WILLIAM BROOKS: What Ives writes about the symphony (but it's more complicated than that, because he didn't actually write it, although there's every reason to believe that he approved of the program notes) is essentially this: "The symphony is an expression of the what, why, and how which the spirit of man asks of life." Then he says that this is particularly the sense of the Prelude. Then he says that the succeeding two movements are the diverse answers with which existence responds. Then, with reference to the third movement, which is the fugue, he says, "This is an expression of the reaction of life into ritualism and formalism."

I'm particularly interested in the fact that, in that description of the piece, Ives starts out by saying that the symphony, *as a whole,* is an expression of the questions, then says particularly the first movement. That means that the second and third movements, although they may be answers to the first movement, are also new questions; and the problem thereby posed by the work is not merely "Which of these is correct?"—which is the line of questioning we fall into when we say, "Is it a parody of a fugue? Is it a good fugue? Is it a bad fugue? What does it mean?" The point is not that it is correct, incorrect, wise, foolish, good, bad, or indifferent. The point is that, in some way or other, it demands that we reconcile it with what came immediately before. And it is because of that demand—a demand that we act upon the material and that we use the material in a way which is appropriate to us and which will bring it together for us in a political and social way which we had not previously been able to achieve—that the work, to my mind, is both an artistic and a political success.

ANDRIESSEN: Actually, perhaps Ives was just somebody who looked around very carefully when he was walking in the streets. It's like the aesthetic that was developed after World War II among painters like Jasper Johns and Robert Rauschenberg and also by such musicians as Cage—just accepting what is in the outside world, also accepting an aesthetic of the outside world in the art world. It does away with the division between art and life. Ives is, in that mentality, a precursor. I think that, for him, it was very simple to put all kinds of things together. He just didn't mind, I think, and that's the marvelous thing about it.

III

On Editing Ives

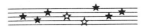

Editors' Experiences

Virtually none of Ives's music was published during his years as an active composer, which ended about 1925. In the 1920s and '30s a few scores were published, e.g., a movement of the Fourth Symphony *in 1927 and the* Set for Theatre or Chamber Orchestra *in 1932 (both in Henry Cowell's New Music Edition), a chamber orchestra version of* Three Places in New England *in 1935, and* Psalm 67 *in 1939. By the 1940s, when Ives's star began to rise and more consistent, intensive publication of his music was possible, his manuscripts were in a dreadful jumble and he was too old and infirm to attend to their preparation for the press by himself. Several able musicians assisted him during his last years, among them Henry Cowell and Lou Harrison, but much of his music was still unpublished at his death, and it became apparent, when his manuscripts were finally gathered together, collated, and catalogued (by John Kirkpatrick in 1960), that there remained much work to be done before proper editions could be arrived at. For many reasons, there is still much work to be done; among them are the facts that Ives's habitual rethinking, revising, rearranging, even recomposing his music has proved a thumb-to-the-nose at the tidy aims of music editors, and that his cheerful offering of all kinds of alternatives to performers extends also to editors, defying them to achieve that "correct" or "definitive" edition they tend to wish for so much.*

Recognition of the special editorial problems of Ives's music led to their becoming one of the main themes of the Festival-Conference. It was addressed in two panel discussions; the one that follows, chaired by Alan Mandel, had as panelists three musicians deeply involved in editing Ives's music (one might almost say three generations of Ives editors): Lou Harrison, John Kirkpatrick, and James Sinclair.

JOHN KIRKPATRICK: I would like to make a few preliminary remarks on problems of editing Ives in general and on my experience with certain pitfalls, certain temptations. They add up to the conviction that one can read between the lines only when one has read the lines very, very thoroughly. The procedure that my own goofs have forced me into is a complete comparison of sources of whatever item I hope to edit. That means a definition of each available source and how the various sources relate to each other. If you're very lucky, you may be able to dope out the chronological order that they represent. You may not be able to. Then you proceed, just like a dutiful grad student, to assemble a kind of parade of thoroughness, and you note that "X has F-sharp" and "Y has F-natural," and so forth. If you're thorough, you compile a kind of assessment of the differences between sources. These may be purely mechanical and may not tell you very much; on the other hand, you also unearth those differences which really do reveal answers to textual questions. You're very lucky if you have been able to dope out the chronology of events, because then you can see that Ives started out, maybe, with this kind of idea, this kind of a flow or a melodic curve, and later on he got fascinated with such-and-such a kind of added dissonance, maybe.

I remember one time he had given me photostats of the end of "Hawthorne," and I faced him with an octave which showed up in the manuscript between two A-sharps in the course of the counterpoint; but in the first printing of *"Concord,"* there was A-sharp against A-natural. I showed him this octave of two sharps in his own hand, and he first tried to say, "Well, that doesn't look like a sharp." I told him, "It looks like this other sharp." He finally burst out, "I couldn't possibly have written that. It makes an octave!" It was perfectly obvious that, in his initial concept, he had accepted the way the two lines of the counterpoint evolved into this momentary octave, but later on he couldn't accept it. Thus between the 1911 ink manuscript of "Hawthorne" and the first private printing in 1920, he decided he wanted this stepped-up dissonance there. To my ears, as the lines naturally evolve the plain octave is much preferable to the stepped-up dissonance. That isn't always the case. Sometimes, those added touches of his are real touches of genius, but sometimes they are his getting in his own way. You have to sort of tread lightly to find out which is which, but you can only do this when you know your sources pretty thoroughly and have done perhaps the inner equivalent of a conscientious and systematic comparison of sources. Then you have a right to try to see behind the notes and, as I naïvely say, "try to make like Charlie."

Now, I have just a few observations on the *"Concord"* Sonata that will string along and perhaps provide something that will listen a little bit like a paper.

First, in approaching *"Concord"* the fact that is inescapable is the vast extent of the source materials. The history of it is something like this. It really all started with Ives's grandmother's enthusiasm for Emerson. She imparted that to her family and her sons, the youngest of whom was Ives's father. He was the kind of musician who went one degree further than Emerson in his application of transcendentalist thought to music. I remember talking with an old violinist in Danbury, who had actually played baseball with Ives on the team called the Alerts, and he told me how, when he was a boy playing under George Ives's direction, he was constantly amazed at how George Ives would be perfectly content to have others conduct, while he sat down among the violins. This man (I can't remember his name and I'm ashamed of myself because I liked him—he's a blessed memory now, of course) couldn't understand how George Ives, being such a consummate musician, could be perfectly happy being conducted by somebody who was so much less a musician. I think that's just part of an acceptance of "life in the round," so to speak—being perfectly happy that somebody else has a chance to have something to do as a springboard toward any kind of growth, and believing that the inner spirit, or what Emerson would call the "over-soul," would operate in all of them appropriately. Of course Ives inherited that, too, and that is really the mainspring of the whole *"Concord" Sonata,* the different mental attitudes and growths and outgrowths of the transcendentalist point of view.

In terms of the actual music, first there were the prototypes. They started in Ives's work with the *Orchard House Overture* of 1902 and '04, probably. All datings in Ives are problematical. It's not that you can't believe a word he says because he was a liar. He was not a liar, but he had a very sly sense of humor and a very acute New England sense of privacy, and often he'd just throw smoke in your face. For instance, after he'd absorbed the fugue on "Greenland's Icy Mountains" into the *Fourth Symphony,* he didn't want anybody to know that it had been in the *First String Quartet,* because that was his own private information; so he took the second, third, and fourth movements of the *First String Quartet* and tried to make the heading "2" look as if it had always been a "1" and tried to make the "3" look as if it had always been a "2," but didn't do so well trying to transform "4" into "3." That was his point of view, and I'm sure that if Charles Ives, in his incarnation, had known that I was going to restore the fugue as the first movement of the *First String Quartet,* he would have been absolutely furious. He'd probably have kicked me out of the house, but I can't help believing that now, as a discarnate soul, he probably feels less angry about it and probably has a sort of affectionate, retrospective view of his youth that cheerfully accepts the way these things happen and the way they contributed to his own growth.

The *Orchard House Overture* is unfortunately entirely lost, except for a half-page of score sketch, and that was the basis for the "Alcotts" movement. Then in 1907, apparently, he embarked on an "Emerson overture" in the medium of a piano concerto, the orchestra being the people and the piano Emerson speaking. That, of course, was recomposed into the "Emerson" movement of *"Concord."* What sketches there were toward orchestral versions of "Hawthorne" and "Thoreau" is anybody's guess. Either it never got beyond an idea or else the sketches are missing. Then in 1910 he got the idea of the *"Concord" Sonata* and started recomposing these things. "Hawthorne" was finished in October of that year, "Emerson" in 1911–12, and in 1912 he was playing the whole thing—but improvising a few passages that hadn't focused yet—for his friend Max Smith, who was a newspaper music critic. By 1915, those improvised passages had focused, and he always dated the "Thoreau" movement as 1915, although of course it was quite a bit earlier. During the convalescence from his heart attack of 1918—that is, in 1919—he finished the ink copy of the whole thing, the clear copy, and also finished the *Essays.* (How much he had done on the *Essays* before that is anybody's guess.) The sonata was engraved in 1920, and the *Essays* appeared in 1920 but the sonata not until 1921. (He wrote—I think it was to Henry Franklin Belknap Gilbert—that he found that proofreading music was harder than proofreading prose.) Those copies of the first printing were out early in 1921. As soon as they were out, he regretted the slight simplifications he had made for the ink copy of 1919 and started to complicate some of them. There are, I think, fourteen copies of that first printing, or fragments of them, with his pencil revisions entered in here and there, all slightly different. They later became the basis of the revised edition, or some of them did—probably as many as he could find, because his music manuscripts were chronically in such a state of disorder that he often couldn't find things. (I remember he told me about certain little revisions that he just couldn't find, and when I finally got to his manuscripts in the summer of 1954, I saw why.)

I think that in 1915 he had already started to experiment with a short piece formed out of the beginning of the "Emerson" movement, more as it had been in the overture; that was the first of the so-called Emerson transcriptions. Shortly after the first printing of the sonata was out, say in 1922 or '23, he added three more.

This is a kind of magazine serial outline of the "Emerson" movement. It's very curious with Ives that once he had achieved this large curve of the "Emerson" movement—and to my ears it's one of his greatest triumphs—there began the adjusting of the old "sonata machine," as Virgil Thomson used to call it, to the material that he had there, vastly diverse and necessarily fairly episodic. Still, the form of the "Emerson" movement is so tight, it's just like the span of steel of an enormous bridge, or like Eero Saarinen's St. Louis arch. Just as soon as he had finished it, however, he was no longer interested in it and he destroyed it and took it apart, just the way he destroyed the profile on him for the *New Yorker* that Lucille Fletcher wrote (and so, unfortunately, her original form of that is no longer extant). Anyway, there are all these different things in the "Emerson" movement.

Then, along in 1916 the "Hawthorne" movement gave rise to the second movement of the *Fourth Symphony* and then, later on, perhaps around 1923 (that's anybody's guess, too), to *The Celestial Railroad,* which was a kind of reworking for piano of elements from "Hawthorne" and also from the *Fourth Symphony,* principally the solo piano part but drawing on other elements from it, too.

That's about all until the various proofs toward the revised edition. Work on that started right after the first public performance of *"Concord"* and Gilman's review in 1939, which pronounced *"Concord"* the greatest music any American had written. There were clamors for a reprint, but Ives, of course, was a little self-conscious about the early printing and wanted to do all kinds of revising on it. He asked me to do it first, but I was so enamored at that time of the first printing that I didn't understand some of the touches that he wanted put in and, being afflicted with a good deal of stasis temperamentally, I just procrastinated. He was very impatient—he was always a person living in the present—and so he did it all himself, with some copying help from George Roberts. There were seven different proofs: I remember around 1942, I think (maybe it was in '40), asking Harrison Kerr how it was coming along, and he told me, with a tremor in his voice, "Mr. Ives has been putting in sharps and flats and taking them out again *all* summer." So those seven proofs toward the revised edition are fairly different. Then, finally, there was the revised edition.

I started out using the old privately printed first edition and some of the variants that Ives wanted me to use, but by the time I'd been playing it a little, it was just the other way around. In 1940, or maybe '41, Mrs. Ives brought me an extra copy of the third proof. That was my bible, so to speak, for a while, and so a year or two after that I was playing from that more, just restoring a few details from the old first printing. You see the multiplicity of sources. With *"Concord,"* there's an awful lot to go on.

I think it is the implicit duty of anybody setting out to learn *"Concord"* to just see for himself. Of course, that may be geographically a difficult and expensive thing to do—to support oneself in New Haven if your home base happens to be someplace like Spokane. It is something to have the luxury of operating like a library bookworm and going through these things and seeing what's what, but, in the ideal picture, it's the only thing to do.

ALAN MANDEL: Photostats of some of the original sources do exist in the Library of Congress in Washington and in the Lincoln Center Library in New York.

KIRKPATRICK: Yes, thank you for that reminder. Unfortunately, photostats are only so much use. The fainter pencil strokes seldom come out with the kind of precision or focus that gives you real confidence in banking on them and deducing from them, particularly where Ives has written something over something else. For instance, when he wrote dates, it was often "September something-or-other, 1894," and that something-or-other might be 24 with maybe 26 written over that and maybe 18 written over *that*. I remember Mrs. Ives telling me that, from time to time, he would have this determination to get things right, and all these multiple datings were on the way toward getting down to getting things right. But he never was really able to. Even before his heart attack he was a composer on nights, weekends, vacations; and after his heart attack he was a sort of semi-invalid. In the thirties he wrote John Becker saying that he wanted to send him a patch of a certain detail in *General Booth,* and he wrote that to copy out those three measures it took him an hour and twenty minutes. He could do only so much, and then he'd have to rest his eyes and himself generally (he always had a couch in his music room), and so it took him that long to copy out those measures in his little "snake tracks." As a result, he never got around to these things. And he had no instinct for weighing the merits of different readings. He had a kind of scorn for what he had done in the past—typical of a person who lives always in the present. For him, the last manuscript or last version of anything was automatically the best. He didn't realize, for instance, that in the *Third Violin Sonata*'s second movement, in those passages which are marked "Repeat if ragged," he had obliterated the original version by his ragged version, which he had sort of scrawled over in heavy ink so that you can no longer see the thing that you were supposed to rag. You have to go back to his first ink manuscript to see what that had been.

MANDEL: How do you feel about the idea that the last version is the best? Do you ever change the versions when you play the *"Concord" Sonata?*

KIRKPATRICK: Yes, and sometimes I find I have just been deaf, dumb, and blind to many details and haven't appreciated them. For instance, there's one place in "Hawthorne," at the end of the third "chaos," where a sequence goes down, and, at the last sixteenth note before the march, the sequence is broken to avoid an anticipation of the F-natural in the march. It goes this way:

"Concord" Sonata, second movement ("Hawthorne"), page 35, measure 2. © 1947 by Associated Music Publishers, Inc. Used by permission.

I always used to think, "Oh, far better just to let the sequence be and let the idea compose Ives, so to speak, rather than have Ives disrupt the normality of the sequence," so I always used to keep the sequence consistent. But then I saw that, really, it was better to play Ives's F-sharp so that the F-natural in the march is fresher.

Why must the F be that fresh? On the other hand, why should the sequence be that consistent? Why not have it with a little quirk before the march sets in? Nowadays I like to keep the original altered sequence and let the F that starts the march be that fresh. But these things are not cut and dried; they're not black and white in any way. Perhaps growth is a matter of "Well, I've done this. Now let's see what this would be like."

MANDEL: Didn't Ives also take that point of view? I remember you told me that sometimes you would play the *"Concord"* Sonata for Ives, and it would be a little frustrating, since he would sometimes change things.

KIRKPATRICK: Yes, but you're flattering me: there was only one time. I started to play *"Concord"* for Ives, desperately wanting, of course, his critique on the way I was doing it. But he didn't want to go back to that old stuff; all he wanted to do was to show me other things that had subsequently grown out of the *"Concord"* material. So he played me *The Anti-Abolitionist Riots* and some of *The Celestial Railroad* and some of "Hawthorne" and other things. I'm not quite sure what they were—probably other cadenzas in the old concerto. It was marvelous—marvelous for the general character of the music—but absolutely no use for what I was trying to do, namely trying to focus the communicability of those four movements so they'd be just as strongly cohesive as possible.

You asked me about the "last version." I do often find that Ives's first idea was best. Painters often say that a sketch, even a pencil sketch toward a painting, is apt to have a freshness that somehow the painting never quite preserves. I think the first state of a musical idea is apt to have that freshness, too, even if it's that kind of simplicity that Ives had no use for subsequently. Once in a conversation with him I inadvertently used the word *simplicity*. There was an explosion that went on for about two minutes, all about simplicity being a cloak for mental laziness, and it ended up, "Argh, damn simplicity!" He could really growl and roar with his voice like that. It was almost frightening sometimes, the intensity that took hold of him, and the intensity with which he took hold of the whole situation. It was as some people tell you, that in a moment of great purpose or great intensity a man's aura can swell to fill a whole room.

MANDEL: I'd like to ask James Sinclair to talk about his work on *Three Places in New England*.

JAMES SINCLAIR: You may know that *Three Places* had its genesis as a symphony for full orchestra. By 1914 there existed a full orchestration, but by 1929 the work still had not been performed this way, even though we have indications that there might have been some contemplation of this, since some string parts with a few markings by Ives on them do exist.

Let me run down the chronology of each of the three movements, since each of them up to a certain point was independent. In 1903, *Country Band March* and the *Overture and March: 1776* were composed separately, possibly as incidental music for *Major John André,* a play by Ives's uncle, Lyman Brewster. We're fairly sure that *1776* was the overture to that, and possibly *Country Band* was to serve as entr'acte music. Both of those works were to end up together later, dovetailed and recomposed into the very popular "Putnam's Camp," the middle movement of *Three Places.*

It wasn't until 1908 that more steps toward *Three Places* were taken. On 30 June 1908, the first day that the Iveses, recently married, were at 70 West 11th Street in New York City, Ives sketched a musical impression that would later be called "The Housatonic at Stockbridge" and become the third movement of *Three Places.* It was based on the experience of hearing church singing across a misty river while on a Sunday morning walk near Stockbridge, Mass., on one of the last days of their honeymoon.

Then, in 1911, Ives began to work on a "black march," a tribute to the first black regiment in the Union Army, the 54th Regiment. Later this was to be titled "The St. Gaudens in Boston Common," referring to the very impressive relief in front of the State House in Boston. In 1912, Ives took the first step toward an orchestral set by orchestrating in full the "St. Gaudens" on oblong score paper. In that same year "Putnam's Camp" was fashioned out of *Country Band* and *1776* into a Fourth of July piece in which the middle section has a dream sequence inspired by material in *1776,* but recomposed. The beginning of "Putnam's Camp" is *Country Band* material, the middle is more or less *1776,* and the very end of the piece is *1776.* It goes back and forth; it's really remarkable how he put them together and how successful it is. Then, in 1913, "The Housatonic at Stockbridge" was orchestrated in full from what had been at first sketches toward some kind of chamber work. It seems to have been for horns, organ, and some violins—a rather small chamber piece, perhaps for use in church. In 1914, "Putnam's Camp" was orchestrated.

The three pieces sat in that state until 1929, when in July Ives wrote to Nicolas Slonimsky to offer a special arrangement of *Three Places in New England* reduced from the full orchestra score. At that time Slonimsky had a fine group of about twenty-four musicians in Boston, so Ives reduced the work to chamber orchestration. The method Ives used to make this successful was to have a pianist take on immense burdens to replace brass parts. By fall, Ives had reworked his orchestration (and made many compositional revisions while doing it). On 16 February 1930, Slonimsky gave a reading of

Three Places before the American Committee of the International Society for Contemporary Music in New York City. The full premiere was on 10 January 1931, when Slonimsky conducted his Boston Chamber Ensemble in the chamber orchestra arrangement of *Three Places*. It was in Town Hall in New York City, and Ives attended. The work was subsequently performed in Boston, Havana, and Paris in that same year. In 1933, Slonimsky persuaded C. C. Birchard to publish the work; it was the first major orchestral work of Ives to be published complete.

The first group to do *Three Places* with full orchestra (using the chamber orchestra score, unfortunately) was the Boston Symphony under Richard Burgin, in 1948. They started the trend of doing it with the full string section, which really puts the work out of balance; I think that the Birchard score sounds best in chamber orchestra.

In August 1972 I came to New Haven and spoke with John Kirkpatrick about what major Ives projects lay ahead, and he suggested I try to restore *Three Places* to its original full-orchestra form. It took fourteen months to ferret out its history and understand all the complications of the revisions that are on top of each other. The sorting of manuscript leaves was a particularly difficult job, because some of them were missing, and what there were showed two histories, one up to 1914, the other after 1929. The history preceding 1914, when Ives copied the work out for himself and had a complete symphony on three separate but similar oblong scores, also included all of the preceding sketch materials, among which were early sketches that were often snippets on one or another leaf of some other work—sometimes a song with a cover page that had been used for a sketch (for example, *The Celestial Country*, which has the first sketch of ideas for "The Housatonic"). And there were scores, typically a pencil score and perhaps an ink version, on three or four staves with a good number of instrumental ideas, which must have been pretty clean in 1914. But when Ives wanted to do the revision for Slonimsky many years later, in 1929, he had gone back to the sketch materials, not the full score—right back to the sketches, with a pencil, sometimes on top of ink, but unfortunately at times pencil. That really confused the issue: new ideas laid right on top of old ones; simple rhythms complicated with rag ideas; single lines now doubled in fourths, now doubled in thirds, now complicated with new lines on top of that; the bass line obfuscated with a half-step doubling or a major seventh; and other things like that. There's a grand C-major chord that appears in "St. Gaudens" toward the end, at one of the climaxes, in which, in the revision of 1929, a B-natural was added in the French horn that makes the chord sound totally different; that's only one example of his adding dissonance during the process of revision.

My whole job, then, was to study all of these revisions and find what related to the later score, and then to make a full description of every page of this material and try to describe what on each page could be considered the earlier version and what was most probably a revision for the later version. Once all of that was done, and once I was satisfied that this material was straightened out historically, then the actual edition was fashioned.

The first movement was in pretty good shape. It's a very lightly scored movement, very profound, low-pitch oriented, with *ostinati* in the bass and very dark sounds, over which a certain amount of melodic material is fairly clear on top. It didn't require many instruments, and when it was reorchestrated for Slonimsky, it was fairly successful in that form and didn't lose a lot of weight. However, here the finest details are extremely important, and an absolute revelation came about when Vivian Perlis discovered, during one of her interviewing sessions, that Goddard Lieberson had the original manuscript full score of "St. Gaudens." I had been working from what remained of Ives's old positives of this score and had never seen several of the pages.

The second movement is a very full orchestra work. Its original full-orchestra score had been somewhat inexplicably cut in many places into small patches which Kirkpatrick has described as being in a state of "lacework"—an advanced state of lacework, as a matter of fact. So the picture is rather incomplete. The music is going along and the horns are playing, and then suddenly the material is gone. You can extend these ideas up to the point where structurally an orchestration would have had to change character; then, if you're lucky, there are a few measures of full score later on, and you can work backward from that point, even though you don't have the original orchestration.

The last movement was also in pretty good shape, although there's a remarkable switch where, in the 1914 version, Ives left a very thin texture. If you know "The Housatonic," you know all of its wandering lines and layered violin lines, watery pictures, and meandering chromatics, all adding up to this great picture of mists and the river's swirls. Those lines are written out in the 1908 sketches in very complete form and yet, for some reason, not worked out in the 1914 version. But they are back in the score in the 1929 revision. One discovery in working with this movement was that a mysterious black hole, so to speak, became apparent: there was a score that there was no real mention of, only notes to the copyist, Mr. Price, to do such-and-such with some material in "The Housatonic." Apparently, having made a rather simplified score of "The Housatonic" in about 1914, Ives almost immediately decided to restore these lines and gave notes to Mr. Price, but we do not have a score. (I've come upon similar notes to Mr. Price, without a score, for the *Second Orchestral Set*—Ives up to his old tricks!) The "Price score" is known only by the memos about it, but I've hypothetically decided what must have been in the score by those memos. It was a revision that must have nearly agreed with the 1929 score, the one that was published in 1933.

So the editing problems of *Three Places* were most difficult in the second movement. The first-movement changes are very delicate, but of course the movement itself is, so they are of major importance even though they are delicate. Since so much of the sound depends on the strings here, I'll give an example of adjusted string writing for the full orchestration. In Slonimsky's group Ives could expect no more than three or four violins on a part, so he had to abandon his original plan of intricate *divisi* and special effects. Out the window went his shading of lighter upper *divisi* against fuller lower lines, three-part solo *divisi* harmonics (transferred to piano), and simultaneous arco and pizzicato. These kinds of orchestral effects, then, are restored to the full score.

In the second movement, all of the brass are restored and what I would call the *con blasto tutti*'s (it's a phrase that Ives used at least once) are very much more powerful, if also thicker. I think that's characteristic, though, and it's a very successful noisy movement. Having been theater orchestra music in the first place (in its first incarnation as *Country Band* and *1776*), "Putnam's Camp" sounds perhaps less fresh than they do; there's less weight, more impact to the small group. But one can hardly deny the infectiousness of the music and that marvelous picture which, in such a short time, goes through such a display of genius, of imagination, of childlike vision.

The last movement also takes a large orchestra, although much of it is successful even in the chamber orchestra version, since the string lines of the chamber score still work out in full orchestra with that same marvelous bed of watery sounds, and the English horn solo over it can be effected well in a small orchestra. However, toward the end, when the waters begin to rush and the spring swells are pictured, the full orchestra makes an immense difference in the amount of sound.

WILLIAM BROOKS: I was interested to hear that you found a kind of "black hole," as you called it, with respect to the *First Orchestral Set,* because I have found a similar one in my work with the *Fourth Symphony.* There is reference to an oblong score—in this case not a score made by a copyist but one made by Ives—which was evidently given to a copyist for use in making a copy, and it disappeared thereafter; that is, it's no longer referred to in connection with later copies. I'm wondering whether this is even more generally a problem than we know. There's at least a remote possibility that some of these black holes may not be so black after all, if we could just track down the copyists, or others, who might still have that material.

KIRKPATRICK: The only copyist I know is George Roberts, and he told me that he never kept anything, he always took everything back to Ives—whatever Ives had given him, including his pencil copy and the beautiful

Three Places in New England, second movement ("Putnam's Camp"), page 27, measures 27–30; full orchestration edition by James Sinclair. © 1976 by Mercury Music Corp. Used by permission.

Three Places in New England, second movement ("Putnam's Camp"), page 27, measures 27–30; chamber scoring by Nicolas Slonimsky. © 1935 by Mercury Music Corp. Used by permission.

copy made by the guy whose name he can't remember (I call him Copyist 18). So, if any of *those* materials are absent, it's simply that Ives destroyed them as no longer necessary. He could do that. He could shilly-shally between being a magpie and being a thrower-away. It was very curious.

QUESTIONER: Balance is one of the great problems that I have found in Ives's orchestral music and I'm terribly interested to hear what Mr. Sinclair has done with *Three Places*. There are many questions that come to mind. Would it be legitimate, for instance, to use a combination of chamber sound and full orchestral sound in performances of such works? For instance, in "Thanksgiving" there's a place where two violins play a solo near the end and the brass are blasting away—as you said before, *con blasto*. It's very difficult to know how to balance this. You can do different things in recordings: you can use a special microphone, for instance, but in concert many of these things are lost on me, and I think on the audience as well. What would you suggest?

SINCLAIR: Well, at moments, perhaps, you could divide your orchestra and use fewer strings; but it's true in all of Ives's works that there are these moments where he has very intentionally made thick fabrics and dense textures out of these many, many little things, not all of which are to be sensed as "first level." He's given ample evidence of his interest in those levels by bringing things up and submerging others at different times. No matter how interesting or amusing those things on the lower levels may be, they are meant to be only part of a lifelike texture. You know that across the street there are typewriters running, even though you don't really hear them. In Ives's mind, there was a similar reality in his music, I'm sure. I'm not enthusiastic about tune-hunting in Ives—that is, trying to bring out the most obvious quotation just because it's there. There may be nonquotational elements on the top that Ives has marked louder than something very familiar below them. I don't believe that changing all of the textures just to bring a tune out is what he wanted. In the *Fourth Symphony,* there are places where he saw fit to indicate the levels, six or so, with letters—A, B, C, D—instead of dynamics; this was a real innovation, by the way. Often a problem of balance is more a problem in our heads than in Ives's; we're trying to get something he didn't necessarily want all the time. I think that, often, simply observing what he asks for will give the sound that he was looking for.

MANDEL: I would like to present the person who did the original work on Ives's *First Piano Sonata:* Lou Harrison.

HARRISON: My whole growth and development in the matter of Ives are very different, I think, from most of those present, because I was geographically in another region. I was growing up in California, in San Francisco, when I had my first contact with the music and the idea and the phenomenon which are Mr. Ives. It came through Henry Cowell, as it did to so many other people—through his beautiful book, the symposium *American Composers on American Music,* a wonderful book to this day, through the publications of *New Music,* through the recording that Mr. Slonimsky made for New Music Recordings, and, as well, through something that Cowell alerted me to— Bernard Herrmann's broadcast of that marvelous fugue.

Then, of course, I became greedy. (All young composers are.) I wanted more of Ives, so I asked Henry how I could get more, and Henry said, "Why don't you write Mr. Ives?" and gave me his address, and I did write to him, and not too long afterward a crate of music arrived. I'm not kidding, it was a crate; in those days there was wood to do these things with. It contained, besides eleven volumes of chamber music, the *Third Symphony,* the *First Quartet,* the *First Piano Sonata,* and a marvelous torn-up version of *"Concord."* (The "Emerson" movement, in a new version, was put into a copy of the remainder of the *"Concord,"* but the original movement had been torn out. I was not to see that.) There were numerous other volumes of music. I was, at this time, mid-adolescent, and I lived with this music as a library. I simply went through it all—at the piano and studying it silently— for year after year. I was living with the material for about a decade, I'd say. Incidentally, when the crate arrived, we read privately the *First Quartet* and I began playing the *"Concord,"* parts of it; the "Emerson" transcription I did at school, San Francisco State College, at noon concerts and the like. There were a few musicians in San Francisco, therefore, outside of the official New Music Society concerts, who did hear some Ives at that time.

Then, when I made my transition to New York, I began working right away on a few of the scores at the insistence of Henry Cowell and Mr. Ives. I was asked to put together *They Are There!* from marked-up, torn-out song material and things like that, and so I did it. There were, as I recall, passages that needed a fair amount of filling in, and, having lived with Mr. Ives's music for a very long time, it did not occur to me that you couldn't do that, so I did it. I simply composed the passages. I don't know what they are any more; I haven't a clue. I'm sure that now we could find out what I did, because now there's so much scholarship around. That would amuse me!

KIRKPATRICK: No fault has ever been found with it.

HARRISON: That's not really what I'm after. Mr. Ives did seem to approve of it, both in letters and in other ways. It did not get played, so I never heard it and didn't know what either of us had done until about a month ago, when the record came out [Columbia M4 32504] and I was able to hear it for the first time. It makes quite an interesting sound. I like it.

The years went by, and I was writing music reviews for the dear, dead *New York Herald Tribune,* and I reviewed a concert by Joseph Barone and the New York Little Symphony in which he had made wrong notes, and I scolded him very severely. The poor man came to me personally (this is one way of doing it), and he asked me if I would conduct something. I said, "Yes, I'd be delighted." I checked my memory and, sure enough, the chamber orchestra forces were strong enough to include all the instruments of the *Third Symphony*, with which I had lived for about ten years. (I've always said that I conducted the Ives *Third* for the first time on a kind of blackmail system.) I also wanted to do Carl Ruggles's *Portals,* and that was possible because we had enough strings. I also decided to do a piece of mine. I told Mr. Ives, through Harmony, what I planned to do, and it was approved. I started copying out the parts of the *Third Symphony* from the oblong photostat which Mr. Ives had included in the crate he sent to San Francisco (and which I still have). Doubtless, this is only one of many versions; by now I am certain of that. My attitude was that this had all arrived and eventually I would do something about it, and bit by bit I did do something about some of it, in its condition as of then. That was fine, I thought, because I also understood from Henry Cowell, and I think quite rightly, that things were variable and always would be. In fact, I would like to make my first refrain here—that Mr. Ives has really left us the most wonderful of playgrounds, a kind of people's park in which we are all arrangers of lovely things.

The *Third Symphony* was well received, as well it might have been, and I adopted the procedure of Henry Cowell, used in the New Music Society, which called for playing any new work twice immediately, so that you get a second round at it. It went well the second time, too, that night.

Then I had my luncheon with Mr. Ives. He asked me during the luncheon to be his eyes—"mine are failing," he said. He wanted me to go through his collected works and help him get them out, which is of course what I had had in mind all the time. However, that proved impossible, because I had a breakdown and so I never did take charge in that way. After my exit from the "halls of readjustment," I had the opportunity to aid in the presentation of the *First Sonata.* That happened when Billy Masselos and I were visiting Ben Weber one night, and Billy Masselos was about to give a concert—he had consulted his astrologer and found that it was a proper day—and he said, "What should I play besides?" (He was going to play some Dane Rudhyar and several other works which I very much wanted to hear.) I said, from my background of ten years' trying it out and working with it, "Why don't you do Mr. Ives's *First Sonata?*" He, of course, did not know of it at that time. So, from Ben Weber's I called the Ives home, and Harmony said, "Just wait a minute, I'll go ask Mr. Ives." (I had, in the meantime, told her that Billy Masselos was a first-rate musician and that it would be done excellently.) She went upstairs and came down with the news: "Yes, do go ahead." They were happy about it. So we did. Night after night, Billy Masselos came over and plied me with sherry and his mother's most excellent cookies and I went through it. I had known this work for ten years and it was among my favorites. The structure of it, the beauty of that haunting thing in the first movement, and what I think is one of the most thrilling of finales, too, in the first movement!

I did what I'm sure many young people are now doing; I traced what Ives called his "snake tracks" for instructions. I will say that the *First Sonata* was in quite good condition. It was not, of course, printed, but there were only a few places in which I had to make choices (which I did with pleasure). There was one really quite difficult passage, however. That was the opening of the fourth movement. In the photostat that I had—I do not know what other sources there may be, since I'm in a state of blissful ignorance about any later source materials—the beginning of the fourth movement consisted of extremely faint instructions, with a note circled here or a chord circled there and then a little line connected with something else. There were verbal instructions, too. I do not know what the state of that passage is now, but, at any rate, what I did was approved by Mr. Ives, although I'm told that he made additions and changes to the version that was finally printed. That's why I say—again my refrain—that he has made us a wonderful people's park and that we will be continuously making beautiful versions for a long, long time.

I was also associated with some of the songs. I don't know how many. Milton Feist and Leonard Feist asked me to prepare them for publication and performance. Those were not difficult, as I recall, simply a matter of making a clear copy and following Mr. Ives's directions. As a matter of fact, I think that probably I'm not the only one who has simply followed Mr. Ives's directions, because they were often very, very clear, if you just paid attention quite seriously to what he said and then just looked where he directed you.

Then, I remember, when the *Second Quartet*'s first performance was coming up, I helped put a few measures of that together. I think that by this time I was getting a little self-conscious, and so I think I only circled and initialed a couple of measures or something. I don't know what else I did, but from my point of view, it was a question of getting the works out.

When questions of revisions of the *First Sonata* came up, at first people seemed to approach me in a sort of accusatory fashion: "But this note isn't what the new edition says"—you know, that sort of thing—and I'd say, "Well, there are probably many versions." I began to reflect that this is likely to go on forever and there may be no definitive version. I think that we might consider making, in the instance of Mr. Ives, a collected edition that would consist of super reproductions with modern photographic enhancements of even the faintest pencil marks—because that, of course, we will need. With modern reproduction processes it is even possible, in those not infrequent instances of a photostat on which pencil marks are written, to get the glint of the original pencil. They might even be illuminated in silver, or some-thing, because the light does that when you look at them, you know. At any rate, a complete edition of Mr. Ives might very well be in the form of en-hanced photographic reproductions of all the original materials. Then the editorial versions—this marvelous playground in which we will all be making beautiful things for the rest of time—would be based on the public version, to which anyone might resort.

MANDEL: I might share with you a little story. Thanks to the work of Lou Harrison, William Masselos performed, and then made a beautiful recording of, the *First Sonata*. Then, ten years later, he was going to make another recording for Columbia. One or two days before he was going to make that recording, John Kirkpatrick said, "Wait a minute. There's a version by Ives, a corrected version in which there are various revisions." He gave it to Bill Masselos, whereupon Bill was confronted with a dilemma: should he cancel the recording or should he go ahead with it? Well, I think he came to a perfectly sound conclusion: he went ahead with it. I had to make a recording, a few years later, of the *First Sonata*, and pretty much the same thing happened. A few months beforehand, Bill Masselos said to me that John Kirkpatrick had given him the corrected version, and he said, "Maybe you should study it." So I did. I rejected certain things in it—every-body has to make that decision for himself—but there were a few beautiful "corrections" which I did use. For example, in the first movement, Ives asks for a few chords to be played "like bells." These cannot be played in per-formance, but I dubbed them into the recording. In the second movement, there's a correction of one note to make an exact quote of "Oh, What a Friend We Have in Jesus." So, I changed that and a few other things.

HARRISON: I'm very happy to know of these new things.

H. WILEY HITCHCOCK: You mentioned a crate full of music—Ives music. Was it original scores or photostats?

HARRISON: They were all photostats. However, it did turn out, and John Kirkpatrick will confirm this, that there was one page of a photostat with actual pencil notations. I was very alarmed to discover that, and I sent it to John. This of course brings up the idea that Ives really gave this to all of us. It's almost like the inventor of Esperanto, if I may say so: he gave the language to the world, you know, and he said, "You can change it and do anything you want with it." There's an Esperanto Academy to take care of that problem, just as Yale and the Ives Society are now taking care of the Ives problem, but it is a gift to the world.

KIRKPATRICK: May I add a footnote? It turned out some years ago that Mr. Harrison actually had in his possession the original manuscripts of the *Trio*—which, I suppose, Ives had turned over to him for some editorial work —and also photostats of the *Trio* manuscripts, some of which had additional

84

pencilings. Mr. Harrison gave all those to the Ives Collection. A couple of years ago, I was in California and what did Mr. Harrison do but turn over all his Ives letters to me for the collection; he was content to keep xerox copies for himself.

HARRISON: Well, of course, that is where they belong. I wouldn't have dreamed of doing otherwise.

Three Realizations of Chromâtimelôdtune

Many compositions by Ives exist in an unfinished state; some are close to completion but have uncertainties or options that leave them open to varied final realizations. Such works pose, of course, special editorial problems—characteristically Ivesian problems. One of these works is Chromâtimelôdtune, *for which Ives wrote out sketches, first perhaps in 1913, then later in 1919, but never put into final form. Gunther Schuller was the first to prepare a realization of* Chromâtimelôdtune *(published by MJQ Music; recorded by Columbia Records). Gerard Schwarz, with the assistance of Keith Brion, made another realization for the American Brass Quintet (recorded by Nonesuch Records). The most recent to probe Ives's four pages of sketches and to realize yet a third version (recorded by Columbia Records) is Kenneth Singleton. One session of the Festival-Conference, chaired by John Kirkpatrick, had these three musicians discussing their varied realizations of* Chromâtimelôdtune.

JOHN KIRKPATRICK: We are concerned with a piece, *Chromâtimelôdtune*, which has four source pages. From them, Kenneth Singleton has transcribed the verbal commentaries by Ives, which, of course, are of the greatest importance in figuring out just what he seems to have meant. [See Plates 1–4 and page 93.]

As usual, Ives's indications are open to a fair amount of different interpretation, and we have three different interpretations of this work. I'm in the particularly fortunate position of not knowing the piece very well. My getting deeply into it has remained wishful thinking, and I'm rather glad it has, because as moderator of this panel I have no particular desire to be in the position of a referee. I only hope to hold to standards of conscientiousness—generally, not specifically.

The first person to have made a realization of *Chromâtimelôdtune* was Gunther Schuller.

GUNTHER SCHULLER: I would like to say just a few sentences to put into context the concept of my reconstruction or, if you will, my interpretation. We have four manuscript pages, and I don't remember now whether it's two and two, but some of the pages date from 1913 and presumably represent Ives's first conception of this piece; the other pages date from 1919 and seem to be a reworking or recasting. Neither effort resulted in a final piece in any sense, and yet there are sections that seem to have been worked out in considerable detail. We have the essential materials, the raw materials of a piece. I took the point of view that had Ives looked at this material a third time and finally worked through to a final composition, he might have done something like what I came up with.

Perhaps I was guilty to some extent of not reading the lines too carefully before I read between the lines, but my approach was what I guess you'd have to call a creative one. I was not thinking of a very accurate, literal transcription or translation of the materials we have. I felt there weren't enough of them to justify that. In order to make them into a real composition, one would have to put in some amount of creative effort, and that, of course, could not be Ives's; it had to be mine. Once I had faced that fact, I then went further. I went so far, in fact, as to try to relate this piece to some other things that Ives had done—for one thing, a superimposition of several musical structures on each other. In my attempts to make something more than a sketch out of the piece—indeed, a real composition which progresses and in which there is a process—in the final section I superimposed the march that had already appeared earlier, but in a different tempo and in a different key, as Ives did in *Three Places in New England* and in the *Fourth Symphony*. This, of course, is a certain degree of interpretive license, but I think it was creative and certainly something that Ives had done on many occasions. Also, what he did very often was to build pieces from a very minimal level of complexity into some gigantic climax and then have a quick fadeout with a leftover quotation of a prayer or a hymn tune. I tried to incorporate some of these ideas in this raw material.

What fascinated me, particularly at that time (it was 1962, at a time when there was not the kind of effort to reconstruct and edit Ives that there is now), was the fact that this is actually an embryonic twelve-tone piece. That is historically interesting, because we've all assumed for many years that Schoenberg was the first to write twelve-tone music, and here Ives, in his marvelous ingenuity and despite the isolation in which he worked, wrote, in essence, a twelve-tone piece as early as 1913. That, to me, was rather staggering, and I must confess that I wanted to bring out the twelve-tone aspect of the piece.

KIRKPATRICK: The next person to realize *Chromâtimelôdtune* was Gerard Schwarz. Mr. Schwarz, would you say something about your interpretation?

Three Realizations of Chromâtimelôdtune

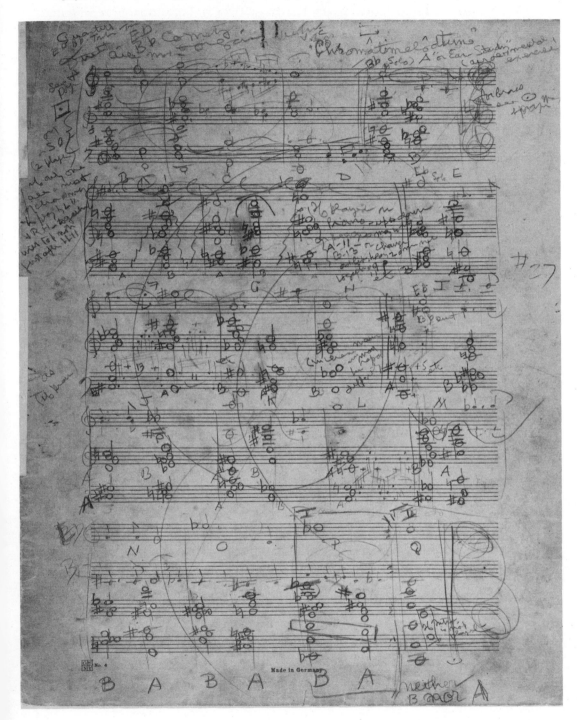

On Editing Ives

Plate 2. Sketch by Ives for *Chromâtimelôdtune* (Kirkpatrick 2795). © 1963, 1967 by MJQ Music, Inc. All rights reserved. Used by permission.

Three Realizations of Chromâtimelôdtune

Plate 4. Sketch by Ives for *Chromâtimelôdtune* (Kirkpatrick 2797). © 1963, 1967 by MJQ Music, Inc. All rights reserved. Used by permission.

Three Realizations of Chromâtimelôdtune

Verbal material from four pages of *Chromâtimelôdtune,* transcribed by Kenneth Singleton.

[*Kirkpatrick 2794:*]

Quartett/ E♭ B♭ Trob, Tu/Duett—E♭ / B♭ Cornets/ & organ/ or violins/ V C/ Bass
  alle mode   "Chromâtimelôdtune"/ "or Ear-Study"/ (aural & mental exercise!)
                B♭ solo   for brass/ see ⊙ [?]/ [?] page
See ∝ / page/ org/ or/ S Q/ (2 players) / if only one/ all or most/ of chords/ may/ be
  play by L.H./ & R H — together/ with top note/ just after L H
If played on/ Piano/ arpeggio/ A-11 B-13 — or/ ad lib/ together 9/ 11/ etc.
  up & down/ may be/ changed/ holdg 2 or more notes   E♭ solo
(as/ if piano)
              (in these meas/〰〰 may be repeat/ differently   B♭ duet
                                                  etc.
                            if Intro/ is not/ played
                            neither/ B nor A

[*Kirkpatrick 2797:*]

or piano may play an up arpeggio & down in different time/or changing beat if play 3
  times

[*Kirkpatrick 2796:*]

Solo/ 2 oct Trumpet   Horn/   See ⊙ /   Trombone (5 lower /
                         or let Trombone start/at ◇ and horn at ⊞
                    oct low / Tuba
When E♭ play/ 1st time alone DC II as coda / ALL/ C[ch]ord
Tuba
        Reverse[?]

[*Kirkpatrick 2795, upper left-hand corner:*] Intro 4 meas
                                     E♭   4 meas
                                     Cor   E♭ Cor
                                     B♭ Cor   or Cl
                                     4   4
                                     ‾‾‾   ‾‾‾
                                     Trombone Intro
                                     Tuba   ad lib
                                                       see
                                                      ⊡
                                                       see
                             for org or/ strings/ or piano/see 1st copy

[*Kirkpatrick 2795, other parts of page:*]

Allegro modo   or   1st Clarinet mp next cor FF
                      1st Time E♭ Cor & trombone / II _____ all _____ _____
              Strings or &/ or Piano & Brass Quartett/ (can be played by 2 pianos—4 players)

II only
2nd Time only / The 3rd time, may be played top tune only Clar p / and drum,
                steady beat & string pizz ♪. pp. as a kind of a/ scherzo or reel/
                      if played 4th time all & drums FF maestoso/
            or Ist time E♭ Cor Tuba
            II   "   B♭ & Tuba (but Trombone first 8 meas)
              III all
better 1st / 1st only & no trombone, till II   I for clar to play
I & II (or only last time)   III
            II or play 3 times as/old copy   "Chromatimel
                                        ◇

Chromâtimelôdtune, reconstruction by Gunther Schuller, pages 11–13, measures 61–66; winds, strings, and snare drum (measures 4–9 of Kirkpatrick 2795) rhythmically superim-

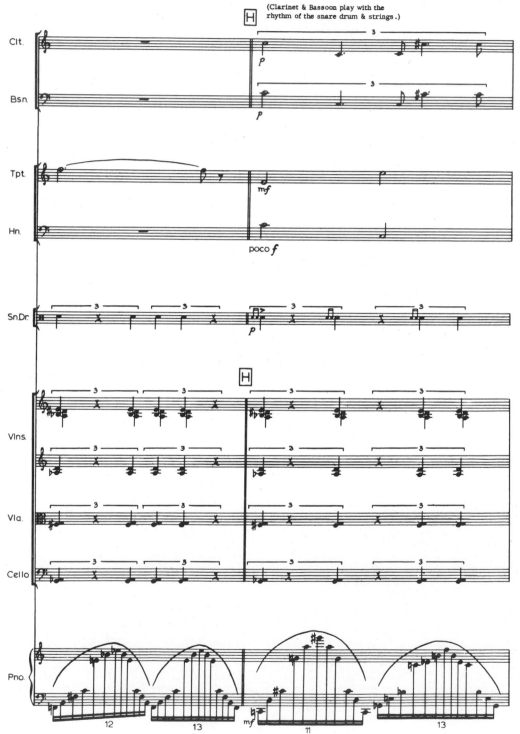

Three Realizations of Chromâtimelôdtune

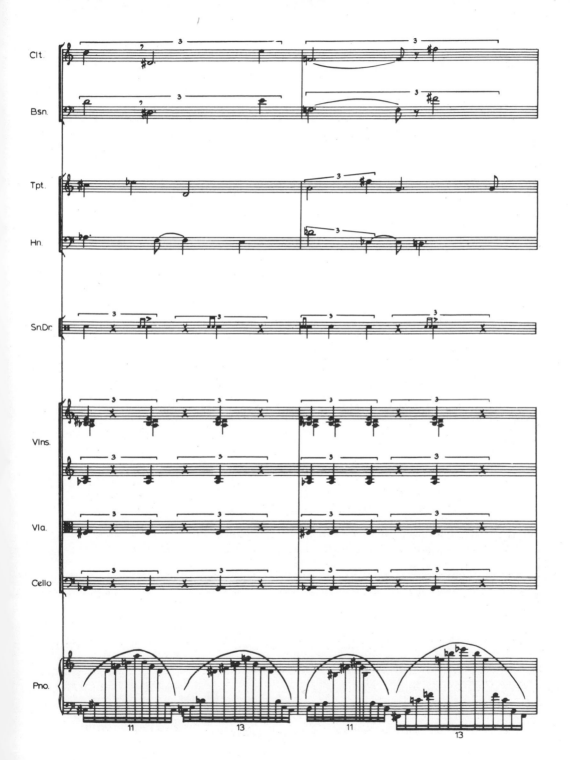

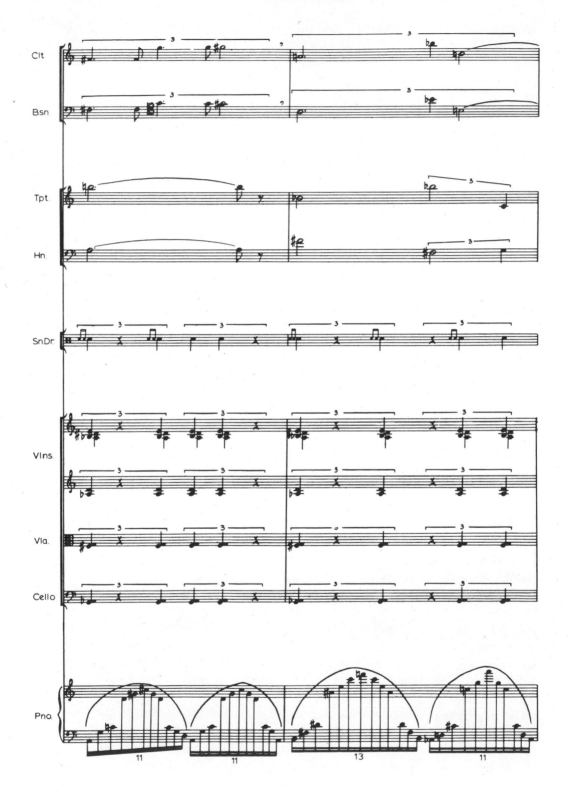

96

Three Realizations of Chromâtimelôdtune

Chromâtimelôdtune, arrangement by Gerard Schwarz, with all four brass in canon; theme stated in trombone (measures 25–28 of Kirkpatrick 2795, third and fourth time through).

GERARD SCHWARZ: If Gunther's approach toward the piece was a creative one, the one that I took might be called an uncreative one. I used to play in the American Brass Quintet, and that's the key to my version. A friend of mine, Keith Brion, brought one of the 1919 pages to me. At the bottom of the page it said that many things could be done to this material. You could add piano or percussion, use clarinets, use strings playing pizzicato like a scherzo—there were many possibilities. If I remember correctly, one of the possibilities was to play it more or less as it was on the page. That was for a brass quartet, with E-flat cornet, B-flat cornet, tenor trombone, and tuba. What I did was just to write down as best I could what I could find from the basic material that Ives gives. I changed one aspect of it: instead of tuba, which I would have preferred, I used a bass trombone, because our group didn't have a tuba. We added percussion because that seemed, at least in my interpretation, required by the music. I thought it would be like a march, a very simple, straightforward piece. I purposely did not take advantage of all the possible creative things that could have been done with the piece. When we played it through in the version that I wrote out, it seemed to work fine. It's a very different piece from Gunther's, but one that we felt was good and which we performed often. The last year or so before I left the quintet, we didn't play it any more, because it was too hard. (It's easier on a record!)

KIRKPATRICK: Kenneth Singleton made a third realization of the work which was premiered early in 1974. Would you describe your approach?

KENNETH SINGLETON: I'm a tuba player, and that should explain why I was attracted to the piece: there aren't that many pieces with tuba, and here was one by Charles Ives, so the excitement was automatically there. Having heard Mr. Schwarz's recording of it, I was very much interested in finding a way that a brass group with tuba could perform it. I started looking at the manuscripts, and it seemed to me that two of the sketches were related; they were meant to be tied together. These are manuscript photostat numbers 2794 and 2795, as found in the Ives Collection at Yale.

Basically, my version uses the introduction (the first three measures of 2794), followed by material from 2795 repeated four times through, as in Mr. Schwarz's recording. Underlying all this are the piano chords that you hear in Mr. Schuller's version; they are also to be found on 2794. All the decisions that were made for this realization are, I believe, implicitly or explicitly explained by Ives on the manuscripts.

KIRKPATRICK: Mr. Schuller, would you like to say more about what you did?

SCHULLER: There was one aspect of the raw materials for the piece that bothered me and still bothers me—it becomes a performance problem as well as a realization problem—that is, the interminable four-bar phrases. I remember trying in some way in my re-creation to deal with that. Ives thought of the piece as being a thirty-two-bar structure, and it is interesting that at least Gerry Schwarz and I felt that it's some kind of a march piece—at least it can be interpreted that way. That's how the drum came into it. Somehow, though, I still felt that there was either something a bit naïve about it or something that Ives would have in some way dealt with differently. I obviously respect him enough to think that. I tried to do that, and I think I did achieve it by the way I interpreted the instrumentation.

There was another problem I saw, which Gerry might wish to speak about. That is, that if you realize *Chromâtimelôdtune* as merely a brass quartet piece there are some almost insoluble endurance problems for the players. That was another reason why I brought in a more varied continuity of instrumentation; that's how the woodwinds got into it. Ives had given me the cue by allowing for the possibility of a clarinet, and I expanded that into a woodwind group.

In regard to the piano part, what I wanted to do was to have that build. The piano part, he says, can also be played by strings or organ, so again I used several of those options, not just one, and I saved the arpeggiation of the piano part until a later stage, adding a rhythmic development to the piece.

In essence, what I really wanted to do, apart from the creative thing I've talked about, was to include in my interpretation the evolutionary process of the piece, because it's clear to me that Ives stumbled on a really primeval concept of twelve-tone music ("embryonic" is already too sophisticated) by realizing that the chromatic scale is in fact a twelve-tone row. The first sketches indicate that that's what he was dealing with, but, as we know, he took some of the notes in the chromatic scale up an octave or down an octave to disguise a little bit the baldness of the scale. In the later sketches of 1919, he took that chromatic scale and really wrote it into a twelve-tone row. I thought it would be nice—and I did it really out of a sense of respect for Ives—to try to include as much of the material that we have available as possible. Therefore, I also wanted to include the evolution of the work from a piece based on a chromatic scale into a twelve-tone piece.

Also, I thought that that little refrain was so touching—it is that marvelously sentimental Ives. In its three bars it postulates a very dissonant kind of idea and then it evaporates and resolves into that beautiful C-major chord. I thought that it was too typical a touch of Ives not to have it appear more than once. I do recall that Ives said somewhere that this could be used several times. I thought also that it would break the four-bar continuity, and therefore I used it in the beginning, as a little refrain in the middle, and then again at the end, superimposing it on the march as an echo in the woodwinds, two-thirds as fast as the basic march.

SCHWARZ: Listening to the three versions of *Chromâtimelôdtune* is interesting. I find that Gunther's version sounds very much like Ives; it really works extremely well. One problem I had in doing it was the same as his: every four bars the piece stopped and nothing ever happened with it. Was the material *that* good, that something shouldn't happen? (Except for the fact that it was something very special in terms of the evolution of music. At least it was very special to me.) I never thought of the piece as being really great, and I never did much with it as a result. What I locked into at the end of those four-bar phrases were the intervals. I started to really get excited by just hearing a good octave, if it were possible, or an augmented fourth or whatever interval was happening in those four bars. Listening to the record that we made, I still lock into the idea that every four bars I hear a particular interval, and I could listen to that beautiful sound for a whole minute.

The puzzling part of the third version [Singleton's] for me is that it's hard to understand, even though I think it is very good and also sounds

Ivesian. The scherzo part sounds good, even though in the pizzicato string part it's hard for me to hear anything of the pizzicato strings. The four against three works well, but I don't hear the chord. Maybe that is the performance, I don't know, but to me it didn't really feel like a scherzo. The problem then for me becomes this: the version that I did, which is very basic, works for me in its simplicity. Ken's version, close as it comes, does not work as well for me, even though in fact it is probably closest to what Ives would have done with the material. To me Gunther's version shows a great imagination as a musician and as a composer. It sounds like Ives and it works well, but it is "Ives-Schuller," obviously.

The fact is that the piece is a puzzle to me. If I thought it were better, maybe I'd try harder to figure it out, but I don't; I'm not completely sold on it.

KIRKPATRICK: Perhaps we could hear more from Ken Singleton about his realization.

SINGLETON: I think Ives gives us a clue on the first of the pages, where he says, "Chromâtimelôdtune or Ear Study (aural and mental exercise)." A lot of his pieces—I think of *From the Steeples and the Mountains* and perhaps the *Tone Roads,* especially *Tone Roads No. 3*—qualify as such, as things that you're never going to sit back and listen to and say, "Oh, isn't that beautiful! Isn't that lovely!" They're designed to make you stand on your feet or your head or whatever you're going to stand on and really listen.

To hear this piece on a recording deflates the possibilities. In the two performances I've been responsible for and involved in, it's been unbelievable what it does to the audience. People really get into it. I think it's the immediacy, the constant drive throughout. It's almost like a rock tune. It is incredibly effective in performance. I would be inclined to agree with Mr. Schwarz, though, since I myself am not that terribly excited by it. It's strange. Maybe it's the overexposure. I've been working off and on with this piece for two years and, you know, you can only copy out that tune so many times before it starts to really wear on you.

I'd like to describe briefly what I did and why I did it. The reason I feel that the strings and/or piano or organ should appear below the bass is that in the righthand margin of one sketchpage [2794] Ives has "for brass / see ⊙." You'll notice that the trumpet part in that measure and in ensuing measures is quite thoroughly crossed out, implying that he wants to use these chords for some other brass. The little circle with the dot in it directs us to the same symbol on another page [2795], where it is next to the brass material. Ives mentions several ways of playing this. He says that the first time you may use E-flat cornet and trombone, and the second time, everyone, but he qualifies that when over the tuba part he says, "better 1st [time]" and ". . . no trombone, till" the second time. He decides it's best to use E-flat cornet and tuba the first time and save the trombone until the second time. Right above the eighth line he says "1st time Eb cor[net and] Tuba"; second time "Eb cor[net], Bb [cornet] & Tuba (but Trombone first eight meas[ures])"; and the third time "all." So he gives an idea there, if you want to do it three times.

In my version, the first time through a clarinet is used, not cornet. I reached that decision recently. In the first measure of sketch page 2795, right above the trumpet part, it says "1st Clarinet." I always thought that meant the first clarinet part, and that the second clarinet part is the next line down, but then I read on. It says "1st Clarinet mp next cor[net] FF," implying that the *first* time through the thirty-two-bar section it should be clarinet, *mezzo piano,* and the *second* time cornet, *fortissimo.* This of course makes it much more practical from an endurance standpoint; the poor trumpet player, who before had to play that through twice on his piccolo trumpet, just about killed himself. Musically it makes more sense; it gives more of a color change. So, both musically and practically, it's much better to use clarinet the first time through. The second time through, use cornet, just as Ives says, *fortissimo,* with everybody else.

Now, to see what Ives had to say about the third time through, you have to look at the third line [on 2795], where he says "the 3rd time, may be played top tune only Clar[inet] p and drum, steady beat & string pizz[icato] ♪. pp. as a kind of a scherzo or reel." The clarinet plays the tune *piano* and the drum is a steady beat. Ives has even written out the drum part there as quarter note, quarter rest, quarter note, quarter rest, etc. The string pizzicato dotted eighth note *pianissimo* I interpreted as meaning that he wants those chords now to go by at time intervals of a dotted eighth note. If so, you have this whole structure that really does sound like a scherzo or reel, and it is something of a relief from what you've been listening to, although I agree with Mr. Schwarz that it begins to wear heavily after a while. (However, as I realize that it begins to wear on me too, I realize that might well be the whole purpose of the piece.)

The last time through, right below where Ives has all that written about the clarinet, it says, "if played 4th time all & drums FF maestoso." So, after you've gone through the scherzo, you throw everybody in, and at that point I chose to double in unison the clarinet and the high cornet part. The piano part I just left as the chords, with a suggestion that the pianist arpeggiate any way he sees fit, since Ives specifies about four different ways of arpeggiating these chords and at the end of each one he says "ad lib." Since he's implying that the pianist may do basically what he wants, I thought it would be nice the last time through to give him free rein. My version ends on the C-major chord very loudly. I agree with Mr. Schuller that the possibility of repeating the intro is actually indicated on both sketches. I chose

Chromâtimelôdtune, realization by Kenneth Singleton, page 14, measures 68–72 with E-flat clarinet playing the theme over pizzicato strings, changing chords every ♪. (measures 1–4 of Kirkpatrick 2795; third time through; rebarred in ¾ to facilitate string performance). © 1963, 1967, 1977 by MJQ Music, Inc. All rights reserved. Used by permission.

not to do so. To me, the three-measure intro is the whole piece in a nutshell. It has the chords labeled A and B, and it resolves on the C-major chord. All the rest of the piece, those thirty-two bars repeated four times, merely restates all those A and B chords alternating; if you end with a big C chord, it seems to me a kind of catharsis at a time when you really need it.

KIRKPATRICK: Would you three gentlemen have questions for each other?

SINGLETON: I have a question for Mr. Schuller. I noticed that you used basically the first and second sketches. Was there any reason why you didn't use the last one? You never have all four voices going in their canon.

SCHULLER: Yes, I do, at the end. I did use material from the last page; indeed, I had to, because it's the only page on which that particular material appears. You've probably studied this exhaustively, which I have not, recently. I went through all that twelve years ago. As I recall, I could not present the entire evolutionary process of the piece, because I felt that the material did not warrant something more than eleven minutes of music. (I think that's the duration of my performance.) I had to eliminate some things, and I guess what I ended up with primarily was the beginning stage, some of the intermediary stage, and the final stage.

JAMES SINCLAIR: Ken, would you explain the A and B chords?

SINGLETON: Yes, I forgot that. You'll notice that the keyboard chords on sketch 2794 are labeled A or B. If you take the A and B chords and add up all the various pitches, you have all twelve notes of the chromatic scale, with a shared tone in each chord, C. The whole piece is in C. You could, I guess, narrow it down another way, because C is the most frequently found pitch. Ives has these A and B chords totally voiced out in the first sketches. He starts to sketch them out, then stops sketching and just writes A, B, A, B for a while, and then even stops that.

SCHULLER: I'd like to add something about those chords. It's fascinating that in the first presentation of them, Ives takes the two chords—one of six notes and one of seven—and during the sixteen bars of the first phrase he always invents a different configuration or inversion, if you will, of those basic chords. As a result, while every pitch always appears in its proper role as a member of either the A chord or the B chord, their positions are constantly reshuffled—a note that may be on top in the first bar is on the bottom in the third bar and in the middle somewhere in the fourth bar. That again shows a kind of concern with the concept of the constancy of the twelve-tone material. That is to say, each bar represents not only the total twelve-tone chromatic but also another concept that Schoenberg was conscientious about —that of total variation. Here Ives did this—and yet, typical of Ives, he then forgot about it. Schoenberg made a school out of it, you see, but Ives just did it, then put it on the shelf and didn't even finish the piece, which is so typical and so marvelous in a way. It's sad, too; one doesn't know what other factors played a part in his not finishing it—his illness, his rejection, other such things.

KIRKPATRICK: So often, Ives didn't go on with these things simply because he didn't have time. Being a nighttime, weekend, vacation composer, he probably had to snatch just enough sleep for the next business day. There was a question from the floor?

WILLIAM BROOKS: I noticed that the three performances are essentially in the same tempo. From the materials we have, the only indication is "allegro mod[erat]o," which is pretty general. I wonder if it's coincidence that they're at the same tempo or whether it's a result of the limitations of the instruments, that perennial problem, or what.

SCHULLER: It has something to do with the arpeggiation in the piano. There's only a certain speed at which you can play that, if you're talking about how fast you can play the piece. If you're talking about how slow you can play it, the trumpet player cannot take it much slower. Indeed, Gerry's version is faster than ours, because the brass have to carry the entire burden.

SCHWARZ: It's even faster at concerts.

SCHULLER: Yes, and I understand that sometimes you didn't even play the fourth chorus.

SCHWARZ: Only once did we do it the fourth time in a concert. Otherwise, only three times.

KIRKPATRICK: I did not find that the three interpretations were in the same tempo. I found Mr. Schuller's slower than Mr. Schwarz's and Mr. Singleton's.

BROOKS: I did, too, but there's nothing in the piece that suggests it couldn't go much faster, except the limitations of the instruments, but nobody's tried to do it.

SINGLETON: But the tempo marking is "allegro moderato."

KIRKPATRICK: As far as I've gathered, "allegro moderato" has differed over the centuries. It's a very different thing in Schubert from what it is in Stephen Foster, for instance.

H. WILEY HITCHCOCK: One reason we thought of organizing this session was to demonstrate (and I think we've done it rather firmly) the many instances in Ives where one cannot really claim ever to produce a definitive single edition. This relates to the work of the Charles Ives Society, which has as its primary aim the preparation of critical editions of the works of Charles Ives, or re-editions along critical and scholarly lines. You can see the kinds of problems we're running into already. I'd like to ask the panelists: do you agree with my view that with *Chromâtimelôdtune* (and quite possibly with many other pieces not so problematic or sketchy as this one) it's perhaps futile to aim for a single definitive edition—that there may be two, three, or even more editions, all based on good, solid, scholarly grounds, all based on the kind of comparison of sources which Mr. Kirkpatrick has spoken of earlier?

SCHULLER: I think there's no choice but to take that point of view. I certainly wouldn't like to claim any definitive priority for my version of *Chromâtimelôdtune*. In fact, as a footnote to that sentence I would say that it was a great American tragedy that a Gunther Schuller, who was not trained in musicology, had to come along in 1962 to make a reconstruction of a work that was written in 1913–19. The sketches for this one were so limited that it had to be really reconstructed, but we know, of course, of many Ives works which were virtually finished and which still were not performed. We also have to be aware of that problem. In any case, I agree that there can be several possible interpretations, given the limitations of the raw materials that we have. On the other hand, we have the same problem with Mahler, let's face it: there have already been three versions of the *Tenth Symphony* and I bet there are going to be some more. And we have the same thing with Mussorgsky's *Boris Godunov*. That is always going to go on. I do think the Ives Society ought to think about this problem a little bit further, though. I think there has to be a limit. I can't say exactly how you do that, but it occurred to me, when I knew I was going to be on this panel, that surely the question would arise here: how is it possible that three persons can do three independent versions? There may even be other people working on this material, because the raw materials are generally available. Must there not be eventually some kind of a limit to this?

KIRKPATRICK: For different works the situation is vastly different. Some are really perfectly crystallized, particularly some of the songs. Others permit about as much variation as *Chromâtimelôdtune*. In "Concord," you have so many choices that Ives wrote me in 1935, "Do whatever seems natural or best to *you*"—and he underlined "you"—"although not necessarily the same way each time." He was determined not to finish that piece because improvising new variants was such fun. So you can't generalize. It's different for each work. Are there some more questions?

QUESTIONER: The problem is very similar to editions of other composers' music. In some of them, if there are ambiguities or variants, the editors add footnotes about the different ways of interpreting the music. It seems to me that possibly in future editions of Ives, or in a complete edition if one will exist, some footnotes might be added to say that it is possible under certain circumstances to add embellishments in the notes, play different versions, and so forth.

KIRKPATRICK: A *variorum* version of "Concord" would be a difficult thing to set up. It would have to be very complicated and fancy in its manner of presentation, but it's probably not absolutely impossible. Other questions?

QUESTIONER: I'm Jeanne Lunn and I'm working on an edition of *The Celestial Railroad*. When I first sent Mr. Kirkpatrick a draft edition of one source that already had four or five different versions of several passages and I included all of them, he wrote back, "At some point or other, you've got to give the performer some indication of what to play." It occurs to me that there is room both for performing editions and for critical editions that give all the variants, but where does one leave off and the other begin?

SCHULLER: I can't help thinking that Charlie would be laughing his head off at our agonizing over all of these meticulous points. I didn't know him, but, you know, he raised more questions than can ever be answered, and it's fascinating. I don't know any composer like this except perhaps Bach (but for different reasons).

KIRKPATRICK: He'd find the right terms with which to make fun of us. He might even enlarge our vocabulary in doing it.

QUESTIONER: I understand that Ives's view of copyright was that it shouldn't exist on his works at all. How do we deal with that in the context of what we're talking about?

KIRKPATRICK: Ives certainly did start out with the idea that he'd like all his music to be in the public domain, that anybody could use it if they were interested. However, later on he went along with the idea of granting copyrights in the normal way, very much as he evolved in his view of the income tax. For many years, he refused to accede to the advice of his income tax lawyer to enumerate deductions, because he felt that if you gave to charity you had no business getting credit for it. He liked to do all these things anonymously, anyway. It was only after years that his lawyer persuaded him that if he did put them down as deductions he'd have more to give away.

JEFFREY WASSON: About a year ago, at the American Musicological Society meetings in Chicago, we got into the problem of multiple editions of single composers' works, and the consensus at that time was that we should not proliferate our resources into many editions. For example, how many editions of the works of Schütz can we stand? Where you run into an individualistic problem, such as *Chromâtimelôdtune*, I think the Ives Society might develop a series of monographs, or a periodical of some sort, in which to present the various versions, so that the material is available but we do not have to go through the engraving process or the expenses of proliferating editions.

KIRKPATRICK: Every now and then grad students write me about Ives subjects for theses and dissertations, and sometimes I tell them, "Yes, so-and-so did a job on that subject, but, even as far as he went into it, the field is still wide open." That's really the reason for going on with other attempts.

QUESTIONER: Ives has been discussed as a person who had an enormous number of centrifugal tendencies in his head, ones so contradictory and paradoxical that it's a real miracle that he managed to hold it together. The effect that he tried to produce in our own heads is in a way very similar, and it seems to me that he succeeded brilliantly not only in his completed works but also in his uncompleted works. It's a very unsettling experience, but I think he would be delighted at how unsettled we are.

SCHULLER: Would he have wanted us to remain unsettled? That is the question.

QUESTIONER: I think he would, in a creative sense. How can you say, in his particular case, that there is going to be *a* style of performance? We have heard during the Festival-Conference the two completely different approaches, both of them most effective, of Mr. Masselos and Mr. Kirkpatrick to Ives's piano music. Mr. Masselos had, it seemed to me, the tremendous "letting it all hang out" power that I felt in Mr. Schuller's attitude toward presentation, and Mr. Kirkpatrick, an almost Mozartian delicacy and control. I recall the recording of Aloys Kontarsky doing *"Concord"* and playing it more or less à la Webern or Stockhausen. I feel that they all were enormously effective and seemed to find a resonance within the music itself, so perhaps *the* style of Ives doesn't really exist.

KIRKPATRICK: I'd like to answer that. Bill Masselos and I are very different kinds of people. He's strong and has big muscles. I have small muscles. I have to make use of gravity for all it's worth, and I aim and bounce. He can hit and hit repeatedly and not get too tired. I would get exhausted. When I was a boy I was a weakling, so I don't have that kind of strength. I have to plan very carefully. I remember Alfred Frankenstein's review of my second recording of *"Concord."* He spoke of its weightlessness. Of course, that's exactly what I intended, that the whole thing sort of dance along and bounce; and that's very different from the kind of thing that the muscularity of Bill can allow him.

QUESTIONER: Did Ives's playing have an influence on your own piano playing?

KIRKPATRICK: The one time I heard Ives play, it was a very flitting kind of playing. He was all over the keyboard, all at once. It was a very deft playing and a very contrapuntal mind—a contrapuntal mind not limited to the scope of ten fingers, but all over the place. His two hands were like what one hears about Chopin's single hand, that while in repose it looked like a narrow hand, in action it stretched over a whole span of the keyboard. Ives's were like that all the time.

To respond to what you asked in a general way, Ives was the most paradoxical man I've ever known, and the greatest paradox was his deep inner consistency and his outer inconsistency. Just the other day, Sidney Cowell was reminding me that no matter where you touched Ives he was exactly the same. He was the same transcendentalist-idealist. Outwardly, you never could tell what would come out of him as a reaction to anything that might happen, or to anything that might have been said. I think he would be happy if he could feel that he had introduced others to the idea of living cheerfully with paradoxicality.

IV

On Conducting and Performing Ives

Conductors' Experiences

Just as Ives's music poses special editorial problems, so does it pose problems of performance—of interpretation, of authenticity, of decisions to be made by players, singers, and conductors. These were explored in the two panel discussions that follow. In the first of these, seven conductors recognized as Ives specialists recount their experiences in a discussion ranging from anecdotal reminiscence to confrontation with specific conducting problems. Two of the conductors, Nicolas Slonimsky and Lehman Engel, were among the first to lead performances of Ives's orchestral and choral works, respectively (in the 1930s). Gregg Smith, Gunther Schuller, and Arthur Weisberg are especially well known "Ivesians" through recordings they have directed. John Mauceri (who moderated the panel) and James Sinclair represent the younger generation of conductors identified with Ives's music.

JOHN MAUCERI: Charles Ives was very much a paradox: the practical man who perhaps wrote impractical music; the man who found highly emotional, universal, and even cosmic content in the everyday object, the daily occurrence, and the half-forgotten memory. His materials are, therefore, romantic in vision and scope and peculiarly American in detail, but his methods are distinctly of the twentieth century, and his message not just for Americans but for the world—in fact, probably for all things in God's universe. In performance, we conductors must face the constant challenge of the music's surface complexity and its inner simplicity and, if you will, mystery. When do we turn on the lights and when do we turn on the smoke machine? How much editorial freedom do we have with this music in relation to other music we conduct? Do we treat it differently from other music with respect to programming, rehearsal techniques, orchestra reaction, and audience reaction? Finally, do we perform this music differently today than we did in the 1940s, '50s, or even in the '60s?

GUNTHER SCHULLER: Those are terribly complex questions and, like one of his pieces, they're unanswerable—I mean, in any absolute way. I don't know that anyone on this panel can say that there is only one way to do Ives. There are enormous problems in dozens of Ives's pieces. For example, take the second movement of the *Fourth Symphony,* where there are immense balance problems and textural problems. I would tend—perhaps it has something to do with the fact that I'm a composer—to be rather literal in the performance of those structures, particularly in the case of *that* score, which I do feel was very carefully edited. It is, in fact, for a publication of 1929 [*New Music,* 2, no. 2], a kind of miracle, considering the enormous, mind-boggling complexity of the score. When, against a massive orchestra, incredible sounds of the brass section, and the percussion section all going in seventeen or so polymetric and polyrhythmic directions, one bassoon is playing "Columbia, the Gem of the Ocean" all by himself, you just wonder what Ives really had in mind. Perhaps there are people who know. I don't happen to, but I know that I'm not going to double that tune in five bassoons and try to make it heard, because even five bassoons can't be heard against that sound. So you're left with an unresolvable question. It is probably one of those little inside jokes that is perhaps more for the bassoonist, who may have been Ives's friend, than it is for the rest of us. In any case, I would lean toward being quite literally accurate in performing that and just let the chips fall where they may. I find that if you do that, the music, even in its most complex structures, comes out with a lean, brittle, hard, clean sound which Ives loved and which is quite a long way away from the typically Germanic sound which he abhorred—the thick, rich sonority. Ives could of course write music that is very sentimental and very warm in a typically, almost native American way, and yet it's never *pretty,* and I don't think it ever *should* be pretty in the normal sense of the word.

MAUCERI: Ives's term would be "nice": when he really hated something, he said it was "nice."

SCHULLER: If you perform a movement like the second movement of the *Fourth Symphony* the way it is published, you'll get a very accurate reading of his intentions, because he worked hard on that score. It will have that hard, uncompromising quality which must not be bent to our personal tastes.

MAUCERI: Yes, but that's a very specific kind of music, that second movement with the marches in very specific rhythm. What do you do with something like the fourth movement, which seems to be much more amorphous, or the last movement of the *Second Orchestral Set,* where in fact a lot of the rhythms—eleven against eight, and the like—seem to be Ives's way of writing only general directions for things.

SCHULLER: Well, I wasn't speaking about rhythms. I was talking about texture and density. If you want to talk about rhythm, that's a whole other panel discussion, but here I would for the moment disagree with you. The man worked too much with the serialization of rhythms and the proportioning of rhythms and the superimposition of rhythms for us to be able to say casually that he probably didn't mean eleven over eight, he probably meant something free. There are instances where he perhaps *did,* but then he makes that clear by some other annotation, and I think the first obligation is to try to take him at face value.

LEHMAN ENGEL: I knew Ives, and he often played sections of his music for me. It's my feeling that he had a sense of improvisation about everything and that nothing was literal. I agree with Gunther that you should do it exactly as he's written it, or as nearly as possible as he's written it, but I think nobody should ever forget that he rarely heard anything that he wrote. Also that, unlike all of us (at least here on this platform), he had had no real experience with music and that everything that he wrote seemed to indicate his feeling about something that had nothing really to do with music. For example, he always told tales about why he wrote things, and those tales had nothing whatsoever to do with music. If he had anything to say about music, it was to talk against all the composers and performers of his early days who wouldn't perform his music. Thus I think that although one should generally play what is on the printed page as well as one can, as accurately as one can, in Ives you're up against something that's quite different. I don't think that he meant things to be so specific. They're really all so mixed up with thousands of footnotes that have nothing to do with music but with politics and opinions. It seems to me that you have to come to grips with what you feel he intended rather than what he actually committed to paper.

NICOLAS SLONIMSKY: I would like to offer, not a rebuttal, but perhaps a marginal comment to both Mr. Schuller and Mr. Engel. It's about the way Ives considered the specifics of his rhythms. I more or less prepared for publication the score of his *Three Places in New England,* and I was simply amazed at the precision of all those overlapping triplets and quintuplets and whatever (there were sometimes eleven, you know), which would all come out synchronized in the middle of a simple 4/4 bar! After all, Ives was a mathematical man; he was extremely precise. In several letters to me, he said, "I like to be precise," and when I, at that time rather young and brash, tried to introduce some new ideas into his scores, so as to make them more readable without changing notes or rhythms, he always had something to say about it.

The main problem for the conductor is to translate Ives's precision into performance and to synchronize notes no matter what overlapping there is. Let me refer specifically to the second movement of *Three Places in New England,* where there is this idea of two marching bands meeting in a town square, but the march movements are in different tempos. I conceived a plan for conducting the two different tempos at the same time, one for the faster march and one for the slower march. I was a terrible showoff at that time, so I thought, "Well, I'll do something that nobody else can do." There are four bars of the faster tempo against three bars of the slower tempo. I must say, for posterity, that I was the one who suggested an *ossia* part to show clearly this relationship, and I had quite a correspondence with Ives on the subject. Finally he consented to the *ossia* part, but he absolutely vetoed my conductor's note. He wrote me: "What I know about conductors, they can't even conduct an upbeat or a downbeat, so this note would be a waste of time, and besides, while I don't mind this conductor's note, since I would not mind insulting most conductors, there are also some intelligent conductors, for instance Goossens." So you see, according to Ives, there were only two good conductors in the world in 1932: one was Eugene Goossens and the other was me (see example on p. 117).

I tried it out in actual performance and it did work. The slower march I conducted with my right hand and the faster march with my left hand, with each bar in the left hand equaling three-fourths of the right hand. One, two, three, one, two, three, one, two, three, one, two, three, and then the left hand finally coinciding again with the other.

ARTHUR WEISBERG: I would like to comment, since maybe the audience doesn't entirely understand. These two tempos are going at the same time, and the problem in the conducting is that we can only take care of the main beats of each tempo. The in-between notes, the notes in the faster march that suddenly starts up against the slower one, are very hard to deal with because they don't fit into any of the values of the slower tempo. Mr. Slonimsky found a very interesting solution to this problem. I remember the first time I did the piece. There's a little trumpet solo in the march in the new faster tempo, and there wasn't any way that the trumpet player could do it except by closing his eyes and listening to the beat produced by the new fast tempo. If he opened his eyes and watched what was happening, he would get completely lost. This is sometimes a very useful way of doing it—just have the player listen, close his eyes, and play it according to what he hears.

JAMES SINCLAIR: That's a solution that Ives himself proposes in some of his other works, where he says things like "It will be easier for the string bass player to watch the piano's left hand."

GREGG SMITH: John Kirkpatrick said to me that he remembers Ives being furious if people tried to change his notation, although he had a very interesting attitude toward an improvisatory character of performance. He kind of liked people to take off once they had worked out what the music was about; then he relished the idea of an instrumentalist even adding his own ideas.

Gunther, you mentioned that solo bassoon. I can't help thinking that

Conductors' Experiences

Three Places in New England, second movement ("Putnam's Camp"), page 35; edition by Nicolas Slonimsky for C. C. Birchard. © 1935 by Mercury Music Corp. Used by permission.

maybe someday a bassoonist will go out into the middle of the audience, sit on some dowager's lap, and play that melody out there, where at least the dowager and a few friends can hear it. We have that kind of problem in *Circus Band,* the second part of it, where at the end it's really a free-for-all. Right in the middle of it, Ives puts in a little note about a Delta Kappa Epsilon fraternity song. When we first performed it, nobody could hear it—there's another guy singing *Riding Down from Bangor on the Midnight Train,* and you can't hear it with that—so we tried many, many solutions. Finally, we just used the idea of going out into the audience and performing it, and it becomes another world.

It seems to me that I never had a case in an Ives score when I wasn't the culprit, rather than Ives. We've all managed to play up the myth so much that we don't realize that almost every single notation that was a mystery or seemed strange finally came out to be a darned good solution. I must say it seems to me that Ives's own notation always proves to be about as wise and musical a notation as it could be. Now that doesn't mean we don't have to make allowances for other things. In *Psalm 90,* there's a bell figure that is a group of nine eighths in 4/4. Well, the real point of it to me is that although the figure starts one eighth note later in each measure, there's a freedom of playing within that figure. You have to start with saying that Ives knew what he was about. He wasn't an amateur; he was a fantastic genius who knew what he was notating, and it's for us to find out what it is about. Then our freedom comes after that.

SCHULLER: I agree. I might just mention one very strong, striking bit of evidence of Ives's precision of thinking about such things. In the second movement of the *Fourth Symphony,* in one very complex section, he actually rates the degrees of importance of the lines. He marks them with A, B, C, D, E, down to F, I believe—five or six levels or degrees of importance. However, we must admit, there are things in the score which he didn't rate at all. Unfortunately, he didn't give us a grading on some of the even *more* complex places in that symphony!

MAUCERI: In certain places—and that, too, is an interesting thing—he really wants specific levels of intensity.

About the programming of the music of Ives and whether his music requires special treatment on a program, or whether, in fact, the music sits very well with music of other periods and from other countries. What are your feelings about how you program Ives? Is it "All-American" night all the time? Have you found that to work?

SCHULLER: I don't think so at all. I think that the problem that I've encountered (we probably all have) is the same one that you encounter with Webern, and that is the extreme brevity of some of the pieces. Sometimes the amount of effort to produce a piece is quite disproportionate to the duration of the piece, at least in terms of a normal concert program. Then there is another curious problem with Ives, which you don't have with many composers—that you may have to repeat a piece because it's a smash success, but it only lasts forty-five seconds, and it goes by so fast that half the audience didn't catch it (they're still putting their umbrellas away and rustling their programs and getting through the first paragraph of their program notes, and the piece is over). I find that I have to allow for that repetition factor because of the shortness of so many pieces. The other side of the coin is that it is sometimes a little difficult to find a place in a normal concert program where Ives is stacked up against standard classics, some mostly lasting the traditional fifteen minutes to half an hour or longer, when you come along with a little piece like *Ann Street* or even something like *In the Cage*. One has to think very carefully about the overall structure of the program.

MAUCERI: Besides the time-duration factor, is there a stylistic one at all?

SCHULLER: I don't know how to answer that, except to say two things. First, it's so varied: you may, in one Ives set, encounter five different Iveses. The corollary to that is that each one of those Iveses takes hold so authoritatively that I don't think there is a stylistic problem as far as the audience goes, although there *is,* sometimes, in Europe, where I've conducted Ives a lot and where they really don't understand the Americana aspect of it or the humor. Generally speaking, European audiences tend to be a little bit humorless when it comes to going to concerts. It's a very dignified matter for them—but Ives didn't see it that way. They're either afraid to laugh or they haven't really gotten the point. Americans, just by being involved in this milieu, get it more readily.

SMITH: The Gregg Smith Singers do tours every year, and we've had a tremendous response no matter what kind of work it is. You talk about variety—it's incredible! Take *Son of a Gambolier:* I've never had a better encore in my life than when we pull out our kazoos during it. The response of the American audience to Ives's music is really quite incredible; it's a kind of gut response. It can occur with a piece like that, which is very direct and certainly stylistically very accessible to the general audience; and yet we can also take a really tough piece and throw it at the audience and the same thing will happen. *General Booth* has just about the same type of breath-taking reaction among our American audiences as *Son of a Gambolier.* Maybe it's because there is so much that's a part of our own selves in it. It's extremely good programming music.

MAUCERI: Do you feel, if you have performed this music in other than American countries, that the response to Ives is much more limited? Does the fact that you can understand these tunes or that you've known them all your life really make a difference in your appreciation of the cosmic elements in this music? It's not, after all, the specific reaction of amusement over hearing "Columbia, the Gem of the Ocean," but a kind of overwhelming deeper reaction. Is that hampered if you do not know these tunes? Let's face it, many of us don't know the hymns Ives knew. We didn't grow up with those melodies, and besides, many of them are buried.

WEISBERG: We may not recognize the specific tunes and the specific hymns, but we recognize the style of these pieces; it's familiar. The melodic intervals are very familiar to us even without knowing the particular work. Some of the hymn tunes would obviously be familiar in the same way to Europeans, but I think *not* some of the folk-type music that Ives uses.

SCHULLER: On the other hand, take Mahler and his *Ländler*. To many people in the United States in the early years when only Bruno Walter and a few others were doing Mahler, this was a music which they really did not fully appreciate, and they did not recognize the *Ländler* (and indeed couldn't), and so half of his uses of *Ländler* went by those audiences. Nevertheless, one could appreciate them for whatever was intrinsically in them—the harmonies and the melodies and the rhythms. When Brahms, for example, imitates (in some of his intermezzos) the zither music of the Vienna *Caféhaus,* one can still appreciate the music without absolutely knowing what Brahms was trying to emulate. It's a question of education, really. In due time, the Europeans will also understand all of the American elements in Ives. In the meantime, they recognize, as Arthur says, the kind of simplistic element that they're hearing. They often wonder at the baldness with which Ives did this, and this is the difference between him and Brahms and Mahler, because Mahler and Brahms integrated tunes into their works in a very subtle way, whereas Ives just laid it out on the table. That is strange for Europeans, because there is nothing in their background as a precedent for that. I think we have to help them with it. I find myself talking to the audiences beforehand and trying to give them a little bit of the sense of what has gone into these pieces.

SINCLAIR: The fact is, it's amazing how really integrated those tunes can be in Ives. Tunes do go by one after another and, for many people, they may seem very much like a potpourri, but Ives's choice of tunes, if one looks at the great works like the *Fourth Symphony* or the *"Concord" Sonata,* is absolutely remarkable. The thematic material of all of those tunes relates them to each other, and there is a fascinating inner growth in the development of their motives—perhaps not as in a traditional development section, but in the tunes' relationships. That is integration and a very complex thing that is not in the least naïve.

ENGEL: Gunther spoke of composers other than Ives. I had an experience at the Turkish State Opera about four years ago, when the State Department asked me to do *Porgy and Bess*. I found that the orchestra at the rehearsals (and I must have had twenty rehearsals with orchestra) couldn't

understand it at all. A dominant ninth chord was enough to set them scream-
ing with laughter. They simply didn't understand it, and they thought the
tunes were excruciatingly funny. Now, if they thought that Gershwin was
funny, what would they think of Ives?

SMITH: I took my group to Europe in 1967, 1971, and just this year,
1974, and it's very interesting to see the change of attitude. They always did
want to hear some Ives, but I always got the feeling that it was only as a kind
of curiosity. This last time, however, it was more like their saying, "We want
to hear Ives because we've finally come around to believing that he is a
great composer."

SCHULLER: I've noticed the same thing.

MAUCERI: We might turn now to the matter of rehearsing Ives's music,
preparing it for performance. Are rehearsal techniques in any way particularly different for Ives than for others? Also, how do your performers react
to rehearsing Ives? What are the major problems that you've found in dealing with the people through whom this music must be heard?

SCHULLER: I think that most conductors might agree that the thing they
find themselves doing at all rehearsals of *all* music is working with rhythmic
problems primarily, and then dynamics. In Ives, the rhythmic problems,
especially in the avant-garde Ives (if we can call him that), are enormous. It's
fair to say that most musicians will never have seen any of those problems
before. They will never have seen some of those delayed overlapping triplets
or quintuplets that start off the beat. In fact, they think it must be a mistake,
and they shove them over one half beat and "correct" them. It's a very
specific performance problem to which, again, there's almost no solution
except talent and imagination and perseverance. I like what Gregg said about
Ives's knowing exactly what he wanted and how to notate it. When he writes
out his concept of that shifted-over rhythm or meter, he is absolutely dead
accurate, as far as I am concerned. However, some of those rhythms are literally unreadable, so you have to take the concept and translate it into the
practical or pragmatic, and that may take a lot of rewriting. Then, you have
to practice it that way to get it accurate, but of course that's not enough.
You must then retranslate it back into the concept. That takes time, and
sometimes you cannot do it in four rehearsals. Sometimes you can't do it in
five concerts. With certain musicians, sometimes you can't do it at all. It
becomes an enormous problem. I would suggest, for whatever it's worth for
the publication of Ives's works, that it would be very helpful to conductors
to have written in the parts (not just in the score, because musicians just
have their individual parts in front of them) the concept that Ives was trying
to get across. Then put in small notes, cue-size notes, the literal translation
that fits the meter that the conductor is conducting. I find I have to take
certain passages in *Three Places in New England,* where the cello section

plays delayed triplets, and rewrite them into every cello part. We might as well do that in the publication process.

Then, there still is the problem of making such a passage play naturally in its own rhythmic contour and not having it translated into incredibly complex syncopations against the conductor's beat, because they're not supposed to sound syncopated. Now that, of course, is the musician's obligation. There is only so much that the conductor can do. He can sing it, he can play it for them, in some way, but in the end it is the musician who is going to do that translation, and that is the biggest performing problem.

MAUCERI: A perfect example is in the *Second Orchestral Set*. There's a place where the violins have a rather simple triplet, except that it's written a sixteenth note off the beat. It's a simple case, but the performers see this horrible thing in front of them. You have to stop and say, "And now you all must do that slightly after the beat to make it sound like that triplet is slightly late." You've taken something like a minute to do that, and that's just one of the many, many problems.

WEISBERG: I've found that for most musicians Ives is practically impossible to play, but I think that young musicians will become better at some of these rhythms, so that they can read them without having actually to rewrite them. I've been teaching classes in just this kind of thing for quite a few years, and I know that it's possible for musicians to learn to play five against four or whatever combination we're talking about. At the same time, some combinations are so difficult that the only way to really play them is to fake them. That's what you're talking about, in a sense—a way, an educated way, of faking some of these rhythms. When you fake them you can achieve much better the flow that Gunther was talking about. When you're really tied down to these complex rhythms, it comes out very angular and very unmusical, usually. I've found that one of the best ways is, first of all, to have a knowledge of how it should be played—a knowledge of how to rewrite it, so to speak—and then if you can't really play that musically, at least you can fake from that knowledge and do quite a good job. The problem is when you have a large section playing, faking together, since the numbers make it difficult; with one person it's fairly easy, but with twenty you have other problems. However, orchestral musicians are really amazing about sticking together, about playing together, in spite of the conductor, in spite of the beat, in spite of anything. They've learned how to stay together, so they can fake together, too.

MAUCERI: I wonder if the verb *to fake* is appropriate in that case. I wonder if, in fact, part of the language of Ives is to actually write mistakes in—to express what might happen if an amateur orchestra or band were playing a certain rhythm. The violins might be late, until they noticed that they were late and finally got the downbeat again, several bars later. In other words, that specific place might be nothing other than late triplets that are suddenly corrected—that kind of human element. We've all sat in church and heard the organist who gets five dollars a week and isn't sure about the C pedal or the G pedal and so the tonics and the dominants are mixed up. There's something kind of marvelous about hearing this simple diatonic melody being completely undermined. It's exactly that, it seems to me, a kind of human element—that kind of interpretive thing that we all do, unconsciously, that makes us human—that Ives loved and frequently wrote into his music. There is even an example John Kirkpatrick told me about in which in fact Ives left in an editor's errors; they seemed to be as good an idea as anyone else's, so why not leave them in? These were exceptions, mind you, but this, it seems to me, is an element of his aesthetic.

ENGEL: I think you've come full circle in explaining what I was trying to say earlier: that everything Ives wrote had a certain explanation in reality. The first thing of his that I ever conducted, which was way back about 1935, was the *67th Psalm*, which is written in two tonalities simultaneously, and I performed it with the Madrigal Singers in the WPA. Ives said right away, "This is the way I always heard the choir at home sing." I cannot believe if he made a remark like that that he really meant that the upper voices should be in C major and the lower voices in G minor. I think he really meant that they should be not quite together. As a result the Madrigal Singers, who never sang quite together, were ideal!

MAUCERI: Nicolas, when you were working up the first performance of *Three Places in New England,* and when you were rehearsing with musicians who had no idea about Ives then, what kind of rehearsal problems were involved?

SLONIMSKY: They said that the man who wrote this music didn't know what he was writing, and that the man who conducted didn't know what he was conducting, and that the whole thing was some sort of a joke on the dignified members of the Boston Symphony Orchestra. (The concertmaster had the most annoying way of announcing, even during the concert, "So far, so good!") The problem was simply to persuade them that their business was to *play* the music. I had much less of a problem with the Berlin Philharmonic, because they accepted it as a challenge. They didn't pass judgment on the music, but the Boston Symphony men—that was forty years ago, so I think it's no reflection on the present Boston Symphony men—just said that it wasn't music. The French were also difficult, but the problem was simply, first, to tell them what to do.

MAUCERI: I would like to point out that the orchestral material is frequently in terrible shape and that one of the horrors of playing the great music of Charles Ives is having to deal with the actual printed music—the parts that the second violinist has or the bassoonist has, which are often illegible. One of the great difficulties in doing things like the *Fourth Symphony* or the *Second Orchestral Set* is stopping and having to say, "Is that an E-flat there? Is that a sixteenth note? What is that rest?" I would hope, as we move toward a more enlightened age, that we can make sure that this situation is alleviated.

I wonder whether there has been a change in performance style over the years, or whether there really is a performance style for Ives. Have we learned something that has affected our performance? Do we conduct the music differently now from the 1930s and '40s?

WEISBERG: I can't talk about Ives thirty years ago, but I think these details that you are talking about are very much up to each conductor's sensibilities and his musicianship. With any piece of music, you look at the melody and you ask yourself, "Is this a soft melody? A hard melody? Is it a rhythmic thing?" I don't see any special thing that's changed. If anything, it's becoming clearer to us because, presumably, musicians are playing the music better, so that we can get a better picture of the music. That's the only change that I've seen.

MAUCERI: Does the recent release of recordings of Ives playing his own music help us in any way?

SINCLAIR: For me, it's provided almost a shocking insight. He's a very romantic pianist. He changes rhythms, he changes many things. Of course, as the composer, he is free to change the materials, and it's very convincing when he does it.

MAUCERI: I wonder if we might have one or two questions from the floor.

ROQUE CORDERO: I would like to offer a short comment and maybe a shorter question. Mr. Mauceri was asking about editing—if it was right to edit Ives before performance—and you spoke about rhythm and many things, but I didn't hear much about the wrong notes in the scores, of which there are many. Listen to Bernstein's recording of the *Second Symphony* [New York Philharmonic; Leonard Bernstein, October 1958] and another recording done by the London Symphony [London Symphony Orchestra; Bernard Herrmann, May 1956], and you will hear that in those two recordings both conductors leave in a mistake of the copyist which was not intended by Ives at all. There are many such little problems that a conductor ought to take into consideration and check his scores to discover, because many of these Ives works that have been printed have been done so quickly that many mistakes are present.

I would like to ask one question of Mr. Sinclair. I see in the program that the *Second Orchestral Set* has been newly edited by you. I have listened to the recording by Morton Gould with the Chicago Symphony, and he has a unison chorus singing at the beginning of the last movement. I have also heard the recording by the London Symphony under Stokowski, in which he has two choral parts, one in the last movement and one in the second movement. Have you taken into consideration the version of Stokowski in your editing? Have you ever found the choral part for that second movement?

SINCLAIR: No. It isn't really intended to be a chorus. That's not Ives's intention there at all.

CORDERO: I'm glad that you didn't put it there because I was the one who wrote that choral part for Maestro Stokowski, so I know the truth.

QUESTIONER: In performing works of Ives, one has, I feel, rather contradictory obligations. One of them, which has been discussed quite a bit, is the obligation to really know what's written and what Ives's intentions were; the other has to do with the improvisatory nature of the music. I was wondering if you also feel the second pull and the contradiction of it? Can you add lines for one concert and take them out at the next? Do you feel performances should change from one concert to the next?

SCHULLER: I don't think this problem is any different with Ives than with *any* composer. There is bound to be, and there should be, the kind of latitude in the performance of Ives that there is in the performance of Brahms or Beethoven or Schoenberg or Stravinsky. None of us can claim to perform any work the same way in successive performances.

MAUCERI: Thank God.

SCHULLER: Yes, I agree, thank God—although the degree of difference is of course the crux of the matter. Also, of course, there are many different interpretations by different conductors, so all that latitude, I think, can be manifested in the terms that Lehman Engel used when he described Ives playing the piano. I wouldn't call it improvisatory; I think that goes too far, as a technical term. It is just that interpretive latitude, that subtle stretching or narrowing or whatever, that we all do whether we want to admit it or not, or whether we're even conscious of it. That, I think, has to happen with Ives; otherwise we're talking about a mechanical monster.

On the other hand, I think—in connection with the question of whether there is *a* performance style for Ives—that it simply is too early. It's premature. We have not yet dealt with Ives performance problems for a long enough time to have arrived at anything like a consensus. Therefore, I think our first obligation is to try, at this point, to be as accurate as we possibly can, based on the scores and on the maximum acquisition of knowledge about Ives in every respect—not only how he dealt with his scores, but a lot about his personality. That always has to come into it. After that, maybe then we have a right to a consciously improvisatory interpretation. But first, we have to be very tight and accurate, because I can't get around the fact that he wanted it precise. He was very precise.

QUESTIONER: On the other hand, you have discussed the single bassoon line in the middle of the full orchestra. Why should we demand of Ives a clarity that he wasn't always interested in giving us? For example, we have composers today, like Takemitsu, who write beautifully melodic lines that are never heard because they just form part of a larger texture. In Takemitsu's case, this is related to an Eastern aesthetic. Isn't it possible that Ives, coming out of a transcendental aesthetic, was intending something similar?

SCHULLER: I hope you understand that that was what I was trying to say. I don't want to double or quintuple that bassoon. I don't want to put it on some dowager's lap. I just want to leave it the way it is. I have no better alternative at this point, and I have to accept Ives's choice. Like all composers who sweat and agonize over every speck on a score, I think Ives did the same thing, and if he left it that way, that's what I'm going to do.

QUESTIONER: I think I was asking something actually beyond just the case of the single bassoon line. As I've heard Ives performed, there seems to be an intention to clarify things, to make each voice sound, and I'm wondering if Ives intended that.

WEISBERG: I would agree with what you're implying—that a lot of Ives is a kind of planned chaos which we shouldn't try to clarify too much. I agree that some of his music is meant to be too much to take in all at once.

MAUCERI: There are many different kinds of music that Ives writes—some very simple, some very polytonal, polyrhythmic. There are times when each conductor has to face up to the questions: What is this music? Do we really want to hear this line? Is this rhythm important or is all not equally important? Should this be mysterious? Should this be clear? Each of us as a performer has to make this decision. In the *Second Orchestral Set,* which right now is preoccupying me, in the second movement there are parts which I feel have to be absolutely clear as far as rhythm is concerned, and other places where it is in fact sort of chaotic. And the last movement is quite amorphous. One has to characterize the music just the way one characterizes *Carmen* or anything else. Ultimately, it seems to me, it comes down to how one deals with any music.

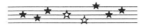

On Performing the Violin Sonatas

In planning a second panel discussion on performance problems in Ives's music, it was thought that his four sonatas for violin and piano, composed between 1902 and 1916, would provide subject matter diverse enough to make discussion valuable, yet homogeneous enough to keep it focused. Three sonata teams addressed the topic: Nancy and Alan Mandel, Eugene Gratovich and Regis Benoit, and Daniel Stepner and John Kirkpatrick. Alan Mandel chaired the panel.

NANCY MANDEL: From his writings, his manuscripts, his philosophy of music, and his music itself, it is obvious that Ives had a very free approach to the performance of his music. He objected to a rigid or slick style of playing and to technical display as an end in itself. For Ives, the most important thing was to express all the inner meanings of his music and to allow each performer to perform the music in his own way, with marked individuality, spontaneity, depth of feeling, and strength of character.

Among the myriad aspects of the sonatas for violin and piano, two elements come to mind. One is a high degree of spirituality, often illuminated in lyrical, melodic violin lines, as in "The Revival" of the *Second Violin Sonata,* the first and third movements of the *Third Sonata,* and the second movement of the *Fourth Sonata,* and in introspective piano passages, such as those found in the first movement of the *Third Sonata.* The other is a unique vigor, vitality, and forcefulness often expressed in complex percussive piano passages and in ragged cross-rhythms and multiple accents in the violin, notably in the second movements of the *Second* and *Third* sonatas and in the first and third movements of the *First Sonata.*

What was Ives's approach to the violin? Obviously, he was never interested in the violin as a showy display instrument. Even though his sonatas demand a high degree of virtuosity from both the pianist and the violinist, it is a uniquely Ivesian virtuosity and represents quite a break with traditions of writing for the violin. The violin is rarely used in a strictly idiomatic sense; Ives's writing is not really "violinistic" in the traditional sense of that term. Nor, on the other hand, does he really exploit the full possibilities of the instrument in the way, for example, that Georges Enesco and Béla Bartók did in their sonatas. Ives writes in his *Essays Before a Sonata:*

> A MS. score is brought to a concert master—he may be a violinist—he is kindly disposed, he looks it over, and casually fastens on a passage: "That's bad for the fiddle—it doesn't hang just right—write it like this, they will play it better." . . . My God! What has sound got to do with music! The waiter brings the only fresh egg he has, but the man at breakfast sends it back because it doesn't fit his eggcup. Why can't music go out in the same way it comes in to a man, without having to crawl over a fence of sounds, thoraxes, catguts, wire, wood, and brass? . . . The instrument!—there is the perennial difficulty—there is music's limitation. Why must the scarecrow of the keyboard—the tyrant in terms of the mechanism (be it Caruso or a Jew's-harp)—stare into every measure?

However, Ives did introduce a distinctly American style of violin playing in his sonatas, namely paraphrases of fiddle music. In the second movement of the *Second Sonata* ("In the Barn") and a little in the first movement of the *Fourth Sonata,* Ives treats the violin as a fiddle rather than as a violin. Or, rather, he presents a parody of country-fiddle music. Consequently, these sections should be performed more in the manner of an old-time country fiddler than in classical concert style. They should have a high degree of spontaneity, vigor, and even roughness. Henry Cowell relates, in *American Composers on American Music* [p. 129], how, as a child, "Ives heard the fiddling to a dance. The fiddler not only did not play in tune with the conventional notion—he did not want to, and it would have been wrong if he had. His idea of music was quite different, and through slips and slides, and slightly off-pitch tones, which could go loosely under the title of 'quartertones,' he created the right and proper music for the village dance."

In other movements of the sonatas, Ives often seems to conceive of the violin either as a spiritual voice or as an actual vocal voice, or as both combined, as in his many hymn quotations and paraphrases—for example, "I Need Thee Every Hour" in the third movement of the *Third Sonata,* "Shall We Gather at the River" in the *Fourth Sonata,* and so on. This sense of an inward, spiritual voice is emphasized at the beginning of "The Revival," the third movement of the *Second Sonata,* by the use of a mute, pianissimo, and also by the use of bitonality in the same section. The first movement of the *Second Sonata* ("Autumn") quotes the hymn tune "Autumn." Material from this movement was soon thereafter developed into a song, *His Exaltation.* This song closely parallels the last section of the first movement of the *First Sonata,* bars 85–111. Similarly, the song *Watchman* evolved from the *First*

Sonata's third movement, and the song *At the River* from the *Fourth Violin Sonata*. This suggests that perhaps his original conception of the violin part was at least partly vocal in nature. Ives remembers [*Memos,* pp. 132–33] how,

> at the outdoor Camp Meeting services in Redding, all the farmers, their families and field hands, for miles around, would come afoot or in their farm wagons. I remember how the great waves of sound used to come through the trees—when things like *Beulah Land, Woodworth, Nearer My God to Thee, The Shining Shore, Nettleton, In the Sweet Bye and Bye* and the like were sung by thousands of "let out" souls. The music notes and words on paper were about as much like what they "were" (at those moments) as the monogram on a man's necktie may be like his face. Father, who led the singing, sometimes with his cornet or his voice, sometimes with both voice and arms, and sometimes in the quieter hymns with a French horn or violin, would always encourage the people to sing their own way. Most of them knew the words and the music (theirs) by heart, and sang it that way. If they threw the poet or the composer around a bit, so much the better for the poetry and the music. There was power and exaltation in these great conclaves of sound from humanity.

This quotation shows how Ives, in his most poignant memories, associated the violin with spiritual exaltation and with hymn singing. It also emphasizes that individuality and freedom of interpretation and performance were most important to Ives. Correctness and literal renditions were furthest from the spirit of the music. Spirituality was what mattered most to him.

ALAN MANDEL: There are certain specific aspects of performing the Ives violin sonatas. First of all, Ives's writing for the piano in the violin sonatas in quite similar to his piano style elsewhere. That is, he uses the piano against itself, in a way in spite of itself. As with the violin, the virtuosity is of a most thorny, craggy nature. There are many points to be made in this respect, but I'll bring up two. First, he uses the piano in a very percussive way in many places—for example, in the climax of the last movement of the *First Sonata.* Perhaps the best example of that is in the *con slugarocko* section of the *Fourth Sonata.* Sometimes, especially in passages of a religious nature, in the piano part he seems to simulate organ textures, as at the beginning of the third movement of the *Third Sonata.* Also, just as he introduces the use of fiddle music in the second movement of the *Second Violin Sonata,* he introduces a uniquely American style into the piano parts, namely ragtime. But he uses the ragtime style molded in his own unique way, as in the second movements of the *Second* and *Third* sonatas. Fragments of ragtime also appear in the violin part.

N. MANDEL: In the second movement of the *Third Sonata,* for example. Another critical matter is that of balance. Ives often writes chains of thick chords, or stormy layers of tone clusters in the piano, and other layered effects, as in the last movement of the *First* and *Second* sonatas, while the violin has a much thinner although vigorous texture. In these sections, the pianist has to take care not to overpower the violin. The technique of "layer music"—namely, the superimposition of independent rhythmic, thematic, and textural ideas—occurs throughout the four sonatas: for example, in the first and third movements of the *First Sonata* and the second movement of the *Fourth Sonata*.

A. MANDEL: There's also the question of rhythm. Ives does not always perceive rhythm within a traditional metrical framework. Rather, as in the previously mentioned case of layering, the rhythmic patterns can be independent yet simultaneous. The largo movement of the *Pre-First Sonata* is a good case in point. Here the piano has a completely different metrical idea and rhythmic idea from the violin; they're independent, yet simultaneous. Another example—this time of three independent patterns—occurs in the first movement of the *Second Sonata*.

N. MANDEL: Ives himself had this to say [*Memos*, p. 125] about his conception of rhythm:

> I have with much practice been able to keep five, and even six, rhythms going in my mind at once, so that I can hear each one naturally by leaning toward it, changing the ear in each measure—and I think this is the more natural way of hearing and learning the use of and feeling for rhythms, than by writing them and playing from them on paper, which shows the exact position of each note in relation to each other, in the eye. The way I did it was to take, for instance, in the left hand a 5—with the left foot, beat a 2—with the right foot, beat a 3—with the right hand, play an 11—and sing a 7. Start with two, gradually add the others—perhaps to begin with, have a slow metronome with a bell play the one-beat, and think of the [measure] as a 2, then a 3, then a 5, then a 7, then an 11—([or] using several metronomes with bells, clicks, to get them going in the mind). . . . Various other rhythms can be held in the mind in this way, and after a while they become as natural as it is for Toscanini to beat down-left-right-up as evenly as a metronome for two hours steadily, and do it nice, with the ladies all tapping time with their feet.

A. MANDEL: The performance of polymetric figures has to be effected by an examination of the manuscripts. For one thing, we see in them that Ives writes his accents or *sforzandos* in certain places in a very emphatic, emotional, excited way. It tells us something of the character of performance desired. For another thing, one is very much struck in the notation of these passages by the feeling of freedom from bar lines in the rhythmic groupings. The manuscript tells us, even more than the printed edition, that

Ives really means the two instrumentalists to think in different meters and different patterns. Although much of Ives is written in a thick texture, there are also examples in the violin sonatas of beautiful counterpoint and imitation written within a much thinner texture, as in the beginning of the last movement of the *Second Sonata* with the hymn tune "Nettleton" and the two instruments imitating each other.

N. MANDEL: In the last analysis, the best approach to the performance of the Ives sonatas is really to perform all of them.

EUGENE GRATOVICH: Performers are usually trained to worship the printed page. With the music of Ives, it is different. The Ives performer must also be an editor-arranger for he is faced with a wealth of sketches, patches, early versions, and copyists' editions. All these sources are important; otherwise the performance version is incomplete. Ives himself, however, sometimes helped to confuse the issue. For example, after talking in Los Angeles to Sol Babitz, who edited the *Third Sonata* with Ingolf Dahl when Ives was still alive, I was able to identify the source Babitz and Dahl used. It turns out that Ives sent them a copyist's version rather than the autograph. As a result, a certain number of differences occurred in the second movement which I will talk about later.

I would now like to give several examples of the types of discrepancies that exist in the published editions, and their possible solutions. For my first example, I would like to look at the second movement ("In the Barn") of the *Second Sonata*. At first, I worked with photostats of the manuscripts, but frequently I found indications by Ives to either use or omit certain pencil directions. The photostats didn't help me to distinguish these differences, so I had to keep coming to Yale to consult the autographs and find out which parts were in pencil and which weren't.

Here is a passage from the second movement—first as it stands in the published edition (Schirmer, p. 17, last line). In the autograph score, Ives put the violin line into the piano part in ink. Both the violin and piano could play this line simultaneously. However, also in the autograph, this violin line is crossed out, and superimposed on it is another musical sketch to be played by the violin. This confusion is alluded to in the published edition: on page 18 of the edition, there is an additional measure above the score marked "First version." It is therefore possible to have the piano play the first version in the left hand and have the violin play the added sketch. This is the version that I prefer to use, because I feel that the violin sketch better matches the style of the section (see examples on pp. 132, 133).

I'd like to enter now into the problem of articulation. Violinists are trained to pay very careful attention to articulation and to bowing directions. When there is confusion in articulation markings, it is disconcerting to the violinist. A sketch helped me to figure out one such problem. The

Second Violin Sonata, second movement ("In the Barn"); Ives's ink version (top half of page), Kirkpatrick 1201. © 1951 by G. Schirmer, Inc. Used by permission.

reason for the confusion in this passage is that Ives went back to the manuscript and redid the articulations and superimposed one on the other, so that one loses track of the proper articulation. But, going back to an earlier version—in fact, one of the incomplete autographs, which might be a sketch—I was able to distinguish between the big slurs as phrasings and the two types of accents used as articulation marks. This is the version for the violin that I was able to come up with (see example on p. 134).

Near the end of this second movement, in the autograph score, Ives asks a second pianist to add a drum part, but again, it's something that he added to the manuscript, and it's at the performer's discretion. Usually, the way it's performed is to have the page-turner do it. I have written out the drum part for a separate player, and that's perhaps the best way to perform it. I find that usually audiences prefer hearing the drum part. (See autograph negative from Sonata No. 2, Q1203: on the right margin in the middle of the page, Ives wrote "Ex. player as drum corp." next to the tone cluster.)

Second Violin Sonata, second movement ("In the Barn"), measures 140–44; as played by Eugene Gratovich. © 1951 by G. Schirmer, Inc. Used by permission.

A. MANDEL: Of course this idea of *ossias* exists in many different Ives pieces, as in the "Thoreau" movement of the *"Concord" Sonata,* where you may either use a flute or not and where there is a viola part which may be used or not, or as in many of the songs where Ives asks that either a flute or violin be added. Or the *Three-Page Sonata,* with its section for another player, either high in the piano or on any one of several different classical instruments.

GRATOVICH: I'd like now to move on to the *Third Sonata,* the rag movement (the second movement). What helped me to work with this was Professor Hitchcock's book, *Music in the United States,* where he talks about different styles of rags. The music that Sol Babitz worked with was a copyist's version, with indications where the performers may rag sections. It's full of pencil markings, repeats, and so on, so that the way it stands now, there is a confusion between the straight version and the rag version. There are sections where you're asked to rag, to alter the rhythms, but you can only do that when you know what the original rhythm is. So, again, you have to go back to the Ives manuscripts. One aspect that made me appreciate this

Second Violin Sonata, second movement ("In the Barn"), measures 145–62; as played by Eugene Gratovich. © 1951 by G. Schirmer, Inc. Used by permission.

movement is that Ives uses in it a hymn that has a basic rag rhythm. When one comes to this hymn, I feel that perhaps one should keep the original rhythm, which is already related to ragtime, and not add a style of bowing, of articulation, of rhythmic changes that might perhaps be related to a later style.

If I may move on to the *Fourth Sonata,* I was happy to hear what Nancy Mandel had to say about a vocal approach to violin writing. I'd like to go even a step further: I think the violinist has to look to the words for phrasing. It's been my experience that the ending of the third movement of the *Fourth Sonata* always baffles audiences: they never know when to applaud, because the movement—that is, the whole sonata—ends at a point where the words ask the question, "Shall we gather?" And that's the way it should sound! Checking with the words and knowing their meaning can help the performer with the phrasing.

Now let me move from the performer as arranger-editor to the performer as analyst. I'd like to look at the second movement of the *Fourth Sonata,* where Ives has a whole page for the violin and several pages for the piano without any meter indications or barlines. You are totally on your own. There is a basic tactus to it. You could operate on an eighth note, certainly, but I feel that's much too rhythmic. If the performer is aware of the three basic motives used there—first the hymn tune that the music is based on, second the original counterpoint to the hymn, and third the motive that the *con slugarocko* section is based on—I think the performer can play the movement with much more freedom.

Regis, do you have anything to say about the piano accompaniment?

REGIS BENOIT: Well, I would only mention that generally the accompaniments of Ives are very rich and that they exploit the piano very well, but you can be led into a lot of traps in Ives by percussive playing. I have found that generally, even in passages that have thick textures and clusters, there's always a melodic component that gives you a sense of line. Any time Ives uses a cluster, there are very often melodic notes in it. I think that voicing such clusters and creating transparency by bringing out the different lines is very important. There's a lot of precision in his clusters and in his chord structures, and I feel they are best perceived if one notes their melodic elements. If one thinks about them that way, it helps put the thing together into an overall structure rather than having just block sounds here and there.

DANIEL STEPNER: I first met Ives's music at Northwestern University some years ago and felt he was important. When I came to Yale as a graduate student, I felt I should try at least to sight-read through one sonata with Mr. Kirkpatrick. I asked him and was surprised to learn that he hadn't played three of them and would be delighted to. I feel very fortunate to have worked with him.

My contribution will be just a few details. For example, the clusters in the piano that have been mentioned have counterparts in the violin part. There are passages in parallel fourths and fifths which I think have the same purpose as a cluster—a resultant tone implied. It's often other than the note itself or else it just strengthens one of the two notes in the double stops.

Another thing: in bowing the parts—and it's been a long process—I find that I'm changing a lot of downbows to upbows. I think it has a lot to do with the kind of phrasing that both Mrs. Mandel and Mr. Gratovich were talking about. Often, at ends of movements, there's that open ended feeling which I think can be enhanced visually and in sound with an upbow. It's hard, in a sense, but it has a kind of tension which I think a downbow doesn't have.

One other thing: there's something very interesting in the *Third Sonata* that has puzzled me for a long time, but I think I've finally worked it out. The low note of each of the figures is on the beat (a sixteenth note on the beat) and a longer chord after the beat. It's sort of awkward. At first it seems like the Hungarian or Scottish "snap," but, having thought about it for a while, I now believe it's Ives's direction on how to play a chord. I think, in essence, that it's a three-note chord, and that what he wants is a very strong bass note in it, so he puts that on the beat, thereby de-emphasizing the top notes (see example on p. 137).

KIRKPATRICK: The four violin sonatas, being all essentially hymn-tune sonatas, used to seem to me to be similar. If you read Ives's program note to the first one and his program note to the third one, you might think they're practically the same piece, but the more I got into them, the more dissimilar they seemed. It seems to me that the first one is more concerned with an experiment that has certain parallels to Debussy, particularly in finding new combinations of old sounds and new combinations of old musical phraseology. It seems to me that Ives is more concerned with the musical materials, with the phrases, and with the hymns as phrases rather than as contours. The second sonata is like a picture of the spontaneity of ordinary people in religious situations or in uninhibited situations like a barn dance. The third sonata is different in focusing its attention on the purpose of the music, on the spiritual exaltation which music is privileged to have as a special prerogative—though, of course, the middle movement is quite different, being essentially a rag. The fourth sonata is, of course, a picture of a child's life. It's sort of Ives's *Scenes from Childhood,* to borrow a title from Schumann—"scenes from childhood" here referring to what the children did on camp-meeting days. So the four sonatas are in fact very different.

Earlier, there was some allusion to the *Three-Page Sonata* and the extra instrument that the second movement of that sonata invites. I think that's optional, just as the flute is in "Thoreau" and as the drum is in the second movement of the *Second Sonata.* I'm not sure that the drum in the *Second Sonata* is really a desirable addition. I can't quite tell from the autograph page whether it was coeval with the rest of what he wrote on that page or whether it was added later, but I do think that, even if it was coeval, it was probably optional. It seems to me that the end of that *Second Sonata* is so rich musically and has such marvelous things happening in the relations of the violin line and the bass line of the left hand that it's a great pity to muddy them by this representation of a drum part at the bottom of the piano or even a real drum. I'm sure that many of you, at some time or other, have experienced the curious frustration of trying to focus a musical texture with something else noisy going on at the same time; and it's not so much that you can't hear it well enough to really focus it, but you feel, "Now, why am I doing this anyway?" I think that Ives, when he had the impulse ("Wouldn't it be fun to add a drum here?"), wasn't counting on that particular aspect of the problem of playing that left-hand part, which is really a very difficult part: you need all the ears you have, both of them, to try and

Third Violin Sonata, first movement; New Music Edition, page 8. © 1951 by Merion Music, Inc. Used by permission.

anticipate just what sounds you're trying to aim for. As a result, I like to think of that drum as optional.

About the flute at the end of "Thoreau." My story about that comes from Howard Boatwright, who told me that years ago when he was studying with Hindemith he was writing a piece for a small group of strings, and he told Hindemith that, at the end of the piece, he wanted to bring in a trumpet. Hindemith said, "No, no, no, no, no. If you do that, you've changed your medium and you've got to recompose the whole thing right from the beginning for strings and trumpet. The thing to do is to make your strings evoke the trumpet." At the end of *"Concord,"* if you bring in a flutist, whether he be onstage or offstage, you change the medium and thereby you focus the attention on the medium instead of the music. Or else you invite the fidgety reactions of many listeners' minds: "What's he been doing all this time?" If he's offstage, "How did he know when to come in?" Or, if he's onstage, "How did he feel standing there like an idiot during the first part of the movement?" and so forth. I thought it was always better to try to make the piano evoke the flute. I've had various degrees of success or failure but, even so, I think it's worth trying.

About clusters, it's true that Ives's clusters always invite one to imagine the voice-leading hidden in them. I remember writing Ives about the clusters in "Emerson"—not exactly clusters, but chords in which things happen and the voices move. (This was before he had sent me any photostats, and I had only the first printed edition of *"Concord."*) I asked him if there were any earlier sketches that would disclose the voice-leading in those chords. He wrote—or asked Edith Ives to write—that when I saw him we could discuss these things. Well, I didn't actually meet him until a few years after that, and in the meantime I had seen how those chords made sense. After he died and it was my privilege to sort his papers, I was interested to find, I think, three different sketches for that letter. He was that conscientious. The first one was long and fulsome and then he thought, evidently, "Oh, no, we'll talk about that when I see the guy." He had put down that, yes, in the middle one of those chords, there is a kind of blur, and it was his idea of the voice-leading. I suppose, to his contrapuntal mind, it was self-evident that a kind of blur was the purpose of the voice-leading. He knew exactly what he had done, I mean G-A-G or G-F-G, or something like that (there are various movements in those chords), but that was what it meant to him, a kind of blur.

When I got going at the *First Violin Sonata,* I was puzzled how much to have reverence for Ives's hybrid spellings of notes. My introduction to that was a conversation I had with him about the song *Maple Leaves,* one of the most beautiful things he did. The phrase "The most are gone now" goes A-sharp, A-sharp, G-sharp, F-natural as can be seen in the example:

Maple Leaves (*114 Songs*, no. 23), measure 4. © 1957 by Associated Music Publishers, Inc. Used by permission.

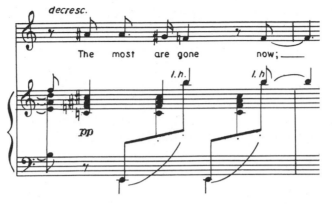

I told him that I thought that my love for that music was all bound up with the beauty of that descending fourth; why not spell it as a fourth? He exploded, and it went on for a long time. "Why the hell when a thing looks like *la, so, mi,* why the hell do you have to spell it *la, so, mi?*" His explosion went on and on, and finally he burst out, "I'd rather die than change a note of that!" At the time, I thought it was sheer nonconformism, but then, the more I got into his music generally, the more it seemed to me that he had unexpected tunings in mind, that actually the core of the passage was probably a real A-sharp reaching up toward B and a slightly low F-natural reaching down toward E—what used to be called a fourth and a comma. From then on, I had great reverence for these things.

When I got into the *First Violin Sonata,* I saw the first version of the opening in sequences of triadic sounds and old-fashioned seventh chords doing very much what Debussy had done with new juxtapositions of old sounds; and all of the triads were spelled as triads and the seventh chords were spelled as good old-fashioned normal seventh chords. However, when Ives transposed it from E minor at the beginning to F minor, he used all hybrid spellings. What had been E-G-B was now spelled F–G-sharp–C-natural, and all of the transposed chords were pretty much that way. Those of you who are familiar with the *Memos* know the story of Franz Milcke's utter consternation when Ives faced him with the *First Sonata* [*Memos,* pp. 70–71], and I can't help suspecting that, even though Milcke was probably a fossilized musician, he was probably thrown off somewhat by the hybrid spellings, as well as by the unexpected associations of good old familiar sounds. That's a department of Ives's music in which I feel you have to tread a mid-course between two exaggerations: either the exaggeration of over-literal reverence or the exaggeration of being unaware of pitch subtleties. Ives said, very justly, that often it's a little futile to try to think of these pitch subtleties when you're operating on a keyboard, but he also said that it's surprising how by subtleties in volume it's possible to suggest subtleties in pitch, and that's perfectly true. For instance, in a chord like an augmented triad you can make any one of the three notes seem like a leading tone by a proportion of emphasis. I've done it and I've heard other people do it.

I was glad that Mr. Gratovich mentioned that place in "In the Barn" with that duplication of the violin in the pianist's left hand. I had never appreciated that until last year. Then I woke up to how marvelous it was. The thing that fascinated me in it was that it was not a literal duplication; at one point, he has a touch of contrary motion, and when Dan and I first rehearsed it, Dan said, "Well, is that really a wrong note there? Don't you think that everybody will assume it's a wrong note?" You see the kind of thing, the touch of contrary motion, and how deftly it goes by. It just makes a little salt and pepper to taste.

Second Violin Sonata, second movement ("In the Barn"); Ives's final ink manuscript. The bass line was added in ink sometime after the original manuscript was made. © 1951 by G. Schirmer, Inc. Used by permission.

V

Ives and Present-Day Musical Thought

The Festival-Conference theme of Ives and Present-Day Musical Thought was approached from several directions. Participants from outside the United States reflected, as we have seen, present-day views of Ives in their respective countries. Two papers that follow here, those by Robert P. Morgan and Allen Forte, approach Ives's music analytically, but from very different viewpoints: Professor Morgan's is a reassessment of Ives's formal procedures in the light of much later musical developments; Professor Forte's is a reassessment of Ives's pitch organization in the light of procedures ordinarily associated with his exact contemporary Arnold Schoenberg. "Five Composers' Views" was an imaginative and provocative panel session, organized by Roger Reynolds, in which five composers of today (many would call them avant-garde composers) interacted. Finally, William Brooks viewed "Ives Today" with a breathtaking interdisciplinary breadth of approach.

Spatial Form in Ives

ROBERT P. MORGAN

My title probably requires some preliminary explanation. Since music is traditionally considered a preeminently temporal art whose relationships are defined within a specifically durational framework, why should one raise the issue of musical space? The question of the ontological status of musical space—the question of its existence and, given that existence, its relation to physical space, our sense perceptions, etc.—is of course one that has consistently interested philosophers and, more especially, aestheticians.[1] But my interest in the matter is not philosophical; it is, rather, musical, analytical, and interpretive. I am not concerned so much with defining a category of musical space as I am with pointing out certain types of musical relationships that suggest the relevance of such a category, at least in much twentieth-century music and especially in the music of Charles Ives.

With this in mind, I will take as my point of departure Lessing's famous distinction between painting, as an art of "figures and color in space," and poetry, as an art of "articulated sounds in time."[2] Substituting here music for poetry, Lessing's distinction will be useful, for it serves to focus attention on the different formal properties inherent in each art and on differences in

---

1. The most comprehensive study of the philosophical questions related to the notion of "musical space" is Edward A. Lippman's *Music and Space,* a doctoral dissertation written for the department of music of Columbia University in 1952. Two well-known recent studies in aesthetics that deal with this problem are Susanne Langer's *Feeling and Form* (New York: Charles Scribner's Sons, 1953) and Victor Zuckerkandl's *Sound and Symbol: Music and the External World* (New York: Pantheon Books, 1956).

2. Gotthold E. Lessing, *Laocoön,* trans. Edward A. McCormick (Indianapolis: Bobbs-Merrill, 1962), p. 78. The general approach to the problems discussed in this paper was suggested by a reading of Andrew Frank's remarkable essay, "Spatial Form in Modern Literature," *Sewanee Review,* 53, nos. 2, 3, 4 (1945), to which it also owes its title. To my knowledge, the earliest mention of spatial effects in music in a specifically analytical, interpretive context occurs in Theodor W. Adorno's *Philosophie der neuen Musik* (Tübingen: J. C. B. Mohr, 1949). Two more recent instances can be found in George Rochberg, "The New Image in Music," *Perspectives of New Music,* 2, no. 1 (1963), and James Drew, "Information, Space, and a New Time-Dialectic," *Journal of Music Theory,* 12, no. 1 (1968), both of which specifically mention Ives, though only briefly.

aesthetic perception resulting from the nature of these properties. Lessing's aim was in part polemical, directed against the strongly pictorial inclination of the poetry of his time; its "intrusion into the domain of the painter" represented to his mind a denial of the true nature of the art.

Turning to Ives, there are aspects of his compositional approach that seem to be designed to minimize the sequential, temporal nature of the music. Or, stated from the listener's point of view, these aspects seem to minimize our experience of time when listening to his work and, correspondingly, to suggest a simultaneous, nontemporal quality, a quality of space. Taking a cue from Lessing, one might say—as in fact many have—that there is a strong pictorial element in Ives's music which results from an application to music of techniques more commonly associated with spatial arts. The point here, however, is not to reproach Ives for having exceeded the limits of his medium. On the contrary, by attempting to negate time as the primary mode of musical expression and experience, Ives developed an important new way of dealing with musical continuity, one that has proved to occupy an increasingly prominent position in later twentieth-century music, particularly that of the post–World War II period.

It may be worth pointing out here that Lessing's reservations about pictorial poetry, as well as allegorical or narrative painting, are representative of a general tendency prominent—really almost exclusively dominant—in the rational framework of Western thought since the Renaissance: to separate the senses into clearly divided areas, each with its own proper art form. Moreover, I think this tendency may explain, at least in part, why so many listeners are puzzled by Ives's music, including many who are drawn to other twentieth-century music, at least that of the first fifty years or so. The frequent accusations of its "awkwardness," for example, stem largely, I suspect, from just those aspects of Ives's music that are experienced as "anti-temporal."

I begin, then, with the assumption that Ives wrote pictorial music—music based largely on relationships that are simultaneous, reciprocal, and reflective in nature rather than successive, sequential, and unidirectional. It is in this sense that I say that these relationships are primarily spatial in nature rather than temporal. If the music is approached in these terms, I think that much that may otherwise seem puzzling in it becomes more readily comprehensible.

At this point I can do no better than to quote the composer himself: "When one tries to use an analogy between the arts as an illustration of some technical matter, he is liable to get in wrong." (I take this as fair warning!) "But the general aim of the plans under discussion is to bring various parts of the music to the ear in their relation to each other, as the perspective of a picture brings each object to the eye." These comments appear in the famous lengthy footnote to the "Conductor's Note" of the second movement of the *Fourth Symphony,* first published in the New Music Edition of 1929,[3] and later published in slightly altered form as an article entitled—significantly—"Music and Its Future."[4] Indeed, almost the entire article is devoted to spatial matters such as the different effects created by varying physical distances between one group of instruments and another, or between instruments and the listener. Ives is also concerned with the specific kind of space that fills this distance—e.g., in the famous passage describing the effect of a horn heard across a lake and that of "a melody [heard] at a distance over the woods," when "the sound acquires a certain vibratory hum as if the pine-needles were the strings of a harp which it swept."[5]

Ives's interest in the role of actual physical space in the musical experience is of course well known, and it is documented in many of his scores which require special seating arrangements: in the division of the orchestra into groups in *The Unanswered Question, Central Park in the Dark,* and the *Fourth Symphony,* and even in a concern for the specific placement of these groups—the "distant choirs" in the first and fourth movements of the *Fourth Symphony,* the distant orchestra in the *Second Orchestral Set,* and the offstage strings in *The Unanswered Question.* Perhaps most suggestive is Ives's description of the projected *Universe Symphony* in his *Memos,* where he speaks of "trying out a parallel way of listening, suggested by looking at a view," and the use of "from five to fourteen groups of instruments or separate orchestras."[6]

It seems to me that Ives's concern with physical space is only a symptom, although certainly an important one, of a more fundamental spatial orientation within the music itself. I would like to turn now to those aspects of his work which, perhaps in a somewhat more metaphorical sense, reflect this

3. The New Music Society of California (Los Angeles, 1929). It also appears in the edition of the complete symphony (New York: Associated Music Publishers, 1965).

4. In *American Composers on American Music,* ed. Henry Cowell (Stanford: Stanford University Press, 1933).

5. Ives quotes the latter passage (from memory?) from the chapter "Sounds" in Thoreau's *Walden.* Thoreau's original: "Sometimes, on Sundays, I heard the bells, the Lincoln, Acton, Bedford, or Concord bell, when the wind was favorable, a faint, sweet, and, as it were, natural melody, worth importing into the wilderness. At a sufficient distance over the woods this sound acquires a certain vibratory hum, as if the pine needles in the horizon were the strings of a harp which it swept. All sound heard at the greatest possible distance produces one and the same effect, a vibration of the universal lyre, just as the intervening atmosphere makes a distant ridge of earth interesting to our eyes by the azure tint it imparts to it."

6. *Charles E. Ives: Memos,* ed. John Kirkpatrick (New York: W. W. Norton, 1972), pp. 106–8. Henry and Sidney Cowell remark in their book *Charles Ives and His Music* (London: Oxford University Press, 1969) that these groups "are to be placed about in valleys, on hillsides, and on mountain tops" (p. 201).

orientation. There are many factors involved, but all share a common attempt to negate as much as possible the succession of temporal sequence as the principal path for establishing musical relationships. They are not all present in all of Ives's compositions, but they are sufficiently common in—and above all characteristic of—his work to form, when taken together, a cluster of related phenomena supplying a helpful rubric for gaining an understanding of his music.

I shall begin with the question of harmonic stasis. The absence of clearly defined, forward, goal-directed motion does much to subvert our awareness of time in listening to music; and there are many passages throughout Ives's later works that are essentially static in pitch structure, and thus appear to suspend the musical motion in time and consequently to locate it in space. The second themes of the first movements of both piano sonatas, for example, are essentially rooted in a single harmonic complex built on an immobile bass. Other examples are the opening of the fourth movement of the *First Piano Sonata* and the entire closing section of the *Fourth Symphony*. Moreover, there are shorter pieces that are entirely grounded in a single harmony, such as the songs *Incantation* and *Serenity*. Even in movements based largely upon functional tonal progressions, Ives frequently truncates the expected progression so that the sense of motion is suspended. This happens with especially telling effect in the first movement of the *Fourth Symphony,* where the bass line, corresponding to the final unanswered question of the text ("Dost thou see its beauteous ray?"), is left hanging on the subdominant.

Thus, even where there is some sense of pitch motion in Ives, its forward (and thus temporal) quality is often minimized. One of Ives's most pervasive techniques for accomplishing this is to make the motion circular—to make it run back on itself, thereby compromising its sense of forward progression and arrival. The most common form of this is a restatement at the end of a movement of the material that initiated it. This can be found in numerous compositions, ranging from such early works as the song *Amphion* (1896) to the first movement of the *Second String Quartet.*

It is important to note that these repetitions have a fundamentally different meaning from the restatement of previous material—recapitulation—in classical forms. The latter brings about a resolution of tonal tension and, equally important, generates a new wave of motion—one destined to stay within the principal key area and thus balance the preceding one. In Ives these restatements are nothing more than brief allusions which link the closing with the opening through explicit association. Whereas in the classical recapitulation there is a confirmation and regeneration of motion, in Ives the repetition is its negation. The piece, at this stage, is not going anywhere; it is over, yet its ending is also its beginning. The musical significance of this seems considerable to me: if the material which initiates a motion can also terminate it, then relative to traditional musical concepts the meaning of motion has been fundamentally altered. Indeed, so have the meanings of beginning and ending, for there is a strong suggestion at the close of these movements that the whole process could begin over again—that is, that they could become truly circular and unending.

There are, as I have indicated, many pieces that one could cite as illustrations of this technique: a number of the songs, the studies numbers 9 and 22, the last movement of the *"Concord" Sonata,* and others. (It occurs in unpitched form in the last movement of the *Fourth Symphony,* where there is a final reversion to the unaccompanied percussion music that opens the movement.) Particularly instructive is the song *At the River* (derived from the *Fourth Violin Sonata*), because it comes so close to being a traditional binary form with normal tonal cadential articulations. The first half consists of an eight-measure period, with a half cadence in the fourth measure and a full cadence in the eighth; and the second half, also eight measures long but somewhat less clearly subdivided, also terminates with a full cadence. This hymn tune, with its bipartite form, is one of Ives's "found objects," and in this case the composer appropriates the borrowed material as a whole. However, he redefines the meaning of the original music not by fragmentation (a common Ives technique that I will discuss below) but by interpolating extraneous material after each of the full cadences. These two inserts are actually taken from earlier portions of the song—they are themselves fragments—and the second one consists essentially of a return to the opening phrase (or its first half), which produces the circular effect. Formally considered, the inserts serve to dislocate the sense of arrival achieved at the preceding cadence—to dissolve the articulation after the fact, as it were, leaving the motion in a state of suspension.

I mentioned Ives's inclination to fragment his material. This technique, which cuts off a musical idea before it is (or seems) finished, is a particularly pervasive one that touches upon virtually all of the composer's mature music. One can perhaps see the technique most clearly in Ives's very personal use of quotation, since here, where the expected continuation is known, one is made particularly aware of any truncation. For the moment, however, I would like to consider the matter in a more general context. One of the most common characteristics of Ives's style is the constant crosscutting from one idea to another, a process that does much to break up the flow of linear continuity in his music. Even so relatively traditional a piece, at least in the pitch area, as *The Things Our Fathers Loved* provides a complex and fully realized example. The entire song seems to grow out of an effort to disappoint the listener's expectations of normal musical continuation. It is almost as if the whole cause-and-effect pattern of traditional tonal music has been turned upside down. This is especially apparent in the phrase relation-ships, which seem to produce no consequents at all, although these are constantly being implied by the ends of previous phrases (their would-be ante-cedents), so that their failure to appear is at once surprising and humorous. In this sense the song appears to be always starting but never reaching any conclusions. Even in the second half of the piece, where the music builds to a large climax suggesting some sort of denouement, perhaps in the form of a return of the opening material now provided with a more conclusive termi-nation, what actually occurs is that the climax is simply broken off, to be superseded by only a fragment of the opening, but one tonally dislocated and even more inconclusive than before.

The resulting fragmentation, produced here by the failure of the phrases to link up with one another in a larger continuity that is progressive in character, contributes effectively to the poignant character of the text. (The latter, written by Ives himself, is equally fragmentary, at least in its first half.) It also affects fundamentally the formal processes experienced by the listener, who is forced to hear the fragments as isolated events rather than in terms of their growth and their implications with respect to one another. The word "isolated" is perhaps misleading, as it seems to imply that the fragments are unrelated to each other. Actually, there is a system of relationships, both tonal and motivic, that spans the entire song and ties it together into a tightly unified complex. The point here has to do with the *type* of relationships involved. Since they deal with fragments, these rela-tionships must be juxtapositional, reflexive, and reciprocal—not sequential, linear, and developmental.

A comparison of Ives's use of fragmentation with that found in tradi-tional music may help to clarify this point, for once again the meaning of Ives's procedure is quite different. In tonal music of the "common-practice" period, fragmentation is normally only forward-directed (and thus not re-ciprocal). This is true in a very specific sense: when a motivic unit is frag-mented—cut in half, for example—it is usually associated with a rhythmic acceleration—namely, the duration of the original figure (be it a measure, two measures, or whatever) is cut in half and thus shortened. The resulting acceleration is almost always associated with a *heightening* of the motion toward a coming point of arrival, a cadence of some sort. In other words, the fragmentation works in a purely unilateral sense, pointing only ahead in an essentially future-oriented temporal context.

In Ives, on the other hand, the result of fragmentation is normally not an acceleration forward but a disruption—a dislocation of one musical event from others immediately surrounding it. Fragmentation is conse-quently not designed to lead from one event to another in sequential suc-cession; rather, it produces a multidimensional framework in which relationships can be established simultaneously in both directions. Thus, although fragments relate backward to previous fragments, they do not do so in the sense of constituting their continuation and completion; although they relate forward to events yet to come, they do not do so in the sense of constituting their preparation. In Ives this can be seen not only at a local level but also within larger formal contexts. A particularly cogent instance of the latter is found in the *"Concord" Sonata,* in that striking passage in the "Hawthorne" movement where the musical momentum, which has been generated by constant rhythmic motion (sixteenth notes or faster) over some four pages, is suddenly interrupted by what might be called a pre-echo of the "Alcotts" music. This "Alcotts" fragment is then itself interrupted in mid-phrase by the return of the faster music, only to reappear again a page later, where it is allowed to continue for some eight measures. This is also eventually interrupted in mid-phrase, however, and the movement then follows its "normal" course until it is again suddenly broken off at its very end for a third appearance of the "Alcotts" music; but now only the first five chords are heard before the faster motion returns to bring the movement to its extraordinarily abrupt close.

The particular manner in which Ives has the first two "Alcotts" fragments emerge from the on-going "Hawthorne" music deserves some comment. In both cases the pedal is held down during the passage immediately preceding the interruption. In the first fragment, the initial major triad is sounded while the accumulated sound of the preceding music is still held by the pedal, so that the new music seems somehow to emerge from the remnants of the old—as if it had always been there but simply could not be heard because of the louder, more aggressive character of the "Hawthorne" music. (In his notes, Ives gives a typically spatial description: "as a hymn is some-times heard over a distant hill just after a heavy storm.") In its second appearance the effect is even more striking: here the first "Alcotts" chord is actually buried within the preceding music sustained by pedal, although one only seems to become consciously aware that it was already there when the pedal is lifted and the chord is repeated.

This is a particularly clear example of a technique that is quite common in Ives, one in which a separate strand of continuity is allowed to be heard only in isolated segments, thus establishing associations which, despite their distance in time, are instantaneous in effect. (Another example is provided by the "distant choirs" in the outer movements of the *Fourth Symphony,* which are only intermittently audible.) The effect is rather like the temporary opening of a window through which one is momentarily able to hear a separate layer of music, always there in some absolute sense yet perceptible only when the window is raised. The association is instantaneous because, as with what one sees through a window, the musical layer seems to occupy the same space as before, a space that is to some degree unaffected by the temporal discontinuity.

The particular form given to these "Alcotts" fragments in the "Hawthorne" movement is admittedly special, even within the context of the "Concord" Sonata; but it is nevertheless closely related to the more general motivic layout of the sonata as a whole, which encompasses a labyrinth of references pointing through all movements in all directions. Thus intimations of the "Alcotts" music are heard, though in a less pure and isolated form than the ones just discussed, throughout the opening movement of the sonata and in the part of the second movement preceding the interruptions. (A fairly lengthy example can be found in an inner voice in the second system of the second page of the score.) Moreover, the "Alcotts" material returns again—and in a relatively complete form, although it is not allowed to end, at least in the sense of reaching a conclusion—near the close of the last movement. Here it forms a separate layer of continuity that is heard in combination with the continuation of the "Thoreau" music which "properly" belongs to this movement. The sense of a separate layer—an independent strand of continuity—is underscored by Ives's suggestion that this passage be played by a flute.

Such connections, tying together extensive spans of time through instantaneous association, are found in relation to all of the principal thematic materials of the "Concord" Sonata. The specific techniques employed are perhaps related to those of thematic transformation in much nineteenth-century music. However, there is something new. Ives's creation, through these means, of a complex web of discontinuous yet interconnecting associations, which stretch over several seemingly independent levels of music activity and integrate them into a single multilinear progression, bespeaks a fundamentally different compositional mentality.

Through this discussion of fragmentation we have arrived at one of Ives's most noted practices: the simultaneous combination of two or more independent, though related, musical continuities. Famous examples, where the technique is especially apparent because the separate strands are so individualized that they have their own tempos, are found in "Putnam's Camp" (the second movement of *Three Places in New England*), in *The Unanswered Question,* and in the second movement of the *Fourth Symphony.* However, a similar approach is evident in varying degrees in almost all of Ives's work, going back at least as far as his Yale days. One thinks of the elaborate thematic juxtapositions near the end of both the *First Symphony* and the *First String Quartet,* both relatively early pieces. (In the latter piece the combined themes are sufficiently individualized to have their own meters, if not tempos.)

The most essential point in the present context is that such passages are texturally, and thus temporally, multidimensional. The absence of a single strand of continuity—what Roger Sessions used to refer to as "the long line"— reflects a basic shift in compositional orientation. Ives works with a number of different yet simultaneous time-movements coexisting in a shared, multilayered universe where each maintains its own individuality while also influencing and being influenced by all others. Here we are very close, I think, to the meaning of Ives's notion, as expressed in the *Fourth Symphony*'s "Conductor's Note," of "bringing various parts of the music to the ear . . . as the perspective of a picture brings each object to the eye." In a passage in his *Memos* he speaks similarly of "trying out a parallel way of listening to music, suggested by looking at a view," so that the listener focuses his ears first on one layer and then on another.[7] It is this that I mean by the multidimensional quality of Ives's work. There is no single point of view defined by the inexorable passage of a single strand of time. It is as if Ives is trying to get outside of time, to enable the listener to walk around the work, to hear it from different angles or perspectives.

In this connection Ives suggests that the music should be played twice to allow for a change of focus. There is no reason why this cannot be done within the context of a single performance; I suspect that this is the way most of us listen to Ives, shifting the main emphasis of our attention back and forth from one layer to another. The organization of the opening movement of the *Piano Trio* is interesting in this regard. Here Ives establishes the layers separately, combining them only after each has been stated as an independent segment. The arrangement is as follows: the cello and right hand (or upper staff) of the piano have a twenty-seven-measure passage alone, after which the violin and left hand play a different passage of similar length; then both are combined for the final twenty-seven measures, followed by a brief, two-measure extension. Thus here each layer *is* played twice, although it is heard in a very different perspective the second time because of the combination.

Another spatial category in Ives can be found in his occasional inclination to serial thinking. Although there are few compositions by him that are explicitly serial in the generally accepted sense, those that are warrant some attention. Several pieces—*Tone Roads No. 1* and *No. 3, Chromâtimelôd-tune,* and *From the Steeples and the Mountains,* for example—have serial aspects, although in all of them the series is (or are, as there may be more than one) only one aspect of the pitch organization. Nevertheless, Ives's serialism is striking. In *From the Steeples and the Mountains* there is a durational series determining the overall rhythmic structure of the piece, effecting first a gradual acceleration of the values from half notes to six-

7. *Memos,* p. 106.

teenths and then, through retrograde, a gradual return to the original values. (The circular character of this motion should be noted.) There is a similar passage in the coda of *Over the Pavements*.

What is principally interesting in terms of spatial thinking in Ives, however, is not his serialism per se, but its status as a particular manifestation of a more general tendency: the inclination to use material that has in some sense been predetermined or preordered. This tendency is evident not only in the use of a series but, more important for Ives, in the use of quotations of already existing musical material. This reflects a radically new attitude toward material—a desire to objectify it, to take it as something given. To the extent that this attitude prevails, the entire compositional process is transformed from one of evolving a work out of the implications of a germ idea to one of placing given materials (objects) in juxtaposition to one another in various combinations and permutations. The whole idea of the motive as germ, as a fecund source from which all subsequent materials grow in orderly succession, obviously assumes a linear temporal framework within which one idea leads logically to the next. It also reflects a particular kind of compositional disposition, one in which emphasis is placed not on the basic motive as something in itself, but rather on its generative or procreative function in respect to temporally subsequent derivations. (This kind of musical development produces, in analogy to organic, biological development, something rather like motivic offspring.) In Ives, on the other hand, the motive—if that is still the correct word—acquires more of an absolute value: it does not point forward, but seems rather to point to itself. Thus its relationships to other motives are essentially combinational rather than progressive in nature. It is for this reason that the structure often seems flat—static and nondevelopmental—when compared with earlier music. The technique involved is very similar to those of collage and cubism in painting, where objects—also frequently borrowed—are placed in abrupt juxtaposition to one another, so that their relations cannot be measured by the spatial-temporal coordinates of the real world but only on the flat surface of the canvas.

The importance of this technique in recent music, whether the musical materials in question are actually borrowed (which of course they often are) or not, can hardly be overestimated. It also plays a significant role in the work of other early twentieth-century composers, notably Stravinsky and Varèse, but in Ives the method receives both its earliest and—except for the recent past—its most radical formulation. It is closely related to those techniques of fragmentation in his music discussed previously and to the combinational structure of the first movement of the *Piano Trio*. Also, the inverted repetition of the music for the opening two verses of *Psalm 54* to accompany its last two verses, where the material previously given to the female voices is traded with that of the male voices, reveals a similar combinational approach.[8] I might also mention here the very special way in which the repetition of the music of the first verse is brought about at the beginning of the second; the process recurs, of course, in verses 7a and 7b. The harmonic motion of the parallel augmented triads in the male voices is arranged in a circular fashion so that it turns back on itself, reaching the original point of departure at the beginning of the second verse. How different this passage is from its traditional formal analog, the period, where the half cadence creates an effect not of gradual rearrival but of interruption, and then of starting over again to complete something previously left unfinished!

The voice exchange in *Psalm 54* is only one instance among many in Ives where the composer creates a specifically spatial effect by the manipulation of registral relationships, perhaps the closest musical analog to physical spatial relationships. Particularly suggestive are the wedge techniques found, for example, in the closing section of *Tone Roads No. 3* and in *Psalm 24*, where the musical idea essentially consists of a registral expansion in both directions from a central axis, followed by a return through contraction to the same point (the motion again being circular). There are even pieces whose entire shape seems to be determined by registral considerations. The overall progress of both voice line and accompaniment in the song *A Farewell to Land*, for example, is framed according to a gradual descent from highest to lowest register, combined with a gradual acceleration of the durations to the song's mid-point and then a corresponding retardation of the values to the end.

Finally, I should refer to those passages, so characteristic of Ives, in which everything seems to happen at once. These passages of unprecedented textural density can perhaps be considered as part of a more general category also encompassing those made up of simultaneous musical layers. In some cases, however, the degree of independence is so great that it becomes difficult to pick out even individual levels within which there is some degree of cooperation. Curiously, in these extreme instances one is forced to reduce everything to one level again: the passages are so complex in regard to their internal relationships that the ear perceives them as a totality—a single sound event bordering on chaos. They *must* be heard simultaneously— spatially—since the ear is unable to differentiate sequential connections among the individual components. Such passages have become common

8. David Wooldridge, *From the Steeples and Mountains* (New York: A. Knopf, 1974), asserts (p. 84) that the music for the last verses is lost and "has been constructed by Gregg Smith, inverting the material used in verses 1/2." However, as is clear in the editors' notes to the score supplied by Smith and John Kirkpatrick, this music was never lost and the inversional idea was Ives's own. (See also Kirkpatrick's review of Wooldridge in *Musical America*, September, 1974, pp. 33–36.)

in recent music (where they are often described as being "statistical" in nature); but Ives was writing them as early as the first decade of the century and no one else composed anything remotely like them for the next fifty years.

In this paper I have focused on many different techniques and drawn examples from a number of different pieces. But what should finally be emphasized is that all are connected with one another and, moreover, that all are consistent with a single compositional attitude which encompasses a wide and varied range of interrelated techniques, none of which can be viewed in isolation. The problem with Ives is not, as is frequently maintained, that he uses a number of different procedures that are perhaps interesting in themselves but are somehow incompatible with one another and thus incapable of producing a unified musical statement. The problem, rather, is that we have not yet found the analytical key for discovering how these procedures relate to one another and, more important, to a unifying compositional vision.

I believe that the notion of spatial form may provide at least one such key to a more inclusive and comprehensive understanding of Ives's work. Before closing, I would like to consider briefly several areas of inquiry related to Ives that might be considered in light of the spatial rubric.

First, of course, is the music itself. I have been able to touch only briefly upon a limited number of examples. I am convinced, however, that more detailed analysis along these same lines, and particularly attempts to analyze comprehensively a single work or movement, would yield valuable and suggestive results.

Second, the question of Ives's position in the history of twentieth-century music is one begging for reconsideration. Musical developments since World War II have seemed to suggest a rather fundamental break with the Western musical tradition, yet the spatial nature of both Ives's music and that of more recent composers suggests the possibility of a new historical alignment, within which Ives would occupy a much more central position than the one currently accorded him.[9]

Equally important is the question of precedence for spatial thinking. The techniques discussed here did not, of course, suddenly appear full-blown in Ives. Certain pieces still reflecting what one might call the older way of musical thinking strongly suggest also, at least in some of their aspects, a spatial point of view—particularly works of the nineteenth century, but also others dating back through the entire common-practice period. (Connections between Ives and Western music predating the functional

9. See my article "Rewriting Music History: Second Thoughts on Ives and Varèse," *Musical Newsletter*, 2, nos. 1, 2 (1973).

tonal period are probably even more patent, but here I am thinking specifically within a linear historical context.)

Finally, there is the question of the psychological roots of Ives's musical thought, both in the personal sense of its relation to the composer's own character and upbringing and in the broader context of its relation to twentieth-century thought in general. In the former case, certainly Ives's attraction to transcendentalism—a philosophy that tends to view time, at least as it is related to external action, as in some sense unreal—is suggestive. In the latter, I might mention the widely held view that one of the characteristic features of twentieth-century consciousness is an altered sense of time, which is no longer experienced as linear. Distinctions between past and present are correspondingly attenuated, so that we often seem to feel closer to the past than to the present, and to the remote past than to the recent past. As a consequence, the causal aspects of time are minimized; the past appears to become part of the present. One sees this clearly in the arts, where allusions to past styles and works have been common throughout the century—in Eliot, Joyce, Picasso, and many others.

I have mentioned Ives's quotations in regard to both his techniques of fragmentation and his tendency to select preordered material. In the light of a new time consciousness, another facet of their use may well be seen as an attempt to abolish time—to minimize distinctions between past and present, between the old music and the new. This is not only a matter of the quotations. In a famous statement, Ives once remarked: " . . . why tonality as such should be thrown out for good, I can't see. Why it should be always present, I can't see. It depends, it seems to me, a good deal—as clothes depend on the thermometer—on what one is trying to do, and on the state of mind, the time of day or other accidents of life."[10] The point here, I think, is that in Ives's music tonality loses its historical context; it is neutralized and can be treated much like nontonal music—with the same kinds of compositional techniques and with similar sonic results. This, finally, is perhaps the most basic sense in which spatial form is atemporal: it enables the composer to ignore historical and stylistic distinctions—or, rather, it enables him to transcend these distinctions through a new kind of formal unity.

In closing I would like to mention briefly two characterizations of Ives's music that I came across while working on this paper. They both seem to me to get to the essence of Ives; and I like to think that they support my arguments. The first is a comment made by the conductor Bernard Herrmann for the Ives Oral History Project at Yale University: he noted that "Ives's music doesn't go on in time and space" and then likened it to "a

10. From "Some 'Quarter-tone' Impressions," reprinted in Ives's *Essays Before a Sonata, The Majority, and Other Writings,* ed. Howard Boatwright (New York: W. W. Norton, 1961), p. 117.

photograph of a happening."[11] The second appears in an article by the German musicologist Elmar Budde on Ives's *Second String Quartet*. After a fairly detailed analysis of the first section of the quartet (mm. 1–15), confined principally to pitch and rhythmic relationships, Budde states: "It might seem that it is a question of motives, but here the figures do not function in respect to the continuity of the entire composition. The relationships are not reducible to binding laws—for example, to a specific system of derivations; they should be interpreted as a net of reminiscences and associations in which each event not only has multiple relationships, but could also be different."[12]

These ideas—of a net of references and cross-references that point in alternate, though not mutually exclusive directions, and of a photograph in which all things are linked in spatial simultaneity—rest at the very heart of Ives's music.

11. Herrmann's remarks appear on the record "Ives Remembered" included in the Columbia album *Charles Ives: The 100th Anniversary* (New York, 1974). Cf. the printed version of the interview, in Vivian Perlis, *Charles Ives Remembered* (New Haven: Yale University Press, 1974), pp. 155–62.

12. Elmar Budde, "Anmerkungen zum Streichquarttet Nr. 2 von Charles E. Ives," in *Bericht über den Internationalen Musikwissenschaftlichen Kongress, Bonn, 1970* (Kassel: Bärenreiter, 1971), p. 306.

Ives and Atonality

ALLEN FORTE

The question of the relation of Ives's music to that of the avant-garde European composers of the so-called atonal school, primarily Schoenberg and his students during the years 1908 through 1920, is an interesting one. I believe that it is central to developing an understanding of Ives's music beyond the superficial level thus far attained, for in dealing with the question one is naturally led to examine with a certain degree of precision basic aspects of the music that have been inadequately, even incorrectly, characterized up to the present time.

Certainly the relation of his music to that of the European moderns was of interest to Ives. Indeed, the *Memos*[1] were initiated by him in 1931 evidently in direct response to the critics who reviewed Slonimsky's 1931 performances of *Three Places in New England*. Prominent among these critics was Henry Prunières, whose *New York Times* review of the Paris concert contained this comment: "There is no doubt that he [Ives] knows his Schoenberg, yet gives the impression that he has not always assimilated the lessons of the Viennese master as well as he might have."[2]

In a letter to the eminent pianist E. Robert Schmitz, Ives wrote the following concerning Prunières's review: "He says that I know my Schoenberg —interesting information to me, as I have never heard nor seen a note of Schoenberg's music. Then he says that I haven't 'applied the lessons as well as I might.' This statement shows almost human intelligence."[3]

It is certain that Ives did not know Schoenberg's music, nor did he know any of the other experimental music being composed in Europe at the time he was writing the *"Concord" Sonata* and other mature works. If Mahler had survived and if he had performed the *Third Symphony*[4] (which

1. *Charles E. Ives: Memos*, ed. John Kirkpatrick (New York: W. W. Norton, 1972).
2. *Memos*, p. 15.
3. *Memos*, p. 27.
4. Mahler took the score of the *Third Symphony* back to Europe with him in 1911, the year of his death. *Memos*, p. 55.

may well have been his intention), things would have been otherwise, of course. In fact, the whole history of modern music in America would have been very different.

The very word *atonality* was, of course, unknown to Ives until long after he had stopped composing. In the past the term has been used to characterize all the post-tonal music of Schoenberg and the music of his students, Webern and Berg. In the present paper the term will be used in the meaning it customarily has now, to refer to the post-tonal and pre–twelve-tone music of Schoenberg and others. To give specific examples, Schoenberg's *Herzgewaechse,* Op. 20 (1911), is an atonal work, whereas his *Moses und Aron* (1932) is a twelve-tone work.

In this connection it should be said that there is no substantial evidence to indicate that Ives's music has anything to do with the development of serial and twelve-tone procedures. The primary connection between Ives and modern European music is through the phenomenon known as atonality, as will be demonstrated.

In order to proceed beyond these introductory comments to a closer study of Ives's music it is necessary to provide a working definition of an atonal composition—a very informal definition, to be sure, but one that will suffice for the present purpose.[5]

An atonal work is characterized, first of all, by the occurrence of musical configurations that are reducible to note collections or sets that normally are not found in traditional tonal music. Moreover, these musical components are not related within the framework of traditional harmonic and contrapuntal structures, but are formed into cohesive musical wholes by a small number of specific types of transformations.

Of these transformations, transposition is the most familiar. Example 1 shows an instance drawn from a Schoenberg song composed in 1909. Notice

Example 1. Schoenberg, *Am Strande,* 1909. © 1966 by Belmont Music Publishers. Used by permission.

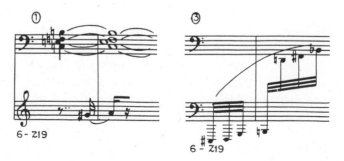

6 - Z19

6 - Z19

<hr />

5. A more detailed treatment is to be found in Allen Forte, *The Structure of Atonal Music* (New Haven: Yale University Press, 1973).

that the sets in this case (and in the Ives examples that will follow) are indicated by a name. The set name says nothing about the mode of occurrence, but is merely a key to a fixed item on a list of sets. Here both sets are of type "6-Z19," the nineteenth hexachord on the list. In addition, the set has the Z-property, which involves special intervallic and complement relations. The two sets are related by transposition, as can be seen by aligning the notes as follows:

$$E \quad F \quad G\sharp \quad A \quad B \quad C$$
$$F\sharp \quad G \quad B\flat \quad B \quad C\sharp \quad D$$

Thus, at one level of analysis, the pitch organization of an atonal work can be described in terms of the sets employed and the operations that relate those sets. In addition, the authentic atonal work exhibits these characteristics throughout, and, although the possibility of local tonal centers is not ruled out, there is no single tonal center analogous to that of the traditional tonal composition. Similarly, an atonal work may include sets that are diatonic in origin—the most obvious example of which is the triad—without being classed as tonal.

This description of atonality, although far from complete, is sufficient for the present purpose. Moreover, it suggests that atonality is not to be characterized negatively with reference to tonality. Rather, the atonal work is an independent composition based upon general procedures essentially different from those of the classic tonal work.

Also, although atonal music can be analyzed systematically, it is not "formula" music. A particular work in the atonal repertory may differ markedly from others in the repertory, although all share the common characteristics just mentioned. It is precisely this degree of flexibility that enables one to examine the music of Ives from the perspective of atonality.

The set-components of an atonal work are sometimes difficult to identify, and, indeed, the identification process requires specific analytical techniques. In addition, in view of the complexity of much atonal music and the fact that a broad spectrum of sets is available, the ear may be misled. Thus, it is not surprising that erroneous statements have been made in the past. A recent example, concerning the music of Ives, appeared in the context of an article by the music critic of the *New York Times*.[6] He compares two passages, one from Ives's *"Concord" Sonata* (the "Hawthorne" movement, p. 41, brace 2) and one from Scriabin's *Ninth Sonata* (p. 185, brace 1), and makes the following observation about the Ives passage: "In figuration and even sound it bears a relationship to the late piano music of Scriabin. . . ." If this comparison pertains to the two passages quoted (which, in all fairness,

6. Harold C. Schonberg, "Natural American, Natural Rebel, Natural Avant-Gardist," *New York Times Magazine,* April 21, 1974, p. 82.

is not clear from the comment), then it is incorrect. Examination of the two passages reveals that they share only one set of the same type (5–24); otherwise, the musical components of the two passages are entirely different. (This probably qualifies our overly zealous critic for Rollo status.)

Did Ives compose atonal music in accord with the description of atonality given? Indeed he did, and the major part of his mature output can be described as atonal. There is, of course, a large number of tonal pieces—for example, many of the songs in the latter part of the collection *114 Songs* (1922) and the tonal movement ("The Alcotts") of the *"Concord" Sonata.* By and large, however, the representative mature works are atonal, and there are some indications that Ives regarded these as superior to those of the formative period (say, prior to 1906). For instance, most of the first thirty songs in *114 Songs* are atonal. Also, in his *Memos* Ives refers to the "slump pieces" (for example, the *Fourth Violin Sonata*),[7] which can be construed as a reference to an unwilling return to the more conventional style of composition. There is also an interesting reference to the "older way of writing and the newer way."[8]

The extent to which Ives employs atonal procedures is extraordinary. As some indication, a number of excerpts from various works will now be displayed and discussed.[9] This will also provide an opportunity to make some comments on aspects of Ives's music that are possibly unique to it and certainly characteristic.

ATONAL SETS

Ives's music abounds in atonal sets, many of which are amply represented in the works of the European atonalists. Example 2 shows an occurrence of set 6-Z24, one of Ives's favorites and one that is often found in the atonal classics—in Berg's *Wozzeck,* to cite one case. Although this excerpt shows an atonal set in the melodic dimension, it should not be assumed that

Example 2. *Duty* (*114 Songs,* no. 9), 1911–13. © 1933 by Merion Music, Inc. Used by permission.

6 - 224

7. *Memos,* p. 70.
8. *Memos,* p. 68.
9. All dates on the musical examples are taken from John Kirkpatrick's *A Temporary Mimeographed Catalogue of the Music Manuscripts and Related Materials of Charles Edward Ives* (New Haven: Library of the Yale School of Music, 1960). Uncertain dates are indicated by ? following the date(s). Alternative dates (after Kirkpatrick) are indicated by /.

this mode of occurrence is typical for sets of the atonal type in Ives's music. On the contrary, melodic lines in Ives tend to be diatonic, chromatic, or whole tone. In contrast to, say, Schoenberg, melodic formations in Ives's music are seldom reducible to atonal sets, although the total musical texture may be atonal.

An atonal set in a far more typical configuration is shown in Example 3. Here the atonal set occurs as a vertical and immediately precedes a section in F major. This obvious juxtaposition of atonal and diatonic sections has far less obvious extensions throughout Ives's music, as will become evident.

One additional comment may be of interest in connection with Example 3. This atonal set, 6-34, is of the same type as the set known as "Scriabin's mystic chord." Ives seems to have been particularly fond of it, for it shows up in many compositions of different types. (Probably he discovered it long before Scriabin.)

Example 3. *Down East* (*114 Songs*, no. 55), 1919; possibly derived from *Down East Overature*, 1897–98. © 1958 by Peer International Corporation. Used by permission.

Large Sets

One of the more obvious, but nonetheless radically innovative, features of atonal music—and one stressed by Schoenberg in his *Harmonielehre*[10]— is the occurrence of chords containing more than the four or five different notes normally found in traditional tonal music.[11] Ives's music shares this feature. An extreme instance is given in Example 4.

Berg asserted that Fritz Heinrich Klein was the first to discover the twelve-note chord or "Mutterakkord."[12] Although the date of Klein's dis-

10. Arnold Schoenberg, *Harmonielehre* (Vienna: Universal Edition, 1911). See the section entitled "Aesthetische Bewertung sechs- und mehrtöniger Akkorde" (Aesthetic Evaluation of Chords of Six or More Notes).

11. In constructing these new sounds both Ives and Schoenberg had to come to terms with prevailing "natural base" theory inherited from Rameau via Helmholtz, Riemann, and others. See *Memos*, p. 50.

12. Willi Reich-Wien, "Alban Berg," *Die Musik*, 22, no. 5 (February, 1930), facing p. 352.

Example 4. *Robert Browning Overture*, 1908–12. © 1959 by Peer International Corporation. Used by permission.

covery has not been ascertained, it would appear that Ives's use of this "universal" sonority here in the *Browning Overture* is the first such instance.[13] Fortunately, there are not many others in the repertory of atonal music.

The origin of these large sets, in the case of Ives, is not difficult to trace. He first used them in hymn interludes played in Center Church during his college days.[14] In particular, Ives used a single eight-note set in these interludes, the set 8-18, which is found throughout the repertory of European atonal music.[15]

A typical instance of a large set in a mature work is shown in Example 5. This eight-note set, which occurs throughout the song, is to be found in much of Ives's music. Why was he so partial to this sonority? How does it relate to other, perhaps more fundamental, pitch components of his music? One answer lies in the complement relation (about which more will be said below).

Example 5. *Nov. 2, 1920 (114 Songs, no. 22)*, 1920. © 1935 by Merion Music, Inc. Used by permission.

13. Among the *Universe Symphony* sketches (negative 03047 in the Ives Collection, John Herrick Jackson Music Library, Yale University) is another such twelve-note chord.

14. *Memos*, p. 120. Kirkpatrick suggests the date 1892 in the *Catalogue*.

15. Ives Collection, negatives 02208, 00974, 03187. It is interesting that the complement of this set, 4-18, is another of Ives's early experimental chords, the "drum chord." See *Memos*, p. 43.

This type of eight-note set is the complement (with respect to the total chromatic) of the four-note set formed by selecting any four consecutive notes from the whole-tone scale. Thus it represents, in expanded form, the intervallic characteristics of the smaller set, which is far more familiar. The following will illustrate.

chromatic scale	C	C♯	D	D♯	E	F	F♯	G	G♯	A	A♯	B
whole-tone scale	C		D		E		F♯		G♯		A♯	
four-note subset (4-21)					E		F♯		G♯		A♯	
eight-note complement	C	C♯	D	D♯		F		G		A		B

The four-note set 4-21 is not the only whole-tone tetrachord. Altogether, the familiar six-note whole-tone scale contains tetrachords of three different types, and Ives uses all three, together with their eight-note complements:

4-21	C	D	E	F♯
4-24	C	D	E	G♯
4-25	C	D	F♯	G♯

We know that the whole-tone scale was not discovered by Ives. (Evidently Liszt was the first to use it compositionally.) However, the use of the large whole-tone set was definitely innovative.

DIATONIC SETS

Just as subsets of the whole-tone scale may be described as whole-tone formations, so may subsets of the diatonic scale be described as diatonic.[16] Sets larger than the diatonic scale may also be described as diatonic if they contain the diatonic scale. For the present purpose, only eight-note sets of this type will be considered, and there are only three of those. Their complements are more familiar:

4-22	C	D	E	G
4-23	C	D	F	G	("chord in 4ths or 5ths")
4-26	C	E♭	F	A♭	("minor 7th chord")[17]

16. Set 4-21, which is a subset of both the whole-tone hexachord and the diatonic seven-note set, normally will be classed as whole-tone, since its complement, 8-21, contains the whole-tone hexachord.

17. The eight-note sets have the same numbers following the hyphens—thus, 8-22, 8-23, and 8-26.

Diatonic and whole-tone components are freely juxtaposed in Ives's atonal music. An uncomplicated instance is shown in Example 6. Here the voice part is based upon the whole-tone segment 5-33, while the accompaniment carries the diatonic set 5-35. The total effect, of course, is atonal, in the sense that no single tonal center is established throughout the song. The atonal effect is considerably heightened in the chamber orchestra piece from which the song is derived. There a number of additional features complicate the musical texture, notably the tritone figure A-D♯ played *ostinato* by the timpani. Ives made the following comment on this work: "Technically this piece is but a study of how chords of 4ths and 5ths may throw melodies away from a set tonality. . . . The principal thing in this movement is to show that a song does not necessarily have to be in any one key to make musical sense. To make music in no particular key has a nice name nowadays—'atonality.' "[18]

Example 6. *The Cage,* 1906. © 1955 by Peer International Corporation. Used by permission.

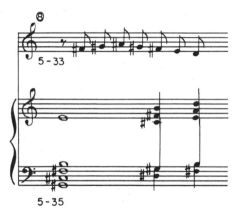

ATONAL SETS

While it was not difficult to characterize whole-tone and diatonic sets for informal descriptive purposes, it is not so easy to categorize atonal sets. The reason for this is that some subsets of the diatonic scale are atonal, in the sense that they never occur in traditional tonal music, being precluded by the operative rules of harmony and counterpoint. Two outstanding instances are provided by the so-called all-interval tetrachords, the only tetrachords in which all interval classes are represented. Whereas one of these (4-Z15) is not contained within the diatonic scale, the other (4-Z29) is repre-

18. *Memos,* pp. 55–56.

sented twice as a subset. Moreover, the whole-tone sets might well be regarded as a special subclass of atonal sets, since except for all but one of the
three-note subsets and one of the four-note subsets (4-21) of the whole-tone
scale, none of its subsets are also contained within the diatonic scale.

Ives was familiar with several of the characteristic atonal sets probably
at least as early as 1892, the date tentatively assigned by Kirkpatrick to some
experimental exercises in the Ives Collection.[19] In the one case (03267), the
exercise consists of ascending major triads set out note for note against a
descending chromatic scale. (Kirkpatrick aptly calls them "wedges.") In the
course of this progression, two common atonal sets are formed, 4-19
(Bb   D   F#   A) and 4-Z29 (A   Eb   G   Bb). In the other case, the wedge
is formed of descending major triads on the upper staff against ascending
major triads on the lower staff. Again, atonal sets are produced, namely,
5-21 and 6-30 (Example 7), as well as the diatonic set 6-33, which Ives uses
often.

Despite all the qualifications mentioned earlier, it seems useful to employ in an informal way the terms *whole-tone, diatonic,* and *atonal* to describe the components of Ives's music.[20] Example 7 will illustrate. This

Example 7. *Three Places in New England,* first movement ("The St. Gaudens in Boston
Common"), 1911–12. © 1935 by Mercury Music Corp. Used by permission.

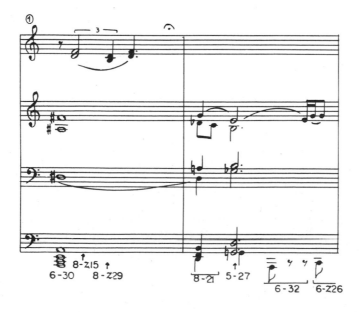

---

19. Negatives 03267 and 02179.

20. These methodological problems disappear in a set-complex analysis. See Forte, *Structure,* part 2.

movement begins with an atonal chord, 6-30.[21] With the introduction of the "Old Black Joe" motive (piano and flute on the upper staff), two eight-note sets are formed. The first of these is 8-Z15, the second 8-Z29, a striking alternation of the two large sets that complement the all-interval tetrachords. The total interval content thus remains constant over the two sets: all interval classes are present in the same number, except for interval class 6 (the tritone), which is represented one more time than any other interval.[22] Both sonorities are found very frequently in the music of the European atonalists.

In the second measure of Example 7 there is a pronounced change to the whole-tone formation 8-21. This is followed immediately by the diatonic set 5-27. When the bass brings in an echo of the "Old Black Joe" motive, with bass notes A and C, there is a corresponding change of harmony from the diatonic set 6-32 (the major hexachord) to the atonal set 6-Z26. (The latter is one of the problematic cases in our categorization, since it is a subset of the diatonic scale, but does not occur in traditional tonal music.) The two diatonic sets 5-27 and 6-32 here relate directly to the quoted tune and may be regarded as verticalizations of segments of that diatonic melody.

The radical fluctuation between atonal, whole-tone, and diatonic components in this passage (Example 7) is typical of Ives's music. It provides a pronounced differentiation of musical content and contributes to the general impression of vigor and roughness that are his hallmarks. In this respect, Ives's music stands in marked contrast to the music of Schoenberg, but it does bear a similarity to some of Berg's music. A familiar instance would be the "Lullaby" music from Act I of *Wozzeck*.

Thus far, examples of large sets have involved mainly vertical formations. A set can be projected over the span of an entire passage, however, as the first excerpt in Example 8 illustrates. This passage recurs throughout the movement, without modification, as a kind of refrain. Although it contains diatonic and chromatic elements, which are most evident in the outer voices, the total configuration reduces to the large whole-tone set 8-21. The verticals indicated by arrows are sets of type 5-34, a diatonic set (familiar in tonal music as a ninth chord) here in the context of a whole-tone formation. This association of whole-tone and diatonic components is manifested in multiple ways throughout the movement. One of the most interesting cases is shown in the second excerpt of Example 8. The diatonic melody first occurs on page 62, as indicated. Subsequently, there is a whole-tone variant on that melody on page 64, and the set projected by the latter is 8-21, the same set

21. A celebrated instance of this set is the "Petrouchka" chord at rehearsal 49 in Stravinsky's score. This set contains two forms of the triad (set 3-11). These two triads are notationally evident in the Stravinsky passage as a C-major triad and an F♯-major triad. Here in the Ives excerpt (Example 7) they are the D♯-minor and the A-minor triads. Both situations are atonal, of course.

22. The interval vector is [555553].

Example 8. *"Concord" Sonata,* fourth movement ("Thoreau"), 1911–15?. © 1947 by Associated Music Publishers, Inc. Used by permission.

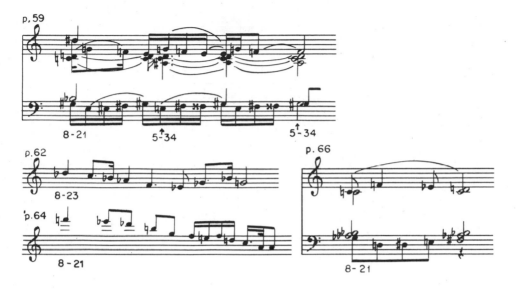

as in the refrain passage just discussed. The final excerpt in Example 8 shows still another occurrence of the whole-tone set 8-21, a compressed variant on the refrain. This method of using a particular set to unify events of different types over long spans of music is very similar to that of Schoenberg in his atonal music.

THE OPERATIONS TRANSPOSITION AND INVERSION

We now know that the operations of inversion and transposition were used by Schoenberg and his students not only from about 1920 on in the twelve-tone compositions, where they were applied to the totally ordered set, with consequent permutation, but also in the earlier atonal works, where they were applied to unordered sets of sizes smaller than twelve.

An uncomplicated instance of Ives's use of transposition is shown in Example 9. Here we have three successive transpositions of the set 5-Z17. A transposition of this type is called an ordered transposition,[23] since the elements of the set remain in the same relative positions.

Two additional comments may be made in connection with this example. First, undue emphasis should not be placed upon the notation here, namely, the partitioning of the set into two trichordal subsets that may be read as triads. Far too much has been made of this aspect of Ives's music, together with the catchwords *polyharmony, polytonality,* and the like. Sec-

23. See Forte, *Structure,* p. 62.

Example 9. *Nov. 2, 1920 (114 Songs,* no. 22), 1920. © 1935 by Merion Music, Inc. Used by permission.

ond, this atonal set, by a historical accident, is the same as the opening sonority in the third movement of Schoenberg's *Five Pieces for Orchestra,* Op. 16.[24]

Example 10 shows transpositionally related sets in a context somewhat more diversified than that of Example 9. The passage begins with three different forms of set 6-31, one of Ives's favorite harmonies, at two levels of transposition (ordered). The fourth vertical, the five-note set 5-32, is directly related to 6-31, as one of its subsets, and the final vertical in the example, 7-32 (the complement of 5-32), contains 6-31 (specifically, as B   C   D♯   E♯   G   G♯). The only sonority that does not directly relate to 6-31 here is 7-34. Although 6-31 is not especially prominent in the repertory of European atonal music, 7-32 is. A familiar example is the "Auguries of Spring" chord in Stravinsky's *Rite of Spring.*

Example 10. *The Majority (114 Songs,* no. 1); derived from *Majority or the Masses,* 1914. © 1935 by Merion Music, Inc. Used by permission.

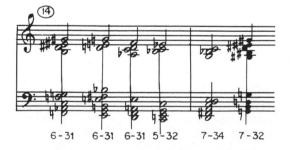

Ordered transpositions are usually very easy to detect in Ives's music; unordered transpositions are not. As one instance of the latter, consider the first two forms of 8-21 in Example 8. The second of these (p. 64) is a transposition of the first (p. 59), yet there is no obvious association between the two set-forms. More specifically, the second set is equivalent to the first set

24. Also borrowed by Berg and used as the first of three chords that form the basis of Act 1, Scene 2, of *Wozzeck.*

transposed up nine half steps. More often than not in Schoenberg's atonal music, two transpositionally related sets generate a contextually significant third set, namely, the set of pitches common to both. It would appear that this aspect of the operation of transposition was not of general concern to Ives, although there is some evidence to the contrary. In the present case, the common pitches (invariants) are C D F G. These notes form the upper part of the first segment (p. 59) and are grouped together in the second segment (p. 64).

Whereas transposition is an operation that atonal music shares with tonal music, inversion of the atonal type (or "symmetric inversion," as Bernard Ziehn called it) is not especially significant to tonal music. Example 11 seems clearly to indicate that Ives was well aware of this operation. Here at

Example 11. *Second String Quartet,* second movement ("Arguments"), 1907. © 1954 by Peer International Corporation. Used by permission.

the opening of the movement are two forms of set 4-12. Not only is the second the inversion of the first, but the sets are deployed in such a way that there is a correspondence of pitches and intervals as follows:

$$
\begin{array}{cccc}
\text{E} & \text{F}\sharp & \text{G} & \text{A}\sharp \\
\text{E} & \text{D} & \text{C}\sharp & \text{B}\flat
\end{array}
$$

That is, the pitches common to both forms are presented first in each case and the remaining pitches form the same interval: the major seventh G-F♯ in the one case and D-C♯ in the other.

The use of inversion in Ives's music is by no means confined to such obvious instances as that shown in Example 11. In Example 12 we find a

Example 12. *First Piano Sonata,* "In the Inn," 1902–10. © 1954 by Peer International Corporation. Used by permission.

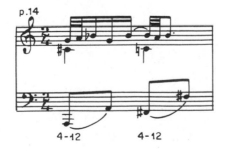

Example 13. *First Piano Sonata,* "In the Inn," 1902–10. © 1954 by Peer International Corporation. Used by permission.

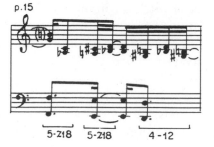

succession of two inversionally related sets in a more complicated and, so to speak, freer situation. Since inversion always involves transposition as well, it is often of interest to see if the particular transposition has any special consequences. That is the case in the excerpt in Example 13. Of the two forms of 5-Z18 here, the second is the inversion of the first transposed by the only interval that will yield entirely new pitches. That is, the second form of 5-Z18 shares none of the pitches of the first form. This is only possible, in general, by means of inversion at one, and only one, transposition level, the one that Ives has used here.[25] This is not intended to indicate that Ives was as systematic as Schoenberg and others of the atonal school, but merely to suggest that from time to time passages in Ives do exemplify those special structural situations that have to do with invariance.

A passage in which transposition is combined with inversion is shown in Example 14. The sets marked B and D, forms of 5-30, are transpositionally related. Examination of the three forms of set 6-33, A, E, and F, shows that set E is the inversion of set A, and set F is the inversion of set E, which

Example 14. *From Paracelsus (114 Songs,* no. 30); derived (according to Kirkpatrick) from *Robert Browning Overture,* 1908–12. © 1935 by Merion Music, Inc. Used by permission.

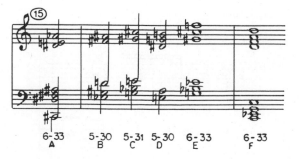

25. The particular level is not fixed, of course, but depends upon the pitches in the set being inverted.

means, of course, that set F is a transposition of set A. In the latter case, the transposition is unordered. Set 6-33 is a characteristically Ivesian formation of the diatonic type, familiar in tonal music as the minor hexachord.

It is worth mentioning here that the set marked F has been (and probably will be again) described as a "polychord,"[26] whereas it is merely an inversion of the notationally less obvious chord marked E, which immediately precedes it and is presumably not a polychord. Terms such as the latter, as well as "dissonant counterpoint" and "tone cluster," are not useful in analytical descriptions, since they do not lead naturally to considerations of relatedness among musical components.

COMPLEMENT-RELATED SETS

The complement relation has been mentioned earlier in connection with the occurrence of large sets in Ives's music—for example, 8-21, the wholetone set. This relation, which is so characteristic of the European atonal music, is far more pervasive in Ives's music than has been realized heretofore. Detailed discussion of the general musical significance of the complement relation would exceed the bounds of this paper. However, it can be said, briefly, that complement-related sets have a specific and unique kind of intervallic relationship.[27] Example 15 provides an instance of two complement-related sets in a local context. Here we find 5-35 (more familiar as the pentatonic scale) immediately followed by its complement 7-35 (the diatonic scale). (Here 5-35 occurs precisely at the end of the first vocal phrase, which carries another form of 5-35.) To avoid any confusion or misunderstanding about the complement-related sets that will be shown in the ex-

Example 15. *The Housatonic at Stockbridge* (*114 Songs,* no. 15); derived from *Three Places in New England,* third movement, 1903–14?. © 1954 by Peer International Corporation. Used by permission.

5-35   7-35

26. Henry and Sidney Cowell, *Charles Ives and His Music* (New York: Oxford University Press, 1955), p. 159. Compare Ives's interesting comment on notation in the *Memos,* p. 195.
27. See Forte, *Structure,* pp. 73 ff.

amples that follow, it should be pointed out that the complement of a set need not be a literal complement in order to qualify. To use the two sets in Example 15 to illustrate, we have the following situation:

5-35	F♯ (G♭)	G♯	B♭ (A♯)	C♯	E♭		
the literal complement	B	C	D	E	F	G	A
the literal complement transposed	D	E♭	F	G	A♭	B♭	C

The transposed form of the complement is, of course, the form of 7-35 that appears in Example 15.

Example 16 shows two pairs of sets in the complement relation. This song begins with a seven-note sonority that Ives has carefully marked "one chord." At the close of the song we find the complement, 5-19, of the opening chord, 7-19. The most obvious pitch link between the two sets is the soprano E in both cases. The other pair of complement-related sets is made up of 7-28 and 5-28, two sets often found in Ives's music (see Example 17). Example 16 also shows that the complement relation can be compounded, so to speak, and operate over different dimensions of the music. Notice, in particular, the two sets 8-9 and 4-9. The set 8-9 is formed at the outset when the low E♭ is introduced; its complement, 4-9, is contained within the final 5-19 as A♯ B E F.

Example 16. *Afterglow* (*114 Songs*, no. 39), 1919. © 1933 by Merion Music, Inc. Used by permission.

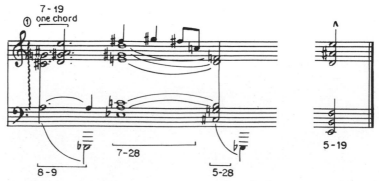

Perhaps even more remarkable are the many instances in which the complement relation is manifested over long spans of music. Example 17 shows the first occurrence of set 5-28 in the *"Concord" Sonata,* a prominent figure in the first measure. The complement of this set is then formed by the flourish at the beginning of the "Thoreau" movement. (Specifically, this is the literal complement transposed up nine half steps.) A few of the later occurrences of 7-28 are also shown in Example 17. All of these are at important points in the music, that is, at either the onset or the termination of a structural motion. The form of 7-28 quoted from page 65 (brace 2) requires a special comment here, since it contains very prominently the hexachord 6-34, also an important set in the music. Indeed, subset and superset relations are of the utmost importance to the organization of Ives's music, and they have been touched upon here in only the most elementary fashion.

A very peculiar and most interesting aspect of the complement relation involves hexachords of the so-called Z type.[28] The complement of a hexachord of this type is not transpositionally or inversionally related to it, and thus these hexachords (fifteen in all) constitute a special case. It happens that Schoenberg and his students, as well as Stravinsky (in his atonal music) and Scriabin, were very partial to these hexachords, perhaps because, for the most part, they are purely atonal sets without tonal associations (except for 6-Z25 and 6-Z26, which are contained within the diatonic scale). Do these hexachords occur in the music of Ives? Indeed they do, and very often.

Example 18 shows the Z hexachord 6-Z24 as the initial sonority of the second part of the second movement of the sonata. There are a number of other statements of the set, not necessarily in the same musical configuration, throughout, and one of these is shown as it appears on page 14 (brace 3).[29]

The complement of 6-Z24, 6-Z46, also occurs prominently in the movement, and two instances are shown in Example 18. The second of these, on page 16 (brace 2), is interesting for yet another reason, since it divides into two sets that are diatonic: 5-34 and 4-20 (more familiar as the major seventh chord). It also contains a reference to "Bringing in the Sheaves" in the bass part. Here we have a more abstruse example of the mixture of tonal and atonal components, but one that is not at all inconsistent with Ives's complicated mode of musical thought.

As is the case with the European atonalists, Ives appears to have favored

28. *Ibid.*, pp. 79 ff.

29. The occurrence of sets in various configurations has been mentioned several times in the previous pages. This type of structuring is typical of Schoenberg's later atonal works, and there is some indication that Ives composed in a similar way. In particular, this passage in the *Memos* is suggestive: "The continuity of this music [the *"Concord" Sonata*] is more a process of natural tonal diversification and distribution than of natural tonal repetition and resolution. Often the roots or the beginnings and end of a passage or cycle are not literally the beginnings and ends—but combinations of tone that can and do stand for them, if not to the eye, to the ear and mind after sufficient familiarity" (p. 195).

Example 17. *"Concord" Sonata,* first movement ("Emerson"), 1907–12, and fourth movement ("Thoreau"), 1911–15?. © 1947 by Associated Music Publishers, Inc. Used by permission.

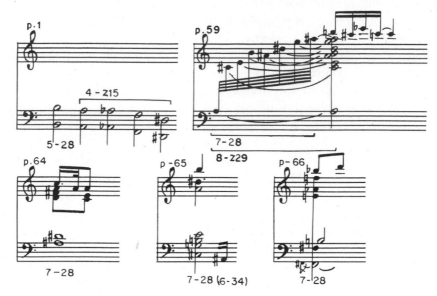

Example 18. *First Piano Sonata,* "In the Inn," 1902–10. © 1954 by Peer International Corporation. Used by permission.

certain sets, several of which have been pointed out. The set 6-Z24 and its complement 6-Z46 are among these. Example 19 shows them as they occur in a variety of musical contexts in the final movement of the *"Concord" Sonata.*

It should be stressed again that Ives uses these sets not only as verticals, but also over longer spans of music. Thus, the two statements of 6-Z46 at the beginning of Example 19 are of the more obvious chordal type, and, incidentally, are associated with the *Fifth Symphony* motive in both cases. The remaining excerpts, however, are not merely chords, but are configurations involving longer spans of music. The statement of 6-Z24 on page 62 (brace 1), for example, comprises the beginning of the new melody and the repeated three-note pattern in the bass, also new. When the repeated bass pattern is resumed on page 63 after intervening music, 6-Z46 replaces 6-Z24 and a whole-tone line replaces the diatonic line in the upper voice (compare Example 8).

Example 19. *"Concord" Sonata,* fourth movement ("Thoreau"), 1911–15?. © 1947 by Associated Music Publishers, Inc. Used by permission.

The next musical example, Example 20, provides an opportunity to review some of the characteristic aspects of Ives's music that have been discussed thus far, as well as to introduce a type of melodic structuring that may be found elsewhere in Ives's music. I refer to the relation between the upper voice of the piano and the violin line over the span of the first phrase. It is evident that they are moving together in a kind of duet, but closer ex-

Example 20. *Second Violin Sonata,* third movement ("The Revival"), 1906, 1909–10. ©
1951 by G. Schirmer, Inc. Used by permission.

amination shows that the relation is even more specific. Indeed, both project the same type of set, 8-27 (the complement of the dominant seventh
chord). Moreover, they both end with the same hexachord, the diatonic/
atonal set 6-Z25. The two sets are inversionally related and the transposition
involved is such that the two forms share seven notes (7-34). For any two
forms of 8-27 this kind of invariance is the maximum possible, and it is only
obtainable by means of a single transposition. Here again we have a case
in which Ives, whether consciously or not, has selected a unique structural
situation. One would not be surprised to find a similar organization in an
atonal work by Schoenberg, although in all likelihood he would not have
used the set 8-27.

The harmonies of the opening phrase (Example 20) are the typical
mixture of whole-tone (6-35), diatonic (5-35), and atonal sets, including the

set 6-34, the Scriabin set mentioned earlier. Notice in particular that the phrase ends with the hexachord 6-Z49,[30] within which there are the two atonal sets, 5-32 and 5-28.

The remainder of Example 20 shows the large sets 8-25 and 8-27 at important points in the music. The set 8-25 is a whole-tone formation, as remarked earlier, and here relates back to the whole-tone hexachord 6-35 at the opening, as well as to the hexachord 6-34, which it contains (four times). In the piano part, a subset of 8-25, 5-30, forms the harmonic basis of the subsequent passage, against which the violin plays a line based on 7-28, the complement of the cadential sonority of the first phrase. This passage culminates in the piano chord identified as 5-16 in Example 20. The total sonority at that point is 8-27, which harks back to the duet between violin and piano in the opening phrase. The final excerpt in Example 20 is merely intended to show again that the large sets, in this case the whole-tone set 8-25, occur in various guises in later parts of the composition.

As a final musical illustration, Example 21 presents a reading of sets in the song *Maple Leaves,* which was selected arbitrarily on the basis of length and the fact that it is atonal. This will give some idea of the way in which Ives organizes a complete composition. For the most part, only the larger sets (hexachords and larger) are given in the chart in Example 21. In discussing these, as well as the smaller sets (as far as space permits), reference will be made to the table of set-complex relations, Example 22. For the present purpose, this table will serve only as a concise display of inclusion relations; it is not necessary here to enter into a detailed exposition of set-complex theory, with its ramifications.[31]

Probably the most characteristic musical component of the song is the single eighth-note figure in the accompaniment. The initial statement of this figure is based on 7-29 (measure 1), and two ordered transpositions of this occur in measures 8 and 9. In measure 2, however, the set 7-30 underlies the figure. The table, Example 22, shows that both these sets contain 6-Z46, the complement of 6-Z24, a set that first occurs in measure 3. The two remaining statements of the figure both involve eight-note sets: 8-24 (whole-tone) in measure 7 and 8-Z15 (the complement of the all-interval tetrachord) in the next to last measure. More will be said later about the relation between these eight-note sets and the seven-note sets, as well as the hexachords.

The chordal accompaniment that begins in measure 3 and extends

30. Set 6-Z49 is also commonly found in Scriabin's music—for example, in measure 6 (and elsewhere) of the "*White Mass*" Sonata (No. 7).

31. See Forte, *Structure,* pp. 93–100. The entry K in the table indicates that the inclusion relation is restriced. For example, the K-relation between 5-Z17 and 4-Z15 means that 8-Z15 (the complement of 4-Z15) contains 5-Z17 and that 7-Z17 contains 4-Z15. The set 5-Z17, however, does not contain 4-Z15. The entry Kh means that all possible inclusions hold between the two sets designated in the table.

23

Maple Leaves

(1920)

*Thomas Bailey Aldrich

© 1957 by Associated Music Publishers, Inc. Used by permission.

Example 21. Chart for *Maple Leaves* (*114 Songs,* no. 23), 1920.
© 1957 by Associated Music Publishers, Inc. Used by permission.

Example 22. Table of set-complex relations for *Maple Leaves*.

	3-11	4-1	4-14	4-Z15	4-24	4-Z29	5-Z17	5-Z18	5-24	5-27	5-28	5-29	5-30	5-33
4-1	K													
4-14	Kh													
4-Z15	K													
4-24	K													
4-Z29	Kh													
5-Z17	Kh		Kh	K										
5-Z18	Kh	K	Kh	K	K	K								
5-24	Kh	K	K	K	K	Kh								
5-27	Kh		Kh	K	K									
5-28	Kh			Kh	K	Kh								
5-29	Kh		Kh	K		K								
5-30	Kh		K	Kh	Kh	K								
5-33	K			K	Kh	K								
6-Z3/36	K	Kh	K	K		K								
6-5	Kh	Kh	Kh	Kh		Kh		Kh						
6-14	Kh		Kh				Kh			Kh				
6-Z24/46	Kh		Kh	Kh	K		K			K		K	K	
6-31	Kh		Kh	Kh	Kh			Kh		Kh			Kh	
6-34	Kh			Kh	Kh	Kh			Kh		Kh		Kh	Kh

through the second line of the poem (measures 4 through 6) brings in a number of new sets. Let us consider these in the order in which they occur.

The first, the whole-tone set 7-33 (measure 3), relates directly to the preceding 6-34, as indicated by the table, Example 22, which shows that 7-33 contains a form of 6-34. (In fact, 7-33 contains two forms of 6-34.) The second vertical, 6-Z3, is somewhat of an anomaly in the piece; there are no other occurrences of it or of its complement, 6-Z36, and it does not relate very directly to any of the other sets. The third set, 6-Z24, however, does occur elsewhere, most notably in the melodic line of the accompaniment in measure 3. Here again is an event similar to a type that is commonly found in the European atonal music: the statement of two forms of the same set vertically and horizontally in the same musical context. In this instance the two forms of 6-Z24 are inversionally related. At the conclusion of the piano passage, on the downbeat of measure 4, we find 5-29, the complement of the accompanimental figure in measure 1 (compare Example 16).

Over the first two quarter-note beats of measure 4 the set 6-31 (also familiar from previous examples) is formed, and this is a transposition of 6-31 in measure 2. Within 6-31 is the tetrachord 4-14, a prominent component of the middle section. The latter also relates back to the previous music, since it is the complement of the set formed by the entire first measure (8-14). The complement-related pair, 5-Z18 and 7-Z18, is also of interest in measure 4 as an instance of "embedded" complement. The hexachord 6-5, like 6-Z3 mentioned above, is not strongly related to many of the other sets in the music. Perhaps its best connections, analytically speaking, are to the all-interval tetrachords 4-Z15 and 4-Z29. (The latter, as a contiguous subset of 6-5, can be seen in the table, Example 22.) With the transposition of 4-14 in the second half of measure 5, a new hexachord, 6-14, is formed—and again, this set is not represented elsewhere in the composition. (Within 6-14, however, is 5-Z17, which has a counterpart in the first measure.)

In the final section of the song, corresponding to the last two lines of verse, there are statements of the hexachords 6-Z24, 6-31, and 6-34, all of which have occurred previously in the music. The statement of 6-34 in the second part of measure 7 is particularly interesting, since it is inversionally related to the form of 6-34 in measure 2 in such a way that there are no pitches shared by the two. This, once again, is a unique situation, one that can be produced by only one level of transposition preceded by inversion.

To return now to the two eight-note sets, 8-24 in measure 7 and 8-Z15 at the end of the song, it is not difficult to show how these relate specifically to the seven-note and six-note sets, as indicated, abstractly, in the table, Example 22. Both 8-24 and 8-Z15 contain 7-30, the set formed by the accompaniment in measure 2. In addition, they contain several of the hexachords that are prominent structural components throughout—in particular, 6-Z24 (and/or its complement, 6-Z46), 6-31, and 6-34. Example 23 displays these inclusion relations. In the case of 8-24 it is interesting to note that two of these sets, 7-30 and 6-Z46, are formed as contiguous subsets. This is another indication of the structuring of sets in terms of subsets, a more detailed aspect of Ives's music that has only been touched upon briefly in the present discussion.[32]

This reading of the main set components of the song by no means constitutes a complete analysis. There are many other features of the music that could and perhaps should be discussed—for example, the fixed pitches E and B in the middle section, the function of the tritone throughout, and the bass line. Also the detailed structure of the melodic lines both in the voice part and in the piano are of interest, since they relate directly to the large sets that govern the large-scale harmonic aspect of the piece. Nonetheless, it is hoped that this analysis, as far as it goes, gives some indication of

32. In the case of vertical structuring in terms of subsets, it is interesting to know that Ives evidently still thought of chords in the traditional way, from the bottom up. This is apparent in one of the *Universe Symphony* sketches, negative 03039.

Example 23. Subsets of 8–24 and 8–Z15 (with reference to sets in *Maple Leaves*).

	F	A	C	B	E	G	C#	D#	
8-24 (m.7)	F	A	C	B	E	G	C#	D#	
7-30	F	A	C	B	E	G		D#	
	F	A	C	B	E	G	C#		(contiguous)
6-Z46	F	A	C		E	G		D#	
		A	C	B	E	G	C#		(contiguous)
6-31	F	A	C		E	G	C#		
		A	C	B	E	G		D#	
6-34	F	A	C			G	C#	D#	
	F	A		B	E	G	C#		
	F	A	C	B		G		D#	
	F	A		B	E	G	C#		

	F#	C#	A#	C	G#	G	F#	F	E
8-Z15 (m.10)	F#	C#	A#	C	G#	G	F#	F	E
7-30	F#	C#	A#	C	G#		F#	F	E
6-Z24			A#	C	G#	G		F	E
6-Z46	F#	C#	A#		G#		F#	F	E
6-31		C#	A#	C	G#			F	E
6-34	F#	C#	A#	C	G#		F#		E
6-5	F#	C#		C		G	F#	F	E
6-Z36	F#	C#.			G#	G	F#	F	E

the developmental character of Ives's music and of the way in which apparently diversified musical components are interrelated.

This paper has endeavored to show, as specifically as possible, the various ways in which Charles Ives's music relates to the music of the European atonal school, to atonality. It seems evident that there are a number of points of intersection, and these have been stressed throughout the foregoing discussion. At the same time, it has not been the intention to pigeonhole Ives's music; it remains a unique and very special phenomenon, one that deserves further attention by musicologists.

———————————

ROQUE CORDERO: Did you mention that Example 2 is an atonal example?

FORTE: Yes. Of course, it's taken out of context, and I realize it looks like it's a possible tonal melody, but the complete song is atonal.

JONATHAN KRAMER: In many of these examples, I notice, Ives uses octave doublings quite freely within his atonal complexes—not only what appear to be doublings of sonorities but also contrapuntal lines coming to the same pitch class. It's something that Schoenberg would probably do far less readily. I wonder if you thought this had anything to do with the way he goes from atonal to tonal configurations very quickly within a piece. Perhaps the octave doublings are suggesting some sort of tonal balance within the atonal world.

FORTE: It's possible. It's an interesting idea.

QUESTIONER: Professor Forte, you have demonstrated fairly clearly, I think, that there are many similarities in Ives's music to the ideas of the Viennese school of the twentieth century, but it seems to me, for instance in Example 15, that analysis of these configurations may be much more simple in terms of just parallel types of bitonal chord streams. You also mentioned that the ear perceives this as an atonal configuration. Hasn't this always been the problem with bitonal configurations—how the ear does, in fact, perceive them? Isn't it a fact that Ives occasionally tried to confuse the issue of what he was really doing by complicating his notation, writing something out in a simple form and then putting it into things like double sharps and unusual keys to make it look more complicated than it was?

FORTE: It seems likely, because there are many cases in which he does have a very complicated notation. I showed you one example here [Example 9].

QUESTIONER: Doesn't Ives in fact just use polyharmony procedures which by 1920 were fairly standard parts of musical expression?

FORTE: Well, there are a couple of things that bother me about that. First of all, I'm not sure that polyharmony or polytonality are really very effective in working out a complete analysis of a piece, since you end up with something that's neither tonal nor atonal. It seems much more effective to put it into the atonal category and deal with the total configuration. The other thing that bothers me is exactly the point you touched upon, namely notation. It's conceivable, for example, to take one of these sections which is not notated in a polyharmonic way or a polytonal way and notate it as a polyharmonic structure. That brings up the whole question of the notational aspects of music versus the sonic, which I think is perhaps a little bit unclear in Ives's case. I personally have taken the viewpoint that it's better to discard the old terminology of polychords and polyharmonies.

ROGER REYNOLDS: I'd like to try to be very cautious about the way I ask Professor Forte what I wish to ask him. First of all, I'll say that momentarily I'm willing to accept the notion that it is useful to talk about pitch content as one of the decisive elements in musical impact. Moving from that, you can, of course, develop a system which will describe that aspect of the musical impact. Within the system you'll have to have labels. To me, the nature of the labels and the system can only become clear and justified by the way in which they illuminate the composer's procedures. We'll get somewhere only if the labels become relevant to the description of the composer's behavior and help us to understand the way he did things and, therefore, the way we might hear them. I would like to know whether, in Professor Forte's book [*Structure*], he treats the question of whether it would be possible to describe any coherent musical expression—that is to say, the work of any composer who has some stylistic base—without finding a statistical system. The second part of my question is: to what degree do you feel that Ives was consciously exercising the kinds of structural principles that you're outlining? I'd like to know whether you feel from your analysis that there is good evidence that he was operating systematically.

FORTE: If I understand the first part of your comment, the statistical aspect, of course, is not relevant at all to the work I've been doing. What I did in this paper, which is merely introductory, was essentially to exemplify a very low level of analysis, namely set-identification and specification of a few relations between those sets. A complete analysis in terms of pitch structure departing from that level would, of course, show a great many other things about a piece like *Maple Leaves,* including, perhaps, information of the kind that you are interested in having—say, the composer's more general procedures.

On the second question, whether Ives was conscious of this, I think it's not really relevant. He may have been playing games occasionally, but my hunch is that these techniques are used so consistently in so many different kinds of pieces and contexts that he must have had some way of going about it. I'm not particularly concerned about whether he did it consciously or not.

Five Composers' Views

Unlike his exact contemporary Arnold Schoenberg, Charles Ives inspired no "Ives school" of American composers; nor was he a teacher of composers. Yet hardly any American composer of today can have avoided a confrontation with his music and his aesthetics. One session of the Festival-Conference, organized by Roger Reynolds, brought together five composers for such a confrontation; besides Reynolds, they included Charles Dodge, Lou Harrison, Salvatore Martirano, and Gordon Mumma. As Reynolds explained, each composer was given only the slimmest of guidelines for preparation of a prerecorded "statement" in musical and visual form. Each statement was prepared independently of the others. The statements were presented by means of a four-channel sound system and a pair of slide projectors, to achieve a controlled counterpoint of spatial, aural, and visual experiences. Exchanges of information among the panelists, between the prerecorded statements, formed effective, improvisatory links between the fixed bits of material in the statements themselves.

ROGER REYNOLDS'S "STATEMENT"

(precipitous, rousing onset; all four loudspeakers in darkness):
—Reeves's "Second Regiment Quickstep"
from "Decoration Day" by Charles Ives*

(fade in gradually):—Mesa *by Gordon Mumma*

(slides of Gordon Mumma at work in festivals and with the Merce Cunningham Dance Company)

* The musical examples heard during Reynolds's statement were excerpts from the works named.

MUMMA: . . . *Information has not to do with whether it's simple or complicated, but whether it's something you need to know. . . .*

(slides of Lou Harrison in his Aptos, California, home)

HARRISON: . . . *What he did was to maintain, in some sense, a very personal composer's workshop that was so far in advance of anybody else that he was talking to himself about things that we all talk about now in common. . . .*
DODGE: . . . *The main interest for me in synthetic speech was how you could have something that sounded quite natural change into something that seemed electronic . . . the continuum between the natural and the . . . I mean, it's how I feel every day. . . . There are times when I feel quite natural and times when I feel completely unreal [audience laughter] . . . and to be able to go in between the two, and search for things that strike resonances. . . .*

(abrupt entrance of synthetic speech composition):
—Speech Songs by Charles Dodge
("A man, a man, . . .
. . . sitting in a cafeteria")

MARTIRANO: *So I began. I bought a Heathkit Analog-Digital Designer, which was one of the first modules to have circuits on [printed circuit] cards, and you could put 22-gauge wire from one hole to another hole and get different effects. A book accompanied it,* Digital Electronics for Scientists. *I was happy with my new-found title and dove in. . . .*

(gradually all four loudspeakers carry independently evolving commentary by panel members; selected slides continue)

MUMMA: *The political and social conditions . . .*

MARTIRANO: . . . *Next . . .*

. . . of working in New York City . . .

came . . .

make it close to impossible . . .

the problem . . .

*to do this kind
of festival . . .*

*of my one
head . . .*

even with . . .

*being much more
sophisticated
than . . .*

*a limitless amount
of money . . .*

*my other
head. . . .*

DODGE: *It was only
two or three years
ago that I became
seriously interested
in . . .*

*. . . the political
and social situation
makes it impossi-
ble to be really
innovative in a
performing sense
in New York. The
reason . . .*

*. . . the important
thing about speech
synthesis is that
each of its
parameters is
independently
variable . . .*

*. . . I knew a lot
about ranges. . . .*

HARRISON: *I
know . . .*

*. . . the nature
and control of
communications
technology . . .*

*It's interesting,
Roger, how we
have grown up
to . . .*

*. . . is finally
approaching the
point where, after
several centuries
of increasingly
elaborate technical
means, but not an
increasingly acces-
sible control of
communications
means, we are now
in a position of
being able to
choose, as individ-
ual artists, whether
we want to work
by ourselves, with
other people, or
with other* systems.

. . . grown around
*to, that point of
view. Not too many
years ago, everyone
expected things to
be on the stage,
and that there was
a certain clarity
in the orchestral
presentation, and
not even more than
at most one or two
levels. . . .
You could have
something in the
foreground and
something in the
background, but
you didn't have*
four or five
levels . . .
*and spread around
everywhere. And,
of course, Mr. Ives
presupposed all
this. . . . It wasn't
careless orchestra-
tion, as is some-
times alleged. . . .*

*The main thing in
speech synthesis is
not speech
synthesis. The
main thing in
speech synthesis is
speech analysis.*

> *. . . he was pain-*
> *fully sensitive to*
> *those delicacies.*

> *(fade in music and slides of exotic instruments):*
> —Concerto in Slendro *by Lou Harrison*

REYNOLDS: *He was discussing a chord in the "Thoreau" movement of the "Concord" Sonata and said: "Of course, one can't hear these special vibratory phenomena by listening to the chord; it's necessary to understand the context and to project that extra resonance onto the experience. . . ."*

HARRISON: *He says about one of those chords: "Now when both the two B's are used in a chord, there is a practical, physical, acoustical difference (overtonal, vibrational beats) which makes it a slightly different chord than the B's of an exact octave—and [even] on the piano the player sees that and feels that, it goes into the general spirit of the music—though on the piano this is missed by the unimaginative"* [Ives, Memos, pp. 189–90].

REYNOLDS: *Isn't that marvelous . . .*

HARRISON: *In short, hallucination is requested.* [laughs]

REYNOLDS: *Yes, yes, exactly. . . .*

MARTIRANO: *. . . That's exactly right. . . .*

> *(begin rapid exchange of questioning and answering exclamations from all four speakers; Martirano spatially fractioned)*

MARTIRANO: *Right? . . . OK? . . . That's right . . . yes . . . yeah . . . You understand what I mean?*

> *(sudden entrance of musico-theatric fragment:*
> HONK [saxophone] YEAH!! YES! [shouting percussionists])
> —Underworld *by Salvatore Martirano*

MARTIRANO: *Can we create circuits that will give out, on the average, beautiful music? The idea of making beautiful music average has been my great ambition. . . .* [audience laughter]

HARRISON: *My thought was that if Mr. Ives could permit himself to do these things, and of course did do them, well then, you could do anything. . . .*

REYNOLDS: *For me it was meaningful to get into the roots of his ideas, in terms of images that are not basically musical but are used, then, as a kind of generative structure or pattern or impulse. . . . I think I sensed that, just listening to his music. . . .*

(opening of four-channel recording with slides of Reynolds answering phone):

—Again *by Roger Reynolds*

REYNOLDS: The general notion of my introductory statement was to suggest the nature of the planning for this session. It was a kind of phantom panel. It consisted only of quotes; that is to say, none of the material was prepared especially for this occasion. The recorded events ranged over the past ten years and took place in various parts of the world. Each panelist was represented by some of his music—fragments only.

It seemed to me, when I was asked to organize this panel, that it was terribly important for it in some way to reflect contemporary musical thought, perhaps more than Ives. (I was sure that Ives was going to get considerable attention in any case.) And it did appear that, since the subject was "Ives *and* [instead of "in"] Present-Day Musical Thought," it would be worthwhile to try to give some sense of the sorts of activities that are going on now. Obviously, this panel is by no means a catholic representation: I had other, largely personal, reasons for selecting the people to participate. Perhaps the main one had to do with a notion that is even more basic in Ives than quotation. It is briefly stated: *incorporation.* The thing that strikes me most about Ives is his willingness to incorporate—to incorporate anything of interest from the real world, whether sounds, or ideas, or images. What we are going to try to do in this session relates to this notion: we are going to wend our way between some prerecorded statements—quotes, in a sense, since they're history—which we shall try to incorporate into a free-flowing discussion.

Let me start out by making a brief comment about how my composition *Again* (heard last on the tape) relates, in my mind at least, to Ives. It has to do with incorporation, the incorporation of materials that are available by means of recording and yet could not reliably be generated in a public situation. In particular, these materials are very complex and unstable instrumental multiphonics, which are the basis of the seemingly electronic sounds in the work. (There are no actual electronic sounds, just transmuted instrumental sounds.) There is also the notion of incorporating ideas. Inherent in the word *again* is the idea of the problem of repetition: trying to do the same thing again and again, and discovering that it cannot be done, that duplication is quite impossible, even if it's a matter of playing back the same sound on tape repeatedly. As the contexts change, the item changes. Yet another way in which *Again* involves incorporation is through encircling the audience. It uses a four-channel tape, and in a real performance the players and loudspeakers ring the audience, so that each listener has quite a different sense of what the "ensemble" is, of what it *means*. This was a very troublesome aspect for the performers, because they were unable to have any sense of the total effect: they were spread around an entire hall and had no sonic picture of what was happening in the middle. (For me, however, this was one of the most attractive aspects of the composition.)

HARRISON: Well, Roger, I very much enjoyed hearing a piece of yours that was new to me, and also seeing Sal's get-up, which looks very much in the back like a meat rack.*

DODGE: To me, more like a spaghetti factory.

HARRISON: Was it a spaghetti factory? With the sauce on. I also very much enjoyed the *Amen*—or what do you call that, Charles?

DODGE: The words are from my song called *A Man Sitting in the Cafeteria*. . . .

REYNOLDS: Are there other comments, or should we proceed?

HARRISON: We can proceed. I was very happy with your introduction.

REYNOLDS: Everybody felt they were . . .

HARRISON: We all liked ourselves.

REYNOLDS: . . . well represented. Of course, one always tries to scheme ahead and imagine what the situation is going to involve, and my notion in doing this introduction was to set the members of the panel at ease and to pique their remembrances. It was a most enjoyable effort to go through large numbers of old tapes and recordings and see what kind of a history this group of people has had—where our paths have crossed in different kinds of ways. And I think it will become clear by the end of this presentation the reasons why the persons on the panel might be said to parallel, at least in some ways, the kinds of activities that Ives engaged in in his day.

CHARLES DODGE'S "STATEMENT"

I will explain a bit about my computer speech synthesis-by-analysis system implemented at Columbia University's Nevis Labs and show some of the musical means to which the system lends itself. I will then play the first third of an operatic dialogue for male and female synthetic voices called The Story of Our Lives, *based on a poem by Mark Strand. While the work was not composed to demonstrate the influence of Ives on my present music, there*

---

* Harrison refers to the hundreds of multicolored wires running from point to point at the rear of Martirano's digital synthesizer (shown in a series of slides during Reynolds's statement).

are several aspects of this part of the work with which Ives might well have felt a kinship.

The synthetic voices are realized by digitizing, analyzing, and resynthesizing recordings of the poem spoken by a man and a woman. In the process of resynthesizing speech, one may alter its separable acoustical properties independently. For example, it is possible to alter speech speed without changing the pitch of the voice. And one may replace the natural pitch contour of the speech with patterns of fixed pitch, thus creating a kind of song or pitched speech. Extensive use of these techniques of alteration is made in the composition.

The parts of the work which have fixed pitch for the vowel portions of the words are most often "sung" in octaves by the male and female voices. Since the voices were recorded singly, with no attempt to record them in the rhythm of the music, they present different stress and durational patterns in their readings of the same text. The rhythm in the octave passages is altered for resynthesis only to make the lengths of the sentences the same for both voices; the speed with which they articulate words or parts of words often differs. This sort of overall coordination of the voices with no attempt to control the small detail is in keeping, I think, with Ives's encouraging a performer to play his part a little out of step with the rest of the ensemble.

My second example is a passage in which three versions of the female voice articulate the pitch of a phrase in contrasting ways, at a much slower speed than that of the original recording. The first version has fixed pitches during the vowel portions of the phrase; the second has the pitch contour of the recording; the third has a continuous change of pitch, a glissando. Sounded together, the three versions have an effect similar, for me, to the passages in Ives's music where he presents, in rapid succession, alternation and/or superimposition contrasting textures and melodies, often in different keys. In this example, the absence of rhythmic differentiation heightens the isolated effect of contrast in pitch articulation.

The part of the work you will now hear consists of the voices of the man and the woman singly, together, and in "choruses"—speaking, "pitch-

From *The Story of Our Lives* by Charles Dodge. © 1974 by Charles Dodge.

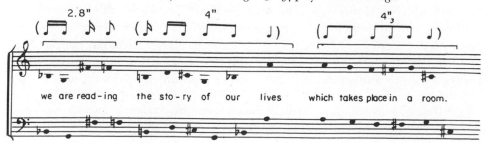

From *The Story of Our Lives* by Charles Dodge. © 1974 by Charles Dodge.

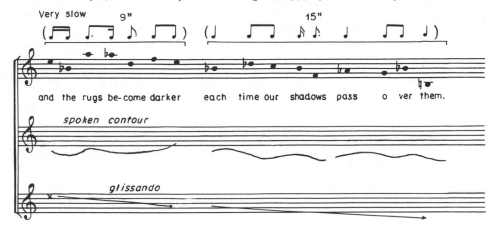

ing," and "glissing" sentences of the poem. *Interruption of one sort of tex-ture and type of pitch articulation by another, and the eventual return of the former (a favorite device of Ives), is here a principal means of continuity.*

—The Story of Our Lives
(first third) by Charles Dodge

MUMMA: Several weeks ago I was in Berlin for Metamusik, one of those glamorous festivals which happen in Europe. There was a considerable representation of music from the United States, and I was performing in the premiere of a work by Christian Wolff called *Exercises*. It is a work in which a number of instruments perform in unison from a notated score. As the exercises progress, they become more and more difficult, until there are sometimes two and three lines at once. I was engaged by the piece, which is extremely difficult for an audience to listen to; it is also difficult for the performers, because of the problem of playing in unison while allowing for the chance heterophony—sometimes the forced heterophony—that is bound to occur, particularly when the ensemble is of a nature that Wolff likes: a mixture of professional and amateur musicians. . . . I was reminded by Charles's work that one of the most enjoyable phenomena to me is heteroph-ony, which we hear very often in folk music in different parts of the world, and that I bemoan the fact that in the way I work with electronics it's very difficult to have any human control of heterophonic phenomena. Now I've heard here, for the first time, a kind of poignant, computer-driven heterophony, and I'm delighted to discover we're getting closer all the time. Ives did it with his resources; Dodge is doing it with his.

DODGE: As you may have gathered, the tapes employ synthetic versions of voices based on recorded models. The rate at which text is spoken into the machine determines the rate at which it comes back out, if I don't choose to alter durations. The heterophony results from controlling longer spans of time but letting the syllables within them occur at the rate at which they were originally spoken, or proportional to the rate at which they were spoken.

REYNOLDS: I've often thought that the repeated words and phrases in Ives's vocal music reflect an effort on his part to allow them, in a continuous stream, to suggest different inflections and different meanings as the accompaniment shifts. And it seems to me that the thing that's so extraordinarily exciting about what Charles is doing is the enlarging of the potential range of coherence within language—that is to say, enlarging the spectrum of contrapuntal complexity yet still retaining phonemic clarity. That's something that lots of people have tried to do in vocal works, but of course it's hard as hell to get singers to understand that they should try very hard to enunciate clearly and yet should not expect at any point to be heard as individuals: their job is to be a corporate unity. With the computer you can handle that easily.

HARRISON: I was thinking how delightful Charles's piece was, and wanted to say that I'm very fond of speech-music in this sense. Of course, I immediately think too of Ives's repetitive use of words—like "round and round and round and round," in one instance [in the song *General William Booth Enters Into Heaven*]. . . . There's a young man on the West Coast of whom you may know, Charles Amirkhanian, who does live speech-music, and this particular work of Charles's, it seems to me, could also be done live, much as Amirkhanian has done in a piece called *Sound Nutrition*. Yours actually could be a live concert piece, Charles, without much trouble; one could learn it from the tape. . . . Speaking of such things, may I interpolate that when I first encountered the difficult cross-metrics in Henry Cowell's *New Musical Resources,* and realized also that they were in the music of Ives which I had then (and still do) . . . well, there was an inner track on a phonograph record (recordings were on shellac in those days, and they were easy to nick) and I took a pin and nicked it in, say, four [equally spaced divisions], and then I would superimpose five nicks over the four—carefully measured, of course—and so on. Then I would put the record on the phonograph and it would go click, click, click in cross-metrics, and I could learn to play them in this way. It's another instance of the possibility of using generated things of this sort as training for live performance.

DODGE: Amirkhanian is producing a recording for the 1750 Arch label—*10 + 2: 12 American Text Sound Pieces*—which has twelve pieces on it.

Ten are as they're usually recorded on discs, but two rely on endless repetition for their effect and are, accordingly, recorded in the spinoff grooves. They're repetitive pieces that go "round and round and round and round."

REYNOLDS: Although I'd promised not to reintroduce any quotes from Ives, I've changed my mind; there is one quote that I wish to incorporate: "Many American composers, I believe, have been interested in working things out for themselves."

MARTIRANO: Well, the fact that the machine is beginning to talk is really an incredible thing. . . .

HARRISON: Frightening, too.

MARTIRANO: I don't remember when someone first lifted the hood of an automobile to look at the engine, but this reminds me of that kind of moment.

REYNOLDS: If we seem to be inter-self-congratulatory, it's because, through my design, nobody knew anything beforehand about what the others were doing in their prerecorded statements. I arranged an order on the basis of casual conversations with the panelists, but we're *all* hearing these things for the first time.

MARTIRANO: And, with all of its clumsiness, isn't it the best time? I get a warm feeling from Number One: it's Baptism.

SALVATORE MARTIRANO'S "STATEMENT"

My first thought when Roger asked me to join the panel was "Oh, is this out of step!" At a time when national identity is being rejected in many private conversations as old hat, society's institutions will find it necessary to bolster simple excellence with national pride and make the celebration an excuse for the music. Poor bedwetting melting-pot America has finally been blessed with an opportunity to celebrate the birthday of one of her artists. Two for one: we should be pleased because we can both believe the music and toast its American character.

Did adopted son Schoenberg have so many celebrations honoring his birth that he didn't need a peculiarly American one? I suppose that during the latter part of his life he was rewarded with a few more performances of his music than was Ives. This can be understood if one considers that Schoenberg had many students on two continents and, in addition, was talked about in more than one language.

At that moment in my wandering thoughts, an idea sprang from my elbow (don't laugh) as I dreamed that Schoenberg, masquerading as a French diseuse, met Ives at a cocktail party and seduced him. Of course the idea seemed ridiculous, irrational, unrealistic, and untrue. "Perfect," I thought, "it belongs to the highly respected artistic institution known in the biz as 'Criminal Art.'" Is the good artist's maxim "Rubar con garbo e a tempo" true? Did anyone ever accuse Verdi of robbing from Mozart the Commendatore's order to repent? or from Bach his Lutheran harmonization of "Domine fallo casto!" (Falstaff, Act III, Part 2)? Why should Ives be punished or praised simply because his inspiration led him to allude to some melodies instead of others?

I reached into my tape bag and found a background for maternity dresses in a fashion show. It featured Ben Johnston, disguised as a psychology prof with a deep distinguished voice, lecturing a student, played by Jerry Hiller, on the subject of an English murderer who had a history of bedwetting. Put it in! The connection is ambiguous enough for an afternoon academic meeting. A touch here and there, a dab of this and that, and in six hours' time the tape was ready for the occasion. A few days around the "Apple" with friends and colleagues? Why not go to this lugubrious birthday party for a great composer? Understand, at home the hero we talk about is Grandpa, not Ives.

Ladies and gentlemen, The Magic Box. *That's the name of this song. Wait, Ives just changed my mind,* and I rename it* Shop Talk.

—Shop Talk *by Salvatore Martirano*

HARRISON: I thought that was fine shop talk, but it made me uneasy as it went along. I had a whole series of reactions to it. The first one was, "Why, this sounds exactly the way composers talk when we're together—about all sorts of materials, and so on." And then, as it went on, I remembered a marvelous piece published in *Caterpillar* some years ago. It was an imitation poem about the translation of a Sumerian tablet; there would be fragments and then there would be a parenthesis—"(at this point the tablet breaks down)"—and so on. And then after a while I began thinking that this lady [intoning in Martirano's piece] sounds much like Cocteau's "The Human Voice"—you begin to think of that communication. Then, finally, I began to get uneasy because I'm almost sure that there are posthypnotic commands buried in the tape of that piece, and I'm afraid to go to sleep tonight.

* (while editing the conversation for publication)

REYNOLDS: I suppose the commands would be more or less threatening depending upon one's circumstances. . . .

HARRISON: I expect it's so.

REYNOLDS: . . . I thought—as has frequently been the case in my re-actions to Sal's music—that it has a good deal to do with the technical pro-cess, modulation, extended in a metaphoric sense. You get the mood or the mode of one form of information transfer being laid subtly over another. In Sal's piece *L's G A* this aspect of modulation is carried to the most glorious ends. This presentation today certainly had that quality, with a gradual realization of the potential inherent in the slight Viennese accent, the lady's way of speaking, the nature of her comprehension of the text (I assume under your guidance, Sal), and then the transference of your aims to her expression, and so on. This has, I think, a lot to do with Ives, too; I don't suggest that you drew it from him, but surely Ives was interested in the modulation of situations—in the way they modulated him and the way his musical contexts might then do it.

Sal mentioned earlier that the matrix being described in his prere-corded statement was, by another fortuitous chance, the matrix organizing *Underworld,* the piece I happened to select to represent him in my intro-ductory statement. The matrix, of course, represents genuine information, again depending upon what you need to hear.

HARRISON: In short, it's a matrix and a model for a composition, right? And, of course, a composition in itself?

MARTIRANO: It's a way of putting the same things together in a lot of different ways on a single sheet of paper. The basic premise states that con-text (with lower or upper case *c*) can be measured. Why reach into the abyss of information and risk coming up with a set of insignificant differences? Given a range, dogs can hear frequencies that humans cannot hear. Why write another opera for a French poodle? I can think my thoughts without airing them. If I choose to communicate, I must find a range that is intelligi-ble to the target. The matrix represents genuine information that I need in order to tell you something that you may or may not need to hear. It's that old progression: logical hypothesis, empirical test, and oscillating evaluation of the arbitrary connection between deductive conclusion and inductive evidence. The matrix is a small finite world of significantly different coup-lings where freedom exists for me to move about easily because I think that you'll know what I am doing. Everyone has a matrix.

REYNOLDS: Your statement also has to do with alternate forms of de-livering messages. That was inherent in the pairs you set up at the very be-ginning: male/female, rational/irrational, sensual/businesslike, etc. Possibly Ives was less into those things; I don't think he was very much into that sort of duplicity. The range in Ives's music stems from a different kind of personality structure, or possibly it was a response to a different sort of social situation.

LOU HARRISON'S "STATEMENT"

Many musicians my age did not have the fortune to grow up from adolescence with a whole library of the music of Charles Ives, as I did after he sent me a whole crate of it. The long-time effect on me has been toward freedom of all kinds. Freedom of intonation is my present subject. I had hoped to present a computer-generated recording of my At the Tomb of Charles Ives, *but this was not possible in time. Still, an example of free style is presented—music composed by the free association of precise intervals as need or desire suggests, and with no gamut in mind:* A Phrase for Arion's Leap. *The metal-strung harps are made by William Colvig.*

That remarkable musician, George Ives, very early indoctrinated his son Charles in the notion that the received opinion about music's intonation was neither divine law nor invariable human necessity. As a result, his son continued to conceive of intonation as variable through the whole of his musical life. And indeed beyond it, for after Charles Ives no longer composed he still, in 1925, published his article "Some 'Quarter-Tone' Impressions." In this article he carefully works out for himself a set of chords, theories, and procedures for composing in a twenty-four-tone, equal-tempered gamut. We remember the image of his father in the thunderstorm, listening to a bell and searching for its lost chord on the piano. Right away, he made a quarter-tone experiment. Still hunting, Charles Ives was seeking the lost chords in 1925. He helped Hans Barth build his quarter-tone piano and was distressed that the instrument was used exploitively and not for the experimenting and studying that Ives himself was hoping for. He was thinking about intonation as a future.

At the turn of the twentieth century, others too were of George Ives's and his son's opinion: Julián Carrillo in the Mexican part of America, Busoni and a few others in the European part of Asia. So that Charles Ives's occasional use in his own pieces of passages and pages in quarter-tones was also normal then.

At about the time that Mr. Ives's compositional end came about, Harry Partch was just beginning the work and the thinking that were to make possible that entry into the future for which Mr. Ives was plainly hopeful. In 1925, the same year in which Charles Ives published his quarter-tone

IN FREE STYLE
Precision Piece: "A Phrase For Arion's Leap"
to Charles Shere from Lou Harrison, 15 Dec., 2517
Poco Agitato
3 Ya Chengs
Metal Strung Harp
E,330
A 440
Troubadour Harp
Block
Percussion
muted gong
l.v.
sweet Jangles
deep Tam Tam
strike with metal spike

article, Harry Partch composed a string quartet in just intonation. And we have found that neither the reinforcement of twelve-tone equal tempera- ment by Arnold Schoenberg nor its compounding to twenty-four-tone equal temperament (or any other number of equal-temperament divisions) was to be the fruitful course. The reaffirmation of just intonation, this kind of re- tuning, was fruitful: besides Harry Partch, and then myself, Ben Johnston, and Kerry Lewis, others are finding this gate which opens into a humanist musical paradise.

—La Koro Sutra *(final mantram) by*
Lou Harrison

REYNOLDS: The thing that strikes me, outside of the obviously marvel- ous sound essence, is the way in which you managed with William Colvig to achieve that resonance in the low register.* It's quite overwhelming. It is difficult enough to get one gong from Bali that will do it, and yet you seem to have a whole array of them which have been made out of considerably less exotic materials. In this situation—in free style, as I understand it— there is certainly an immense extension of Ives's mode of thought. Not only is there variety within references but one can reestablish a point of departure with each action. So that instead of having chains of actions all of which are related to a common reference (and then possibly having several references moving at the same time) you have the ability to move across a pond on stones that are being overcome with the floodtide as you go.

HARRISON: It's a wonderful description. . . .

REYNOLDS: . . . a reaction. Are there others? There may be a lot of feelings, but perhaps not things that want to be spoken.

MUMMA: I have only a beginning, in my own work, of a special kind of sympathy for this concern with intonation. I don't approach the matter of intonation with the same materials that Lou and Harry Partch have used, because I don't work with instruments of fixed tuning. But in the work that I've done with electronics for some years (even when, at the outset, it was on a fairly unsophisticated basis), I have come to a similar way of "ear think- ing" through my concern for the sonorities I have had to control. Whether it was a matter of using just intonation or some other kind of non-equal- tempered but acoustically sensible procedure, it was arrived at on my own, without systematization, simply by an intuitive working with pitches in various kinds of conglomerates or chords, or whatever you want to call them, that *sound* right. Their sonorities are more focused because they are tuned

---

* With a few exceptions the instruments in *La Koro Sutra* were designed and made by William Colvig in consultation with Lou Harrison.

in ways that have to do with a natural acoustical intonation, rather than an equal-tempered or a logarithmically structured intonation. I'm expecting a growing concern on the part of many other composers (and in the near future, I suspect) with the control of sonority. I suspect that soon the literature will be full of articles dealing with these kinds of tunings.

HARRISON: May I recommend one? It's *Xen Harmonicon,* a new journal; in the current issue will be found my *At the Tomb of Charles Ives,* which is also in free style.

DODGE: I was interested in Lou's statement that he had hoped to present a computer-generated tape of *At the Tomb of Charles Ives.* It is a very encouraging sign to see Lou Harrison, who has made the study of intonation systems an integral part of his compositional thought, taking advantage of the control and accuracy of intonation made possible by computers.

HARRISON: Apropros of that: I found a young man with a T-shirt in Santa Cruz, and it had a big square marked off in blue and inside of it it said "ACOUSTIC"; I'm waiting for the electric persons to have "ELECTRIC."

REYNOLDS: Intonation is relevant to a lot of work that is being done now—certainly to the work that I'm doing, though that has nothing to do with formal systems; it has to do with obeying the facts that are presented by real situations, as Gordon said. I find myself having to deal with instrumental multiphonics, for example, in which one instrument produces two or more pitches at the same time by complex modes of vibration. Frequently, in fact almost inevitably, they're not "properly" tuned. Yet they're always interesting and, strangely enough, they almost always seem consonant. I have found it necessary to build the pieces in such a way that they accommodate the notion of such natural multiphonic events. The composition that I'm working on now has to do with *transients;* it has involved numerous trips to junkyards and elsewhere to get large and unlikely shapes of metal and striking them and getting glorious sounds which are not quite bell-like but surely, again, relate to the fascination of Ives and so many other composers with natural, sounding objects. That obliges you to take a new attitude toward listening and tuning.

GORDON MUMMA'S "STATEMENT"

—Some Voltage Drop
by Gordon Mumma

*with minimum obtrusiveness
and adjusting to circumstances*

203

remove teakettle and plastic canteen
from backpack under panel table

fill teakettle with water from plastic canteen
and afix whistle-top to teakettle spout

remove compact gasoline stove from backpack
and place on panel table

prepare stove for lighting (prime burner element
with gasoline drawn from tank with pipette, etc.)

light backpack stove with flint and steel
and adjust flame to appropriate height

place teakettle on backpack stove

interrupt remains of panel discussion
to announce slides of old wind-up train—"Ives Railroad"—
being projected on wall behind panel

remove crosscut saw and violin bow
from case under panel table

tighten and prepare bow with rosin

as the whistle-drone begins from the teakettle
and the slide projection is completed,
introduce a single, high-pitched sustained sound
from the bowed crosscut saw
in ensemble with the teakettle drone

establish a specific interval
including the possibility of a unison
and gradually increase the loudness of the bowed saw
to equal that of the teakettle drone

after an appropriate time
interrupt suddenly
the teakettle drone and bowed-saw ensemble
with the three-minute tape composition
Wooden Pajamas (Salvador Allende: "de aquí
sólo me sacarán en pijama de madera")
played at maximum, but undistorted, loudness
from loudspeakers surrounding the audience.

REYNOLDS: Gordon is extraordinarily responsive to local conditions, which is to say he is a dedicated observer of things. And I think this is a characteristic aspect of many American composers, perhaps all of the American composers who are of interest to me personally. They have this quality: extraordinarily responsive pragmatism. They work with what there is and overcome obstacles. Gordon's presentation was an example of that conception: translate an aim into relevant action without much interest in the historical roots. . . .

MUMMA: Who, me? You mean I'm not much interested in historical roots?

REYNOLDS: . . . that your actions don't necessarily depend upon them.

MUMMA: I was talking with Sherman Van Solkema last night. I haven't seen Sherman in many years, so we don't have a sense of continuity in terms of our profession. In our conversation the matter of "what Ives means to me" came up. We both felt that this was very hard to describe because it was not a matter of direct influences, of the sort that can be traced from one composer to another in a given school of composition.

My first contact with "Ives" was that model railroad train you saw in the projected slides of my presentation. It was a hand-me-down, wind-up electric train given to me when I was only a few years old. Shortly after receiving a communication from Roger asking me to join this panel, I happened to be visiting my parents' home in Massachusetts. They reminded me that they still had the train. Now I wasn't discussing this panel with them at all; and I had forgotten all about the train, forgotten that its name was "Ives Railroad." It was just one of those things that goes into the back of your memory, and when you see it again there's that Proustian response of more than *déjà vu;* it becomes a mystical kind of experience. And so I took a few pictures of it, assuming it would get thrown out eventually. (After all, I am a grown boy.)

HARRISON: I was delighted by the sound of the rhythm tape, and by the train too, and I did not notice that it was the "Ives Railroad." Of course, this is the "Terrestrial Railroad." . . . But I'm somewhat alarmed at a "wind-up electric train"—that's what you said.

MUMMA: Is that what I said? But, you see, that's perfectly understandable. It's part of my mixed-up heritage. I was a kid during World War II, and we couldn't buy dry-cell batteries to make paper-clip motors and all those experiments you can do, and that's affected my life very much: I'm still playing with those toys that I couldn't have. . . .

HARRISON: . . . electrically deprived . . .

MUMMA: It's all mixed up. . . . Whether I heated this kettle on an electric hot plate or with some solid-state heat transfer . . . there are any number of ways one could have done it. . . .

HARRISON: I liked that steam drone section because it titillated me but did not cross my pain threshold, which is very low. It had a nice contour—just right. It also, of course, makes a political comment, just as Mr. Ives did and all of us have to, sooner or later.

DODGE: One March day, I was walking down the street (this was in Manhattan) and came across a man playing a musical saw, sort of tucked back in a doorway, out of the wind. I was with my six-year-old daughter, who was just of an age to get a big kick out of such things. So we went and gave the man a quarter to play a song, but we didn't have time to stay for the entire song since we were waiting for a bus, and the bus was coming. He played the first part of the song and then, as we were leaving, he said, "Well, the next time I see you, I'll play the whole song." And of course I haven't seen him since. I feel now, though, that having paid the price for the piece I've gotten my money's worth this way.

MUMMA: Ives has really been a spiritual influence on all of us, even though we're all quite different composers. I've had a thought, a concern about Ives, which is now being reinforced, particularly by people like Frank Rossiter and Robert Crunden, who are looking into the nature of his life. I have the feeling that the man was undernourished, that he was not able to do, or chose not to do, the kind of experimenting that, say, Gustav Mahler did with *his* resources. A great deal of Ives's interest in ideas such as having more than twelve notes within an octave really remained very conceptual—celestial, if you will. In that sense, I feel we're all somewhat alike in that we're all quite different from Ives: we have apparently made the commitment to try it all out with the materials we have at hand. He used the materials he had at hand but, in fact, perhaps in some sort of laboratory sense, very consciously put himself apart from living with them. The reasons for that are undoubtedly very complex. But in that sense, I think, we stand apart from him. Now, I'm sticking my neck out here . . .

HARRISON: It's always a good thing to do.

MUMMA: . . . because I have the feeling that, in some respects, he didn't go on with things that *I* wish he had gone on with. He chose something else, in his ornery way, and . . .

HARRISON: . . . and that leaves us a bigger playground, too.

MUMMA: Yes, we have a bigger playground because he didn't nail it all down for us and tell us what to do. There's no "school of Ives," bless him.

REYNOLDS: Very few of us, I feel confident in saying, are in any scholarly sense aware of Ives. We're aware of him in a curious metaphoric and spiritual sense, and that is the force and variegated nature of his impact on present-day American musical practice. It is not an impact derived primarily from study of his scores, and frequently not even with aural contact except for a few works—*The Unanswered Question*, the *"Concord" Sonata*,

General William Booth Enters Into Heaven—certain formative things, that were available.

Why don't we open it up now for comments or questions from the audience?

QUESTIONER: What if there had been no Ives? Would you be doing the same thing?

MUMMA: There were others. It's really a whole era. . . . One day, years ago, in a Boston music store I ran across thirty or forty volumes of Cowell's *New Music* (which Ives was one of the persons responsible for) and came across all those other names in that uncanny music—that was when I realized that I had friends. I wasn't doing what they were doing, but there I found a nation with which I felt some affinity. And so, if there hadn't been an Ives . . . well, I don't know. There would have been a Ruggles, and there would have been . . .

REYNOLDS: Cage . . .

MUMMA: . . . Brown. There would have been a Nancarrow, and all the rest of them. It was all there and it's an incredible resource. That's my answer.

REYNOLDS: I'd answer the same way, that it's that direct pragmatic inclusion. "Use what you've got"—and they all did it.

HARRISON: Well, I'm plump and a materialist and I encountered Ives so early that I'm inextricably connected, and happy about the connection. Also *New Music* I had very early contact with. In fact, it was through Henry Cowell that I first encountered Ives.

MUMMA: *New Music* is a spiritual resource that is apparently not easy for people to get to. Some libraries have the collection, but it's still extremely rare. It ought to be reprinted—without any editorializing, any removing of anything, just reprint the whole thing. It's not that we should make a sacred event of it, but it is a perspective of the time, of music particularly in the United States. It was a period of incredible ferment which suffered the same disruption that European music suffered because of World War II, that kind of strange historical continuity gap. It disappeared and is now essentially unknown. I don't mind breaks of continuity—after all, that's the story of life nowadays—but that particular break is a great loss to many people.

HARRISON: But don't you think, Gordon, that the pattern of the small intellectual magazine, to which *New Music* was related, was continued in, for example, *Source* and now *Soundings?*

MUMMA: Absolutely.

REYNOLDS: There can't be too many nations that are faced with this heady state of being: of having such tremendous resources available, and still discovering our own stuff. It's really an incredible phenomenon.

QUESTIONER: Are you finding in the electronic medium that kind of feeling that Ives talks about when he says that music does not have to be what you hear it to be. . . ?

HARRISON: "My God! What has sound got to do with music!" Unquote, Ives.

MUMMA: That's an interesting question. If Ives had had electronic resources, would he have worked with them in the same way he did with his acoustical resources? I'm sure he would have. There are some interesting people between Ives and us—for example, the composer Conlon Nancarrow, who, in his own quirky way, works with player pianos with procedures that are essentially related to what Charles Dodge is doing with digital computers. Player pianos were the resource Nancarrow had at hand. . . . I'm sure that it's just a matter of working with what you've got.

MARTIRANO: About that Ives quote, "What has sound got to do with music!" If I recognize the A-flat (I used to think this thought and I am only now remembering the thought I used to think) at the conclusion of the second appearance of the A theme in the slow movement of the Beethoven Third as being an A-flat by the oboe, then there's something wrong with the performance or my chair. That's sound. If, on the other hand, I do not notice its A-flatness and am led around by the nose, sensitive to every twist of the melody and never bothering to reflect, then the performance and my chair are both fine. That's music.

Back to influences: In the music that I composed during my teens and twenties, the influences are obvious—Mom, Dad, guitar, southern Italian folk music played at home; Schicchitani, Bach, Beethoven, Verdi, Bartók, Berg, Elwell, Rogers, Dallapiccola, and others from music lessons; Parker, Young, Monk, and others on the jazz scene of the 1940s. In my thirties, I tailored pieces for friends. In recent years, after a short course in digital electronics, I designed digital control and data-generating circuitry for musical parameters in a hybrid system dubbed the Sal-Mar Construction. The analog circuitry was designed by Franco; Borovec designed a fast multiplexer for sound distribution; DiVilbiss contributed much on all fronts. My effort was purely selfish. I now have a composition that I can play myself in public exploitively for a fee. I have so far resisted the temptation to make a tape for public distribution, in order to preserve integrity in my presently firm belief that it is real time, and not the past, that is the most important concern. Influences are come-what-may and, in my opinion, should be loved, not made sacred.

I agree with Gordon's observation (and Roger said the same sort of thing earlier) that it's a matter of working with what you've got, and only wish to add a quote from the enlightened old sage who said, "God bless the child who has his own spiritual resource as well."

Ives Today

WILLIAM BROOKS

For some reason, when I began this paper I had the impression that my assignment, so to speak, was to connect Ives's work to present-day American culture, to indicate what there is about Ives's music that attracts us to it. But I found this a very uncongenial task, and eventually realized that the difficulty lay in the view of history it embodied.

The starting point for historical studies, it seems to me, must be the preoccupations that animate our interest; that is, we must begin not with the properties of historical objects, which are forever inaccessible to us, but rather with the uses to which we wish to put their present manifestations as historical artifacts. When we make historical judgments, we are engaging in present-day activity: history is not a phenomenon which lies somehow outside our permanent transience. We make our histories from materials drawn from the sea of artifacts that surrounds us. Certain bits of flotsam catch our eye, and around these we weave our stories, while others drift by unnoticed. We choose among these drifting bits in ways that reflect our current cultural attitudes; we structure them using the same techniques we employ to structure the entire environment. Their value or pertinence is not inherent in them, but rather depends on the extent to which they match the matrix we use to sort out our current lives. Their value thus changes from time to time, as the paradigms which govern our thinking change.

My question, therefore, is not "What is there about Ives's work that is of interest to us today?" but rather "What is there about the way we structure our world today that draws Ives's work to our attention?" Articulating the question this way implies that subsequent questions properly concern *use* rather than *value*. What is it that we wish to use Ives's music for, now that we have picked it from the debris? We should also realize that since the way we phrase our questions is itself a reflection of the way we structure our world, we can expect the forms of the questions to be partial examples of their answers.

There have been two prominent metadisciplinary paradigmatic changes in recent years. The first of these can be summarized as a shift from object to system: Western thought has increasingly become concerned with the relationships between objects rather than the properties of the objects themselves. In the physical sciences, attention has shifted to the statistical analysis of complex phenomena and to the interactions of objects whose boundaries and behaviors are fuzzy. In the biological sciences, taxonomic concerns have largely been replaced by ecological ones; it is now assumed that an organism interacts with its environment rather than acting upon it.

In the humanities, the most persuasive and inclusive efforts to investigate systems rather than isolated behaviors have been grouped under the term *structuralism*. In essence, the structuralist argues that the relationships between behaviorial events may reveal more clearly the workings of an individual or culture than the contents or characteristics of the events taken by themselves. Structuralist procedures have by now been applied to a wide variety of fields, with varying degrees of success. Those areas in which the structuralist approach appears to have been most fruitful seem to share two characteristics.

First, these congenial fields all contain a bounded universe of objects or events and therefore a limited, though perhaps very large, number of relationships. The procedures which can be applied to such a field are primarily those of selection and permutation. They do not generally involve the creation of new objects or relationships to accord with mental images; that is, they do not stipulate an ideal and then deduce precisely the optimal means for achieving that ideal. They rather pick and choose among the possibilities at hand, using their choices in whatever way seems most sensible.

Second, the areas in which structuralist thought is most comfortable tend to de-emphasize the importance of chronological or causal relationships. Of course, causality is a perfectly legitimate relationship between objects, and it is thus a reasonable component in structuralist analyses. However, it is only one component among many, and not necessarily to be preferred; structuralism therefore tends to treat synchronically objects which have usually been arranged diachronically, such as the events in a story, the lines of a poem, or the rules governing inheritance.

These two characteristics—the arrangement of objects chosen from a bounded universe and an emphasis on synchronicity rather than causality—are precisely the characteristics I emphasized in my opening remarks about history. From these I was induced to reformulate my original question as "What is there about the way we structure our world today that draws Ives's work to our attention?" We can now see that the reformulation was itself an example of the way of thinking we inquired for and that the structuralist approach to the humanities is both a motivation for and a partial reply to the question. Let us ask, then, "Since we now appear to be preoccupied to some extent with structuralist concerns, in what ways is Ives's work an apt focus for those concerns?"

Claude Lévi-Strauss is one of the foremost structural anthropologists, and in one of his most famous passages a distinction is made between the making of myth and the making of science. The metaphor Lévi-Strauss uses for the myth-maker is that of the *bricoleur,* that peculiar kind of handyman native to France. *Bricolage,* which is what the bricoleur does, has no real English equivalent, but it has some properties in common with "Yankee ingenuity." Both have to do with devising solutions with efficiency and even elegance from the materials at hand; both imply the reuse, in unexpected contexts, of prosaic materials and techniques whose original functions are often far removed from the new situation. Let us quote at length from Lévi-Strauss's own description of the bricoleur's activity:

> . . . the rules of [the bricoleur's] game are always to make do with "whatever is at hand," that is to say with a set of tools and materials which is always finite and is also heterogeneous because what it contains bears no relation to the current project, or indeed to any particular project, but is the contingent result of all the occasions there have been to renew or enrich the stock or to maintain it with the remains of previous constructions or destructions. . . . [The set] is to be defined only by its potential use . . . or because the elements are collected or retained on the principle that "they may always come in handy." . . .
>
> Consider [the bricoleur] at work and excited by his project. His first practical step is retrospective. He has to turn back to an already existent set made up of tools and materials, to consider or reconsider what it contains and, finally and above all, to engage in a sort of dialogue with it and, before choosing between them, to index the possible answers which the whole set can offer to his problem. He interrogates all the heterogeneous objects of which his treasury is composed to discover what each of them could . . . contribute to the definition of a set which has yet to materialize but which will ultimately differ from the instrumental set only in the internal disposition of its parts. . . . But the possibilities always remain limited by the particular history of each piece and by those of its features which are already determined by the use for which it was originally intended or the modifications it has undergone for other purposes. . . . The decision as to what to put in each place also depends on the possibility of putting a different element here instead, so that each choice which is made will involve a complete reorganization of the structure, which will never be the same as one vaguely imagined, nor as some other which might have been preferred to it.[1]

1. Claude Lévi-Strauss, *The Savage Mind* (Chicago: University of Chicago Press, 1966), pp. 17–19.

Now, the features which characterize the activities of a bricoleur in this description are precisely those features which characterize Charles Ives's music. Like bricolage, Ives's works are built from materials at hand; the project is defined in part by the nature of the elements which have been collected. To be sure, these elements include the exotic and experimental as well as the conventional, but even the least colloquial of these were acquired experientially, not theoretically. Ives's tuning experiments, for example, sprang from observations of the inharmonic partials of bells; the polymetric constructions were rooted in village band performances. Thus these and other so-called innovative techniques were collected in precisely the same way as were the quotations of stylistic parodies.

Imagine Ives at work, then, as we did the bricoleur. His first step, too, is retrospective. Having in his mind the substance of the project at hand, he turns to his preexisting set of tools and materials to choose the manner in which the project will be realized. The completed work will be a recombination and permutation of elements drawn from this set, in which the particular characteristics of any one element will persist but will not necessarily be conventionally employed. Moreover, this completed work will be only one of many possible solutions to the problem; it will in no way be an optimal solution, and others might even have been preferred, had circumstances brought them about. The compositional process involved is one of establishing new relationships among a heterogeneous, circumstantially assembled collection of elements. The elements are drawn from a tangible and limited universe rather than constructed to accord with an ideational and infinite one; their fixed properties are relevant to the solution only by virtue of the way in which they are related.

For Lévi-Strauss, bricolage is an analog to the making of myths; he writes: " . . . the characteristic feature of mythical thought, as of 'bricolage' on the practical plane, is that it builds up structured sets, not directly with other structured sets but by using the remains and debris of events: . . . odds and ends, . . . fossilized evidence of the history of an individual or a society. The relation between the diachronic and the synchronic is therefore in a sense reversed."[2]

The elements used in Ives's work are also "odds and ends," the "remains and debris" left behind after a priori valuative judgments are made. Ives worked almost exclusively with acoustic phenomena that his more scientific contemporaries dismissed as vulgar or chaotic. From them he built structures which in effect freeze history; by compacting an individual or social lifetime into a single event, they summarize synchronically the oppositions and relations that history organizes chronologically. Ives's works

2. *Ibid.*, pp. 21–22.

thus become mythic representations of the fundamental dichotomies which underlay the American society he knew.

Again we find that we have circled back to our original assertions about history. The processes Ives employed in building his works are the same processes we used in formulating our original question. We have chosen Ives from the valueless debris that surrounds us to be an element in the structure we call history in precisely the same way that Ives chose *his* elements from the acoustic debris that surrounded *him*. We can thus conclude that we turn our attention to Ives because Ives's work is a manifestation of the process by which we turn our attention to him. From this consistency we can conclude that the dialectic which is embodied in Ives's mythical representations still animates our society. Ives is of use to us in making our own myths today.

Earlier I asserted that there were two metadisciplinary paradigmatic changes of special interest in recent years. Our investigation of the first of these, which has to do with a change of emphasis from object to structure, has brought us to a recursive formulation that is an excellent example of the second, which concerns closed, self-referential, and possibly paradoxical systems. In its simplest form, this second change asserts that the observer must be included in that which is observed, that the builder of structures is enmeshed in the structures built.

The dramatic embodiment of this position in the Heisenberg uncertainty principle has become so familiar in the physical sciences that its influence is no longer a subject of controversy. In the biological sciences, new ecological disciplines have made it increasingly clear that the observer is inseparable from the observed. Similarly, as biological and cybernetic advances have made the problem of modeling the mind ever more important, the circularity implied by the fact that it is the modeler who is being modeled has become inescapable. Linguistics finds itself increasingly preoccupied with the parallel problem: language can only be described by language.

In the humanities, the structuralist movement occupies a curious kind of halfway position with respect to the problem of self-reference. On the one hand, by emphasizing the interrelationships between objects rather than the properties of objects in isolation, the structuralist movement has continually drawn into the web of study manifestations and behaviors that were formerly separate, some of which had been isolated because they were attributed to so-called observers. On the other hand, the structuralists themselves have generally maintained a rigorous distance between their persons and their work; the models they have built do not usually include themselves in the relationships defined. In large part, structuralists have been concerned with the relationships between one object and another, but not those between an object and themselves, an object and itself, or themselves and themselves.

The separation between the builder and that which is built persists in the phenomenon of bricolage. The bricoleur is in no sense a part of his materials, nor do the results of his work become in any consistent way a part of him. Each project is undertaken independently of its predecessors; if a particular procedure discovered earlier is reemployed, the repetition is fortuitous, not the result of the parallel application of a single system. The tools and materials of the bricoleur continually change in an alogical fashion; those which are used up in one project are replaced almost haphazardly en route to the next. Both the tools and the finished projects remain separate from the bricoleur himself and are left behind or acquired as the occasion provides. The bricoleur neither remains in one place nor moves systematically to another; rather, he sort of muddles along in an ever-changing but always pragmatically satisfactory fashion. If we imagine him lost in a forest, we might expect that he would wander as inclination suggested, neither returning to his original location nor tracing a direct path toward a distant goal.

In these respects Ives's work differs greatly from that of the bricoleur. The acoustic objects Ives built became as much a part of his tools and materials as those he found among the debris of his contemporaries' music. Ives's music constantly refers to itself when considered as a whole; very few pieces can be treated as isolated objects and fewer still "use up" the materials of which they are made. At the same time, Ives's works do not form a sequence in which certain crucial materials or problems are systematically clarified; rather, they seem to point in many directions at once, reusing previous solutions in ways quite inconsistent with the original materials' functions. If Ives is a bricoleur, he is a special kind, one who constantly interrogates his own products and his own self in an effort to begin again in new ways with that which he has already finished.

It is instructive to compare Ives's sketches with, say, Beethoven's. In the latter case, the systematic, line-by-line "improvement" of previous material is absolutely explicit, while in Ives's case, the materials remain unchanged while their permutations are constantly adjusted to bring into the circle of possibilities all the juxtapositions which had previously been employed. Were Beethoven lost in the same forest as our bricoleur, one might expect the straightest of lines to be traced, most probably directly toward the tallest tree. Imagining Ives in the same situation, one visualizes an ever-widening circle, the interior of which is always known and available for use in extending the territory to the next radial increment. The forest may never be escaped, but somehow that doesn't seem the point.

The self-referentially inclusive character of Ives's work leads to a seemingly impossible situation in which both progress and stasis seem to coexist. The circle widens, but the center remains the same. Thus, while there is a clear progression of sorts through the major orchestral works, there is rarely if ever the sense that earlier works have been left behind; and in the songs the continual recrossing of familiar but ever-expanding territory is even more obvious. The same intimate interplay between centered homeostasis and linear change underlies even isolated pieces such as the *Second String Quartet* and the *Fourth Symphony*.

The impossibility of progress and stasis coexisting in the same work is only apparent. The paradox results in part from an exclusive emphasis on naming the states of a system rather than describing the processes by which the states are reached. In a very real sense, to return to a state is to find a new one, and recent efforts to account for paradox in logical terms actually postulate the impossibility of recurrence.[3] Each recrossing of an ever-widening circle places even the most familiar objects in a new context; the perspective from which a phenomenon is viewed inevitably shifts, whether desired or not. Ives described the situation as follows:

> A natural procedure in a piece of music, be it a song or a week's symphony, may have something in common [with]—I won't say analogous to—a walk up a mountain. There's the mountain, its foot, its summit— there's the valley—the climber looks, turns, and looks down or up. He sees the valley, but not exactly the same angle he saw it at [in] the last look—and the summit is changing with every step—and the sky. Even if he stands on the same rock at the top, and looks toward Heaven and Earth, he is not in just the same key he started in, or in the same moment of existence.[4]

The emphasis in the foregoing is on *process*—the act of climbing, the crossing and the recrossing. Process partakes of both progress and stasis. Like progress, it requires temporal analysis; like stasis, it implies no particular goal. When a world view that is rooted in process is frozen by being partitioned into a limited number of named states, paradox results. In a sense, we find ourselves trapped by the structuralist procedures we want to employ; our difficulties arise only when diachronic phenomena are reduced to lists of synchronicities. Process can adequately be described only by verbs, not by nouns.

However, our language is dominated by nouns, and paradox therefore becomes a necessary tool for explaining self-referential processes. It is no wonder, then, that so many of Ives's writings are permeated with contradictions. The essential assertion is, almost always, that diversity is coextensive

3. See, for example, G. Spencer Brown, *Laws of Form* (London: George Allen and Unwin, 1969).

4. *Charles E. Ives: Memos,* ed. John Kirkpatrick (New York: W. W. Norton, 1972), p. 196.

with unity; the world is seen simultaneously as a totality and as a collection of highly distinct individualities. Opposites have to be seen as nonopposites, and it is through the understanding of process that this reconciliation is achieved.

Both in this general position and in many details which follow from it, Ives is very much akin to a near contemporary of his, Buckminster Fuller [b. 1895]. In fact, even the superficial aspects of both men's careers evidence striking resemblances. Both men received an intense but unorthodox education and did only mediocre work in traditional academic surroundings. Both worked in relative isolation for a large part of their careers. Both found themselves compelled to interweave the problems of society with their disciplines, and both developed an eccentric and distinctive prose style to express this mixture. Both were supported throughout their lives by a deep but unconventional faith and by strong, devoted wives. Both began to be recognized at about the same time, and both were simultaneously acclaimed as geniuses and ridiculed as eccentrics. Both reached a peak of influence of sorts in the 1960s, when their work was adopted by a generation whose lifestyle and behaviors differed radically from their own, and both have prophesied the future in ways which our own experience begins to confirm.

However, there are more deeply rooted similarities between Ives and Fuller. Both men apply a self-referential perspective to a spectrum of problems which range from the intensely personal to the universal. Individually, for example, Fuller's work, like that of Ives, is all of a piece; Fuller too is a bricoleur whose activities draw together bits and pieces of the technological universe that surrounds him. Like Ives, Fuller also includes his own projects in the bits and pieces on which he draws: like the Quaker on the oatmeal box, he constantly offers us a view of himself on an earlier or smaller scale.

Both men have an intricate and apparently self-contradictory attitude toward technology. Ives's antagonism toward airplanes, power plants, and other technological innovations is the subject of many anecdotes. On the other hand, Ives also argues that direct government has been made feasible by, among other things, "the fact that today a man can sit down and talk to his brother in San Francisco, receive a co-daily message from Cape Town, and hear the voice of a dead man make a speech on modern business efficiency—and all in the same three minutes."[5] Similarly, Buckminster Fuller goes to some length to berate much of present-day technology while clearly advocating technological solutions to a host of contemporary problems.

In Fuller's case, the resolution of the apparent inconsistency can be found in the notion of *design*. Fuller argues, essentially, that just because

5. Charles E. Ives, "The Majority," in *Essays Before a Sonata, The Majority, and Other Writings*, ed. Howard Boatwright (New York: W. W. Norton, 1962), p. 162.

all elements in a given universe are interrelated it is not true that all technological solutions to a particular problem are equivalent. That one is superior for which the web of interconnections with its surroundings most precisely matches the preexistent web from which its materials were drawn. A new solution is not built upon the debris of its predecessors but rather fades into them, transmuting them as it comes into being. The principles of design are those which govern this process. Thus a technology is not measured by the objects which it generates but by the process by which it regulates itself, altering both its solutions and its procedures to more perfectly match the changing universe in which it is embedded. The goal of such a process is not an edifice but emptiness; the visionary technology toward which Fuller's design tends is invisible.

It is suggestive, in this context, that the technological advances Ives cites approvingly also tend toward invisibility. They have to do with the intangible transmission of information, not with the physical construction of objects. Ives, like Fuller, sees that the purpose of a specific solution is to so illumine the future that it itself becomes unnecessary; the building of objects limits rather than encourages the process by which design continues. Ives is most insistent when he discusses the technology of music; he writes, "The instrument!—there is the perennial difficulty—there is music's limitation."[6] He looks forward to a time when this technology too will have been perfected to invisibility: " . . . the day will come when every man while digging his potatoes will breathe his own epics, his own symphonies. . . ."[7]

For both men, the possibility of such recursive, self-effacing design is a consequence of the recursive structure of the world itself. Fuller argues that the world is organized according to certain recurrent structural devices, like tetrahedrons and domes, which can be used to build a well-designed technology; elemental patterns pervade the universe at all levels, in all places. Similarly, Ives quotes the transcendentalists approvingly: "All things in their variety are of one essence and are limited only by themselves."[8] The world reveals itself in its elements; each fragment is both itself and a model of the whole. The elements of the world are related not merely to each other but also to the totality of which they are a part, and progress or design consists essentially in transferring attention from the former sort of relationships to the latter.

Moreover, Ives uses precisely the same model to describe social and political systems. In essence, he asserts that every person's thought is both unique to that individual and an aspect of the universal mind. It is the rela-

6. Ives, "Essays Before a Sonata," in *Essays,* p. 84.
7. Ives, "Postface to *114 Songs,*" in *Essays,* p. 128.
8. Ives, "Conductor's Note" to *Symphony No. 4* (New York: Associated Music Publishers, 1965), p. 14.

tionship between each person and the larger unit of which he is a part that is of interest to Ives; neither he nor Fuller devotes much concern to regulating a priori the relationships between one individual and another.

Thus neither is primarily concerned with specific issues of behavior or morality. Ives requires only that such issues be decided in a way that is consistent with the relationship between individual and collective thought; *any* decision, so reached, acquires a validity entirely apart from its practical or ethical consequences. "It must be assumed," he writes, "in the final analysis and consideration of all social phenomena, that the Majority, right or wrong, are always right."[9] Only through such a paradoxical formulation can language succinctly express the distinction between a rightness based on specific judgments and the rightness of a process.

The process Ives advocates is essentially democratic, taking as its starting point the procedures outlined in the American Constitution; it is not, however, *merely* the procedures outlined in the Constitution. Ives envisions the application of these same procedures to *themselves* in a way which makes them simultaneously more pervasive and less visible: "Representative government, as I see it, is not an organic state or institution in itself. It is a practical and expedient part of a process, which has given popular government a start."[10] This process, by being applied to itself recursively, becomes both more continuous and less obtrusive. In this sense, it is like technological processes, which, we have already observed, become more extensive and less visible when applied to themselves. As we have seen, it is also to this increasingly invisible technology that Ives looked for the practical solutions to recursive democracy: " . . . the public store of reason is gradually taking the place of the once needed leader. From the Chaldean tablet to the wireless message, the public store has been wonderfully opened."[11]

Precisely the same position has been espoused by Buckminster Fuller. Typically, Fuller's remarks are more concrete:

> Democracy must be structurally modernized
> must be mechanically implemented
> to give it a one-individual-to-another
> speed and spontaneity of reaction
> commensurate with the speed and scope
> of broadcast news
> now world-wide in seconds. . . .
> Devise a mechanical means
> for nation-wide voting
> daily and secretly

9. Ives, "The Majority," p. 163.
10. Ives, "Correspondence with William H. Taft," in *Essays*, p. 211.
11. Ives, "The Majority," p. 160.

by each adult citizen
of Uncle Sam's family. . . .
This is a simple mechanical problem
involving but fractional effort
of that involved in distributing
the daily mails to the nation.[12]

In this excerpt, Fuller proposes voting once a day, but there is nothing conceptually impossible in imagining a reduction in the periodicity of this process to half a day, an hour, a minute, or less. As recursive, collective decision-making becomes more and more pervasive, it becomes more and more perfectly coextensive with day-to-day life. At the point when the process of collective government becomes instantaneous, anarchy and order are joined: all is government and nothing is government. The paradox in Thoreau's famous epigram, "That government is best which governs not at all," can be resolved by regarding government not as a fixed set of regulations, but as a process of this sort, in which self-extension and self-limitation coexist.

There is, however, one important limitation which must be placed on self-referential social processes. Possibilities that would lock the process irrevocably into a particular consequence must be proscribed. Faith in the future cannot be based on the certainty that specific decisions will be made. "If the people . . . make fools of themselves," Ives writes, "they *make* fools of themselves, and we all will have to stand for it."[13] In fact, it is only the certainty of uncertainty that justifies such a faith; only if the outcomes of specific decisions are uncertain can we argue that the collective intelligence of future generations will continue to make them.

Thus, continuing recursive processes can legitimately alter themselves only insofar as they do not eliminate uncertainty about the future. The only exception to this principle occurs when restrictive processes are applied to themselves in a way which results immediately or eventually in their own denial; but this circumstance also increases uncertainty by eliminating processes which allow for only a limited set of outcomes. Thus it is perfectly reasonable to proscribe legally a proscriptive legal process, despite the self-referential paradox, but it is altogether untenable to use that process to proscribe only future self-alterations, leaving intact and untouchable present proscriptions. More generally, the proper recursive use of constraints is to constrain themselves, not to constrain the constraining of themselves. The latter procedure in effect skips a cycle, resulting in a situation in which the

12. R. Buckminster Fuller, *No More Secondhand God* (Carbondale: Southern Illinois University Press, 1963), pp. 12–13. © 1963, R. Buckminster Fuller. Used by permission.
13. Ives, "The Majority," p. 176.

infinite regression grows ever more rigid, rather than fading with each repetiton.

The distinction just made can be generalized to a distinction between two fundamental types of self-reference. In the first, a process asserts its own validity; the prototypical example of this is the assertion "this sentence is true." In the second, a process denies itself; its prototype is the assertion "this sentence is false." It is with this second type that Ives was primarily concerned.

The first implicitly denies the passage of time. Consideration of the utterance "this sentence is true" leads to a logic of the form "this sentence is true, therefore it's true, therefore it's true, therefore it's true. . . ." All points in the logic are the same; no iteration can be distinguished from any other. The formulation also eliminates any reference to concepts outside itself; there is no falsity in it. Applied to itself recursively, it generates only a larger and larger body of assertions, each identical and each formulated from the same apparent starting point.

The second, in contrast, requires temporal distinctions. Its logic follows the form "this sentence is false, therefore it's true, therefore it's false, therefore it's true. . . ." Each clause depends on the preceding one; only by using the concept of temporal succession can any one clause be correctly formulated. The initial utterance requires immediately the introduction of a new concept; the process is inclusive, rather than exclusive. The string of clauses generated is balanced: each negates its predecessor. The process is homeostatic, not linearly accumulative.

In recent years, this form of self-reference has become increasingly important to Western thought. We find ourselves today faced with the necessity of converting from a linear to a homeostatic culture. Our logics, which have been previously dedicated to constructing more and more magnificent edifices of truth, must now begin to encompass and usefully employ falsity. The processes that have governed our lives have been based on the assumptions that temporal boundaries do not exist and that therefore we can begin at every moment as though an infinity lay before us. We must replace these processes with ones which recognize cyclical finitude and which are designed to aid us to close each cycle appropriately with the start of the next. The alternative is termination.

At the outset of this discussion, I asked, "What is it about the way we structure our world today that draws Ives's work to our attention?" We found a partial answer to that question in the nature of the question itself. Ives's work usefully illuminates the same structural concerns that generated the query. We now find that the self-referential process embedded in our approach to that question provides the second principal reason for our interest in Ives today. We are engaged in a pressing search for tools to aid us in a self-transformation which will align that which is recursive in our thinking with cyclic rather than linear processes. In Ives's music we hope to have found such a tool.

WILLIAM AUSTIN: I enjoyed following the whirling thoughts of Mr. Brooks. I enjoy sharing his final hope that Ives's music may be a helpful tool. My question is about his use of the term "we." Who are "we"? Am *I* free to join your "we" or to leave it?

WILLIAM BROOKS: It's definitely an invitational "we," and if you would like to exclude yourself—you or anyone else—feel free to do so.

FRANK ROSSITER: In choosing from the flotsam and jetsam of Ives's life what you've chosen, would you exclude transcendentalism as being not particularly useful to what we're interested in, or would you find a way to work that in? I was particularly disturbed by your comments on the electoral process. I can't quite feel that Ives saw it that way. I feel that he had a kind of transcendentalist faith that it would turn out in a certain way, not that it was completely undetermined.

BROOKS: I think he probably did have such a faith, but at least in his explicit prose he asserts that he'd be willing to deal with it if it didn't, which I think is an important observation. Speaking of the transcendentalists in general, I was struck by your remark earlier that among the transcendentalists or among the people of that persuasion, Thoreau and Garrison are the ones to turn to for analogies. I think that that's essentially the case.

ROSSITER: Your analysis doesn't exclude transcendentalism, then?

BROOKS: No.

QUESTIONER: I like the idea of the bricoleur as an analogy for the process Mr. Brooks describes, and the climb to the top of the mountain as being not a relationship of objects but of process, but it seems to me also that another very important aspect of that is reaching the top of the mountain.

BROOKS: I agree. It's an important distinction to realize that when one climbs a mountain one does get to the top, and that the process is therefore terminated in a way in which the processes that I was talking about are not. With respect to the bricoleur, I am more of the persuasion that's been expressed earlier that in a very real sense all of Ives's music is program music and is explicitly or implicitly concerned with social values. In that sense, one could argue that he was building objects with a purpose analogous to that with which a bricoleur might build objects; that is, he was building objects which he hoped would have a function, would be useful to society, just as the bricoleur might build a wagon or whatever was necessary.

QUESTIONER: Just a very brief and perhaps obvious comment concerning the mountain-climbing experience. In at least some of Ives's works—many, perhaps—we do have the mountain top in view as the climb is being made. We're fairly sure of what the final goal is going to be, but not at all of how we are going to arrive there. On the way up we may take different paths and see different objects, and we may focus upon those individual objects as we ascend, but both the process and the means of attaining the final goal are in view and perceived. I'm thinking mainly of works in which there is a hymn tune as the ultimate outcome: you're fairly sure it is going to come, and it does, but how it's arrived at is unknown.

CARLETON SPRAGUE SMITH: It seems to me that the speaker was expressing much more of himself, and structuralism, and the fact that we have to move from a cumulative to a homeostatic culture, than he was really giving us Ives as Ives was from a historical point of view. I suggest that beauty is really in the eye of the beholder and that this kind of analysis is more pertinent to ideas of the twentieth century—of the 1970s, perhaps—than to what Ives was originally himself thinking and doing.

BROOKS: Well, one of the points I hoped to make was that when we argue historical data, we are arguing essentially from the point of view of use. That's often not explicit in our discussion of the data, but it is nevertheless always there. When I extract certain phenomena from the body of material we associate with Ives and use them as the basis for judgments, I am making those judgments to achieve some present purpose, and that present purpose involves a set of values. If we were to assert that Ives could be investigated as he was at the time, which is an assertion I wouldn't share, and were the phenomena to be analyzed from that point of view, that would still embody a present purpose and a present set of values. I wouldn't want to try to articulate what those values are, because I don't share the position well enough to feel sympathetic to it; I'm afraid that I might end up criticizing it. But I think it's important to realize that when anyone talks about Ives, you can't leave the person who's talking out of the equation—out of the discussion of what's being said.

ROSSITER: I have an answer to that, too. I think that if we considered Ives's music in terms of the values of his own time, we would have to consider it as useless music, because it was so considered at the time when he wrote it. So, necessarily, we have to take into account our point of view today—reflecting the whole discovery of Ives and then the slow coming around to thinking of him as a great composer. In his own time—perhaps even to a certain extent in his own mind—his music was a very different sort of thing. You can't get away from the present point of view, I would agree.

QUESTIONER: I found Professor Brooks's presentation very interesting, helpful, and provocative. However, regarding the key terms *organic, synchronic, cyclic, mythic, total, universal, the individual,* and *the whole,* although we may indeed be able to relate them to Lévi-Strauss, structuralism, process, and Buckminster Fuller, they can all also be related to the transcendentalists. I would think that in order to relate Ives to Buckminster Fuller and to Lévi-Strauss even more convincingly, it might be valuable, perhaps even necessary, to try to make a contrast with the transcendentalists. In other words, can we say that Ives's composition is more like the structuralists than it is like organic form? That would seem to be a necessary contrast or comparison before one could fully make the point.

BROOKS: I must have slipped somewhere. I tried to avoid the word *organic,* but the other ones I have no quibble with. I personally don't see any profit in making that distinction. What use would it be to us to cut down the relationship between Ives and the transcendentalists?

QUESTIONER: Well, I wouldn't want to cut down the relationship. I would be interested in the implication that Ives may be very close to the transcendentalists and perhaps not all that close to the modernists that you're referring to. If we don't make a distinction, then it's tantamount to saying that the transcendentalists and Lévi-Strauss, Buckminster Fuller, process, and structuralism are close to being the same, and they're not.

BROOKS: I think there's a connection.

LOU HARRISON: I address myself to the concept that Mr. Brooks brought up—the changing view of Ives. It seems to me there is a very good prototypical analysis in Lévi-Strauss's *The Raw and the Cooked*—the overture section of it. It seems to me that the musical fraternity in earlier decades thought of Mr. Ives in connection with what Lévi-Strauss calls code, that is to say, in connection with the technical procedures by which one could make music; there was utter fascination, of course, with Ives's wide range of technical achievements. Interest shifted then, it seems to me and many others, to be concerned with what Lévi-Strauss calls message; and we are now here discussing him as myth. It seems to me that he's covered quite a broad range —and the reevaluation is of course, as Mr. Brooks points out, in ourselves.

Appendixes

Essays by Foreign Participants

Anachrony I and Charles Ives

LOUIS ANDRIESSEN

I wrote *Anachrony I* (the title might be translated "Time in Contradiction") in 1965–66. Many techniques of composition used in the past fifty years are used in this piece, often by way of contrast.

Many techniques are being commented upon while used here: a twelve-tone sequence is concluded tonally; a fragment in late-Romantic style disintegrates into a cluster. Most of the time, however, the different styles are left intact, kept for what they are worth but sometimes combined with another style or used at the same time. Six composers are cited literally in the third minute of the work, but more often a composer or a style is merely referred to. The literal citation of fragments from other composers must be seen as a far-reaching consequence of the "style" of this work: the lack of a style. If fragments in Penderecki style, French film-music style, Boulez style, etc., appear in a work, it is, in that sense of the word *style,* without style. It contains too many styles to have a style of its own. That is not, however, the purpose of *Anachrony I.* It is much more a mirror, in which the musical reality of today is reflected; thus, even a fragment of pop music is included.

With these references to styles I go back to 1874, when the first composer was born for whom musical style was not the same as personality: Charles Ives. He wrote, long before Schoenberg, twelve-tone music; he infringed the laws Schoenberg was yet to set. Unaware of the European tradition of elite music, he used brass band music, chorales, and folk hymns without making a caricature of them—as rich musical sources, one totality of musical events. For the first time in the history of music, someone used the musical reality.

Anachrony I is dedicated to Charles Ives, one of the few composers who thought music more interesting than himself.

Ives and Our Music Today

GUIDO BAGGIANI

It is certainly true that the fortunes of Charles Ives are rising rapidly in Italy: not by chance did a well-known Italian author say, more or less, "In our country we are always quick to go to the aid of a winner."

If we attempt to chart the interest in Ives at RAI (the Italian radio network), for example, we find the following. In 1957, Bruno Maderna first conducted *The Unanswered Question* and *Tone Roads 1* and *3*. After 1957, there are no performances reported until 1963, when Leibowitz and also Pradella conducted *Three Places in New England* in public concerts; in the same year, Ives's *Second Symphony* was conducted by Leibowitz. A brief table of radio performances may conveniently be given for the years thereafter:

1964 *Fourth Symphony*, cond. Ozawa
1965 *"Holidays" Symphony*, cond. Maderna
1966 *Sonata for Violin and Piano* [No. 2?], Redditi and Cardini
1967 *Central Park in the Dark*, cond. La Rosa-Parodi
  Third Symphony, cond. Dennis Burkh
1968 *From the Steeples and the Mountains*, cond. Foss
  Fourth Symphony, cond. Ozawa
  Fourth Symphony, cond. Bertini
1969 *Robert Browning Overture*, cond. Maderna
1971 *"Holidays" Symphony*, cond. Ferro
  "Concord" Sonata, R. Trythall
  Second String Quartet, Iowa String Quartet
1973 *Three Places in New England*, cond. Cerha
1974 *Robert Browning Overture*, cond. Panni

This table indicates, first, the increasing frequency with which Ives's music is being performed in Italy and, second, the first shy (and as yet sporadic) attempts at performance of Ives by interpreters not specifically associated with contemporary music. (One should add that the numerous Ives works which offer obstacles to performance because of their unusual instrumental requirements are still so many dead letters.)

It is not difficult to find vital aspects of Ives's work flourishing in all directions in today's music. Before reviewing them, let me quote the program notes written by Luciano Berio to elucidate the third movement of his *Sinfonia*, composed in 1968 for the 125th anniversary of the New York Philharmonic. They seem to indicate a deliberately assumed Ivesian poetics, even though Berio says he is referring to Mahler, specifically to the scherzo of Mahler's *Second Symphony*, treated like a container within which a large number of references is proliferated, which are related to the flow of Mahlerian discourse. Berio writes:

The references range from Bach, Schoenberg, Debussy, Ravel, Strauss, Berlioz, [etc.] to Boulez, Stockhausen, Globokar, Pousseur, Ives, myself and beyond

. . . assembled to make possible the mutual transformation of the component parts. . . . The juxtaposition of contrasting elements, in fact, is part of the whole point of this section of *Sinfonia.* . . . If I were to describe the presence of Mahler's "scherzo" in *Sinfonia,* the image that comes most spontaneously to mind is that of a river, going through a constantly changing landscape, sometimes going underground and emerging in another, altogether different, place, sometimes very evident in its journey, sometimes disappearing completely, present either as a fully recognizable form or as small details lost in the surrounding host of musical presences [jacket notes, Columbia MS-7268].

The technique of quotation, using the glasses of memory as an autonomous parameter, is a debt which our music gladly acknowledges to Ives rather than to Stravinsky or even Mahler himself. What, in fact, is this technique? It is a compositional procedure essential to us. From his earliest years (see the second movement of the *Second Symphony),* Ives's musical objects, always the same yet always different, are not developed by means of a progressive expansion of agogic possibilities but are instead immersed continually in different atmospheres, illuminated by changing colors, in the magic lantern of his harmony.

We read in *Essays Before a Sonata,* apropos of Emerson, that "his underlying plan of work seems based on a large unity of a series of particular aspects of a subject rather than on the continuity of its expression. . . . Orderly reason does not always have to be a visible part of all great things" [*Essays,* p. 22].

It is not improbable that when John Cage went to Darmstadt to shatter the sacred image of the tone row he brought with him some memory of Ives. Multiplicity, the conflicting coexistence of many disparate elements, is one of the phenomena with which contemporary music is concerned. What then interests us in Ives today: his polyphony, or better yet his heterophony, where it pullulates with resonant material, as in the second and third movements of *Three Places in New England* or in the second and fourth movements of the *Fourth Symphony.* These are the teachings which are vital to us.

In 1968, at the beginning of my career as a composer, I wrote a score for strings, *Metaphora;* it was the second and last closed score of my life. I remember that my great concern was to have different sound materials all present at the same time from beginning to end; the progression of the piece consisted only in the varying degrees of presence of different elements in relationship to one another, in a perpetual moving away and drawing near.

I do not wish to speak in detail about my music (all the more so since everyone considered that score boring) but only to underline the fact that the first problem to be confronted today by anyone who sets about an artistic endeavor is still the disquieting negation of the principle of identity, the enlargement of the area which our reason must struggle to comprehend. And Ives has made his contribution to this condition.

What about Ives does *not* interest us? His strange attachment to the fugue, for example. It is said that another composer who also bestrode two centuries and was similarly removed from the usual social position of the professional musician—Gesualdo, Prince of Venosa—was concerned with justifying the seriousness of his musical intentions to "those of the trade." Could there be something similar in Ives? A fugue implanted in such a masterpiece as the *Fourth Symphony* seems to me justifiable only if considered as the necessary shadowy zone, the negative movement of a man who is perhaps too positive.

Yet it is in this same *Fourth Symphony* that we find the ultimate consequences of the multiplicity of events which interests us: *the multivalence of the space parameter.* Certainly we owe the elaboration of sound in space to the electronic means that have been put at our disposal, but if we consider this spatial multivalence in terms of the differentiation of sound activities—such an important idea in the work of American composers (Earle Brown as well as Cage) and still today a most fertile ground for many European composers (Bertoncini, Boucourechliev, and others, as well as Stockhausen)—here too we find a precursor in Ives, if not indeed in his father (since it was George Edward Ives who had the idea one fine morning of having two brass bands march through the streets of Danbury, starting from opposite sides of the town and playing different music).

Let me mention finally a double aspect of Ives's personality, contradictory at first glance but in reality typical of any musician who in some way lives through a crisis of evolution: (a) On the one hand, interest in pure sound *previous to its organization* in some form: thus evidence and priority of the timbre parameter (its harmonic richness often appears as the result of Ives's need to construct his own timbres: fundamental plus overtones). (b) On the other hand, interest in the original organization of a sound structure—such as, for example, the magnificent arc of the *"Concord" Sonata.* It is then that Ives is able to write, "My God! What has sound got to do with music!"—a phrase which should be engraved in gold letters from the moment when writing music means setting out one's presuppositions, drawing conclusions, and seeing what happens. The only works worth writing are those in which one has no idea at all what the final result will be, despite the fact that people generally are anxious to consider as *real* composers only those who know exactly a priori what their completed work will be like.

Ives did not suffer from this anxiety, luckily for him and for us.

Reflections on Ives

JOHN BECKWITH

This is an account, from memory, of various episodes by which a Toronto musician, through the 1960s, became more and more aware of the music of Ives.

In the opening season (Fall 1962) of a remarkably vital, though short-lived, series called Ten Centuries Concerts, we wanted to do some of the Ives repertoire. A friend of one of the series' board members, then at Yale, copied by hand for us the score of *From the Steeples and the Mountains.* I still have this copy. The piece was, evidently, not then yet in print. The performance was to feature four noted composers playing the four spaced-out chime parts, but we ended up using professional percussionists, since the parts were not, after all, quite so easy. The brass parts were divided, with two players spelling each other on each line. The performance came at the end of a program, and the long final resonance made a stunning, magical effect. The sound, reproduced since in an exercise I have tried with students, consists of formulas from change-ringing, in an "enriched" C major, the bell scales a semitone adjacent on either side lending qualities of age and distance by their "out-of-tune-ness"—akin to the informal heterophony of tribal singing.

In 1964 the Canadian Broadcasting Corporation commissioned a radio documentary on Ives from the composer R. Murray Schafer. It included a résumé of biographical, literary, and musical materials and also, valuably, original contributions by Cage, Copland, Bernard Herrmann, and others who had been close to Ives in one sense or another. (Cage's contribution appears in his book *A Year from Monday*.)

In 1966 the Toronto Symphony under Seiji Ozawa performed the *Fourth Symphony* (in the one-conductor version, and without a chorus). The experience of preparing and rehearsing the "primo" of the four-handed orchestral piano part was, to start with, unsettling. "There's so much going on; you can't hear," the players were saying; and the conductor said he was resigned to selecting from moment to moment the parts he himself wanted to make audible. By comparison with merely overwritten orchestral music, this seemed unrefined and unpunctuated. Disturbing, powerful, at times repellent, it was also, deeply and simply, moving. The Columbia recording could not yet serve as a guide, though any recording would have to be selective in a more arbitrary way than Ozawa's ear, as the CBC pickup of this performance indeed proved. There is an Ives orchestral sound (or so the experience suggested to me) which is (a) centered in almost continuous dissonant piano meanderings and (b) deadset against ordinary notions of clarity and euphony. (Significantly, in the early 1970s analysts of orchestration and texture started taking it seriously, instead of continuing to maintain that Ives was naïve and did not know the orchestra.)

In 1969 three of us in the faculty of music of the University of Toronto organized an all-Ives concert with student performers. The program consisted of *The Unanswered Question, The Gong on the Hook and Ladder* (which we played twice), the *Second String Quartet,* and about eight of the songs, including *General William Booth, On the Antipodes,* and *An Election*. Some of our practical discoveries may be usefully mentioned. The C-extension string bass makes an admirable substitute for the thirty-two-foot organ-pedal C at the end of *On the Antipodes* (a stunner, to compare with the end of *From the Steeples*). *The Gong on the Hook and Ladder* contains obvious disagreements between printed score and parts. It has to be conducted in a very slow two, except for a few bars. I believe there was no recording at that time, although the work had been in print since 1960.

The preparations for the all-Ives concert either established or confirmed two areas of general impression about Ives's music (again from memory): (1) Such "editorial" songs as *An Election* are embarrassing only if considered from a conventional aesthetic standpoint. While they do not "sing," they do communicate and have even the effect (again) of unsettling one's thoughts. Was it George Ives who said of such music, "What it sounds like may not be what it *is*"? (2) The quotations, always much discussed, are different in intent and in treatment from those in, say, Mozart, or Schumann, or Satie. *The Gong on the Hook and Ladder* refers characteristically to "Clementine" and "Columbia, the Gem of the Ocean" —characteristically, that is, by floating bits of these tunes into, and out of, a continuous, dreamlike, musical texture. The pre-echoes of the first few intervals, the frequent choice of a mid-phrase starting point, and the chromatic blur at the conclusion are all deliberate features representing the shredded edges of the quotation. In performance, whether thin or heavily underlined in the score, the quotations always make their effect—i.e., make hearers conscious momentarily of their presence. "Clear" in a conventional orchestration-class sense they are not; available for aural selection they are.

On Charles Ives and "Wild Gardening"

J. BERNLEF

As a poet who would have liked to be a composer (as so many poets did and do), my discovery of Charles Ives's music came as a shock of recognition. In the *"Concord" Sonata,* "The Fourth of July," the *Fourth Symphony,* and other works I recognized the same voice I had heard before in the poetry of William Carlos Williams and, in another way, in that of Marianne Moore.

The 1960s were for me and many other artists the period in which we experimented with what we then called "open forms." Listening to Ives's music, I learned a great deal what such forms were about, their advantages and disadvantages. The borderline between art and life seemed highly artificial to me; Ives erased it with athletic gusto. He was a shining example for me of artistic freedom and daring. His music excited me in the same way as Williams's great poem *Paterson* did: it gave me the notion that the raw material of poetry in all its rawness should be sought outside the rules of the sonnet, so to speak. So-called free form is, however, dangerous. Only a driving force, a character and an imagination as strong and many-sided as that of Ives, can hold the paradox together.

Later on I learned to know Ives as a writer, and as a great American one too. It is amazing that both John Cage and Charles Ives are missing from anthologies of American literature. For also in the field of literature Ives is original and full of life, with his "notes jotted down in the midst of action" (as Williams put it once, speaking about his own poetry).

The importance of Ives's music and writing lies, I think today, in its belonging to what I would call "the critical tradition." Although Ives may never have intentionally wished to express it, his works function for me (besides all the sheer pleasure they give) as a critical examination of music and the deadly habit-forming of the musical world. In the same way that Marcel Duchamp is "actual," in a way still with us, Ives is living and will be living as a creative and a critical force for a long time to come.

What Ives has meant and means to me can best be expressed in poetry. In 1966 I published a collection of poems called *The Shoes of the Conductor*. One of the poems, using many quotations, is called "Wild Gardening" and is based on the music and writings of Ives. "Wild gardening" may be an apt description of Ives's music at its best: it is not nature but a man-made garden which in its arrangement tries to "imitate nature in her manner of operation," as Cage once put it.

Wild Gardening[1]

(Dedicated to the memory of Charles Ives)

"Four different people playing
tennis together does not always
destroy personality," Ives wrote,
a man who let two brass bands
intermingle.

things seen from the corner of the eye
and behind one's back

<blockquote>

a silent insult behind the victim's back
may be ruled unintentional, even if it
is seen reflected in a mirror or a window.
Time.
</blockquote>

belong to it
when one at least looks at
silence as sound

<blockquote>

John Cage discovered silence to be made
of two sounds: a high-pitched one, that
of our nervous system in action, and a
lower one, the sound of our blood in
circulation.
</blockquote>

and poetry as a magic of intervals
  in which everything happens
but with precision
like a glass of water, being
just that and some more

<blockquote>

How does the water taste?
Rather like water, I'm afraid.
The Drug Experience, Grove Press.
</blockquote>

1. © 1966 by J. Bernlef. Used by permission.

The love of the silver fox for its brood
disappears at once when a plane roaring
over drowns out their squeaking

and so I always see what I don't see: the mark in
the shoes of the hitchhiker last seen near Orly,
a dance step long forgotten returns as an acquaintance from the tropics at a party; changed but
nevertheless still the same

four different people
playing tennis, one serves,
number two kneels down, number three
waves to somebody in the teahouse and
number four, sweating, freezes in a smash
in our eyes
maybe in a philosophical way
four people play tennis together
on our deceptive retina

at the corner insensible to movement
like a frog sitting between dead flies
starving, waiting for a vision

                                     a frog does not recognize a motionless fly
                                     as desirable food, but is quite indifferent
                                     to it: it is, so to speak, "intellectually
                                     blind." *Encyclopaedia Britannica, Ltd.*

the trip by train proves it:
looking outside, the proud cathedral
flies from the centre to the left
to make room for a poor man's garden
but from the right-hand corner of the
window already a stationcar full of
newspapers drives into my point of
view and pushes the cathedral
out of my eyes and into my brain:
vision is a question of infatuation

four different people
playing tennis
surrounded by a fence
behind it little boys look
for old and weatherbeaten tennisballs

the game is a question of rules
the court has certain dimensions

It seems that it is primarily the
existence of borders which are signaled
to the brain, while regions of constant
intensity do not need much information.
R. L. Gregory: *Eye and Brain,* Hutchinson.

some of the net's mazes are broken
the ball slips through sometimes

languidly, on his toes, a
player raises his racket and smashes:

he has nothing to say and
he says it—perfectly

the court with its holidaycoloured gravel
and its fading white lines is
a place where things are

This is not a composition. It is a place
where things are, as on a table or in a
town seen from the air: any one of them
could be removed and another come into
its place through circumstances analogous
to birth and death, travel, housecleaning,
or cluttering. John Cage: *Silence,*
Wesleyan University Press.

four different people playing tennis
exchange positions
as on a table someone puts down
a tin of sardines and forgets about it;
mumbling he goes looking for it in the
kitchen, pushing aside a plate, shoving
a box of thumbtacks behind the refrigerator

the game overrules its rules
the court its dimensions

the little boys find a slip
bind it to a stick and
storm into the rosary
where girls hiding behind sunglasses
rime with loveliness

If the weather sours during an exterior,
the line "It's wonderful weather" is
replaced by "No rain is going to drown
our love." *Time.*

235

four different people playing
tennis but where
a hypothesis: somewhere tennis
is being played

familiar to the point of invisibility.
A. R. Salomon: *On Jasper Johns.*

tennis balls are far more than
patterns of stimulation: they
have pasts and futures;
when we know its past
or can guess its future,
a tennisball transcends experience
and becomes an embodiment of knowledge
and expectation without which life
of even the simplest kind is impossible

the fur of a new tennisball
belongs neither to the ball
nor to the surroundings

to lose the possibility of recognizing
2 similar objects. Marcel Duchamp.

we would find them in babycarriages
in trees building nests

the same for the rackets
four different people
playing tennis: the game
only to recognize in its
disappearance

the court is a place
just as empty, just as filled
as the glass on the table

into which at any moment anything
may be poured. John Cage: *Silence.*

beer
a coke
a handful of gravel
2 wasps flying through the net
score, unseen

how often we are blind

Whenever we blink we are blind, but

we are not aware of it. R. L. Gregory:
Eye and Brain.

the park plays tennis
high sits the referee
with outstretched hand
above the trees: a statue
at its foot some boys
are looking for fading balls and
find underwear, dead birds, plastic cups
all changing the result

four people
    how will I express it
maybe they don't exist
    there is no game
called tennis
    no court

what's the result more
than the image of what we
don't know: four people
playing tennis the description
of the invisible

The song of the black-throated warbler,
Bradford Torrey translates it as "trees,
trees, murmuring trees," a pleasing, dreamy,
drawling, reedlike lay; others change
it to "cheese, cheese, a little more
cheese"; and Dr. C. W. Townsend sets it
down as "Hear me Saint Theresa."
The New Yorker.

that's to say: the inability to
involve the park into the game;
the sweating boys looking around
the ducks quacking
the grazed knees and small
publicity planes, the pregnant
girls, sometimes with their husbands
but mostly eating, alone

I have written what I saw
but this is not a composition
not a poem about four people
playing tennis together on the

deceptive retina of my eye they
came and into my head

in this head
    that is a rustling park
where paths follow footsteps
and chance lies around like
a ripe footnote
    one thought was born:

four different people
playing tennis together
does not always destroy personality:

                a means of experiencing nothing.
                John Cage: *Silence*.

and with words I have nothing to say
and I say it

                In fact I have not written a book at all.
                I have merely cleaned house. All that
                is left is out on the clothes-line.
                Charles Ives.

Charles Ives, or America of the "First Romance"

MARTINE CADIEU

I first heard music by Ives in Italy. (France was unaware of him for a long time.) It was *Three Places in New England*. I had published two novels and had heard a great deal of music (especially, in my childhood, Debussy). I liked Varèse, Nono, Boulez, Berio. I knew younger composers much better than this patriarch of American music. My attraction for America had come through literature—Melville, discovered in my adolescence; then Thoreau, whom I loved; Hawthorne, whose puritanism annoyed me; Whitman, moving and visionary. I had devoured Faulkner, Fitzgerald, Hemingway (the last far from Ives, truly at the opposite pole). In [American] music, apart from Cage, I found nothing: the offerings of Copland or Gershwin erected something of a barrier. I was fond of jazz—not as a specialist, just as a frequent listener.

    Cesare Pavese was very precious to me. His discovery of America entranced me —that America of the "first romance," as Massimo Mila, critic and friend of Pavese, wrote of it. To me, there seemed to exist in music no phenomenon analogous to those found in American movies and literature by the generation of Pavese. For many European intellectuals, America presented a very peculiar cultural image, as American musicians came to Europe for their models, their nourishment. In music, only the popular genre—which mixed together in the same pot Negro worksongs, prayers, games, dances—asserted itself . . . jazz. We did not know that the musical equivalent of Thoreau, Emerson, Whitman—the musical equivalent of the movies of King Vidor and Chaplin—existed, on the library shelves of Yale University. Then, once we began to realize it—thanks to efforts of various Americans, to the pianist John Kirkpatrick, to energetic persons at Yale— I raced everywhere I could to hear Ives . . . and I heard him even more in Italy (Venice, Bergamo, Brescia, Como) than in France.

In France, where he is now recognized and performed, I sometimes have to fight the stereotyped notion, all too easily accepted by the [French] mentality (that famous Cartesian mentality with its tendency to label things permanently), of Ives as a "Sunday musician," disorganized, a bit naïve, for many a sort of Henri Rousseau *le douanier* of music—a genius furiously intuitive, savagely original, whose technical and stylistic innovations were piled up prodigiously in the *"Concord"* Sonata.

Another label is that of a musician *exclusively* daring. But it seems to me that the audacity of the means employed, the discoveries (like the clusters in *"Concord"* produced by a piece of wood which determines precisely the keys to be depressed, etc.), matter less than that energetic, shimmering, immediate evocation of the places (space), the events (time), and the spiritual substance (memory) of the great nineteenth-century American minds, those who made of Concord and Orchard House a sort of American Athens.

France had Debussy. In his crystalline analyses, Boulez often rejects the notion of "impressionism" (just as nowadays one rejects certain exaggerations linked with the term "Romantic"). He reveals the modernity of Debussy, the pervasiveness of the "nuclear motive," and—marvelously—underscores that search for freedom which characterizes Debussy's whole output. The same search for freedom is found in Ives—a rejection of schemata, an acceptance and even a highlighting of contradictions, and—as in Debussy's *Jeux*—a profound sense of irreversible time. *Jeux* is the fountainhead of a kind of musical form which alters our hearing: this form, which renews itself *instantaneously,* implies an instantaneous mode of listening. Orchestrational invention, individualization of timbre, "initial alchemy, not eventual chemistry" (Boulez)—these are true of Ives as well as Debussy. But in the ceaseless flickering of light (as with Claude Monet) and the mysterious marriage of shadow and sparkle (as with Cezanne), Debussy escapes into the forms, made and unmade, of clouds, of water, of nocturnal aromas, of sounds in the air. Ives, on the contrary, allies himself with human life, and he sees all of it, down to the smallest detail (like Proust and Joyce); the rays of his music illuminate equally a patriotic statue in Boston Common, a child playing near a statue of Liberty (a child trembling in memory), trumpet calls on the Fourth of July, General Putnam's camp at Redding . . . even a little boy outside a wild-animal cage ("Is life anything like that?"). All Ives's strength comes out of his love for man, a love concrete, sensual, vast. His music thus mingles militant hymns and cowboy songs, the sweat of workingmen, cries of joy or of grief, sadness, passion. All is inseparable, coexistent.

Whereas Hemingway expresses himself like a reporter—clear-cut, a realist viewing life as terminated definitively by death—Ives, with his fresh view (indirectional music, like that of Debussy and, later, Boulez) and absolutely unspoiled eye, discovers and reports but opens out on an idealistic world, on the spirituality of the transcendentalists.

If Proust comes to mind, it is because of the art that Ives possesses of getting to the deepest layers of memory, also because of a certain slender thread that runs through all his works. Contrast, in Ives, the persistent, vigorous idealism and the secret pessimism. This cauldron, this whirlwind of colors, this sudden joking, sometimes even this disorder . . . and then, at bottom, under all that—slender, taut, tenacious as Ariadne's thread or as true love—this melancholy. Expressive moments, emotions, are always there but squeezed in between gray shafts of sadness. The ideal, already distant, seems always to recede further. A yearning of the spirit is constant, inextinguishable. There remains in the foreground popular American life, holidays, children's songs; but melancholy underlies the music, and we should pay attention to it: it is a rejection of the world as it is. There is also this thread of memory, this perpetual return to a child's view, to the first sight of something, the first romance. This underground current, as with Proust, is also the magical source of Ives's creative power: musical continuity, creative continuity. Ives—like Proust, like Joyce—is a "work in progress" (but closer to Joyce in his *indirection,* for Proust transfixes time).

"Genius . . . comes less from intellectual gifts and a social refinement superior to those of others than from the faculty of transforming or transposing these things. . . . [It belongs to] those who, ceasing to live for themselves, have the ability to make a mirror of their personality; consequently their life, however ordinary it may be socially or even intellectually, can be reflected in the mirror, since genius consists in the power to reflect and not in the intrinsic value of the thing reflected" (Proust, *A l'ombre des jeunes filles en fleurs,* characterization of Bergotte [trans. Justin O'Brien]).

The identification of human experience with the life of music is the hallmark of time understood as "duration," according to Bergson. (Bergson, even before Proust, influenced my studies and those of many young French of my generation.) I am always struck in Ives by the sense of remembrance. What is met in life of grandeur, beauty, strength of emotion does not come from outside but springs from the very heart of him who accepts them. Thus a new "I" never ceases to flourish. One recalls Goethe's remark (November 1823): "There exists no past for one to yearn to return to; there exists only a perpetual present, fashioned from the ever-expanding elements of the past." This is very apparent in Ives.

I am often uneasy in the presence of young artists who sell themselves. The present system of subventions, commissions, broadcasts, and recordings, which hastens success for young musicians (or rejection, for those who burn themselves out quickly), is useful up to a certain point. For myself, I have always preferred to have a second occupation rather than being a professional writer: I wish to write freely, not on assignment or under any pressure besides my own internal need. I am thus especially struck by Ives's attitude as a youth in choosing *de-*

liberately (a fact some of my compatriots are unaware of, as they bemoan the "poor Sunday musician" and his "blocked creativity") another profession than that of a musician and then composing—with the fervor and intensity born of necessity—evenings and weekends, after having wished and waited for those free moments.

An immense power of *solitude* in Ives, a solitude without bitterness, is one of the secrets of his music. He did not wish to "reduce art to a trade" (Mila), and he put into practice the advice that John Erskine was later to give young American writers—"If you wish to write, learn a trade and don't depend on writing for your livelihood." Ives did not shut himself up in an ivory tower: his business practice also nourished his art since it satisfied a humanitarian need. (When Boulez began his career as a conductor, he told me that it would be a terrific safety valve for him as a composer.) That Ives cared nothing about promoting performances of his music, that he gave his scores free to anyone who wished them, that he renounced his copyright privileges and in his writings fought for the full-flowering life of a *free* man (outside of capitalism, outside of communism) in a manner perhaps utopian but finely and furiously—all this makes him, like Thoreau, the forefather of a young generation which rejects the world as it is, with its false values of materialism and that sad confusion presently existing between progress and prosperity. The thought of Ives's music, linked with his personal actions and his extraordinary faithfulness to himself (the shock of the war on him!), remains for many a vital inspiration. [Translated from the French by H. Wiley Hitchcock.]

Charles Ives Here-and-Now-and-After
AUSTIN CLARKSON

The celebration of his 100th birthday with an international, interurban festival-conference would likely have provoked Charles Ives to transports of scornful laughter and inspired invective. Nevertheless, we must honor him the best way we know how, and a five-day symposium makes a fine beginning. But how do we continue to be adequate to his memory? He despised all familiar and comfortable categories and distrusted professionals and academics. I suspect he would have dismissed most of us as so many Rollos, Nice Old Ladies of whatever sex who love "nice" music, Prof. $5000s, Mus. Docks, g—— d—— saps!—takin' money for emasculating music and students—permanent-wave conductors, and performers with mollycoddle minds. And he would have set about finding a music that would challenge the bases of our hearing until we came to reckon with the fundamental meanings of his life and art.

But Ives has no say now, and we must see that we do justice to his greatness, even though it may be at the expense of some well-loved traditions and institutions. He forces us to reexamine our attachments to technological materialism and analytic scientism, to our gapless histories and our axiomatized musical syntaxes, wherever they damp response to the live values of our own (not to mention other peoples') music. Ives challenges us "to hear the world with new ears," and his devotees should spread his musical thought wherever conformity is preferred to creativity, learning is measured objectively, cognitive development is prized over affective, perceptual, or imaginative development, and achievement is judged normatively rather than individually.

Had Ives possessed a more conventional aesthetic, he would have been readily socialized into the standard roles of composer, performer, musical essayist, and teacher. His outstanding musical gifts, his remarkable intellect, and his immense capacity for work would have led him to the forefront of whatever profession he selected. Had he chosen, he might even have succeeded in the academy as an eminent professor of composition at a distinguished university, admiringly imitated by successive generations of students. However, his aesthetic was composed of more ardent stuff that bred antipathy to academics and professionals and other purveyors of arbitrary rules and conventions that stifle the imagination. It arose not out of feelings of inferiority, but out of a profoundly mystical idealism whose consequences have not been fully appreciated.

Ives's music exceeds most analytic and critical categories of our day (not to mention his), and it adheres to no one stylistic idiom, but his extraordinary exploration of musical devices demonstrates the incisive logic, and at the same time the imaginative freedom, of his mind. He was thoroughly familiar with the traditional lore of harmony, counterpoint, and form, as he was with instrumentation and current interpretive idioms. He simply chose to ignore them. Ives was no child playing alone; he was a young warrior on his visionary quest, departing into the wilderness to seek his song of power. He found his song abundantly in the solitude of a hermetic musical life—song that is, in essence, a mantra of the cosmos, that resonates with life at all levels of consciousness, Augustine's *carmen universitatis*. In a fundamental sense, Ives's compositions have the quality of charms (= *carmina*). This is evident in his method of quoting the music of his milieu. He introduces the sounds of his culture not out of a naïve eclecticism, nor as quasi-literary allusions, but because his music calls for the power that adheres to these acoustic images and that engenders a *participation mystique* through the mechanism of sympathetic magic. Jerome Rothenberg, poet and anthologist of tribal song texts, points out that to produce these effects, the tribal singer requires "special languages, extraordinary in their nature and effect, and uniting the user with the beings and things he's trying to influence or connect with for a sharing of power, participation in a life beyond his own, beyond the human." Such special languages, he continues, are a small but nearly universal aspect of primitive and archaic poetry and may involve purely invented, meaningless sounds, distortion of ordinary words and syntax, ancient words, and words borrowed from other languages (*Technicians of the Sacred*, 1968, p. 386).

Ives's powerful intuition drew him to this bedrock of the creative imagination, where utterances invoke systems of belief rather than systems of grammar or rhetoric; but the tension between the special language he invented from the sounds of his world and the conventional language of his professional contemporaries was often unbearable ("If you want something played, write something you don't want played"). Despite massive although often well-meaning discouragement, he persisted in the faith of the "poet-magus" that his sounds have the power to move the listener toward specific ends. Note why Ives quotes Beethoven in the *"Concord" Sonata:* "There is an 'oracle' at the beginning of the *Fifth Symphony;* in those four notes lies one of Beethoven's greatest messages. We would place its translation above the relentlessness of fate knocking at the door, above the greater human message of destiny, and strive to bring it towards the spiritual message of Emerson's revelations, even to the 'common heart' of Concord—the soul of humanity knocking at the door of the divine mysteries, radiant in the faith that it *will* be opened—and the human become the divine!" (*Essays,* 1961 ed., p. 36).

The quotation from Beethoven is an "ancient word" borrowed for Ives's own special language, and it informs the movement with the quality of a charm that draws the hearer by its mysterious power to a heightened understanding of Emerson and his optimistic program for mankind. Whenever Ives quotes the songs of the Yankee town and countryside, he is the tribal singer drawing on the power of the commonweal to lead the listener on to higher knowledge. Even an Apache war dance may be used—*if* it "comes nearest to his [the musician's] soul" and thus "has a part in his spiritual consciousness": "With this assurance, his music will have everything it should of sincerity, nobility, strength, and beauty, no matter how it sounds; and if, with this, he is true to none but the highest of American ideals (that is, the ideals only that coincide with his spiritual consciousness), his music will be true to itself and incidentally American, and it will be so even after it is proved that all our Indians came from Asia" (*ibid.,* p. 80).

From the transcendentalist experience Ives developed an aesthetic that disapproved of the notion of compositions as property, of performers as automatons, of scores as finished products, of sound as everything ("What has sound got to do with music!"). His music is grounded in participation between composer, performer, listener, utterance, and world. His scores are sketches for a music of the spirit in which the performer is urged to join in the creative act and the listener is charged to transcend ordinary consciousness and achieve states of mystical awareness. If we listen closely, we will find the power in his music, and in the music of those who explored this path after him, to adapt ourselves and our musical institutions so that we may become more effective agents for transmitting higher states of moral and spiritual, as well as aesthetic, consciousness. Charles Ives would, I believe, accept that prospect as a fitting centennial offering.

On Charles Ives

PETER DICKINSON

There are two changes in perspective, particularly evident during the last decade, which may account for the growing relevance of American music of all kinds to audiences outside America.

The first concerns the relationship between Europe and the United States. In his recent book, *Love-Hate Relations,* Stephen Spender explores the increasingly significant contribution of American writers to literature in the English language. He concludes that during this century balance has shifted in favor of the United States, and contrasts what Emerson called "the immense advantage" enjoyed by England with its almost complete reversal today: "European thoughts are American thoughts." The situation is more complex than this, but it does help to explain European interest in American arts, an interest which more recently includes serious music and creates a climate in which there is an audience for America's first major composer.

The second change is in what might be called the balance of power between classical music and the music of the present century. Ives met opposition at a time when the Austro-German tradition was supreme, but in this century horizons have widened with injections of folk culture, through Stravinsky and Bartók, and the influence of Oriental music and thought on composers as different as Messiaen, Britten, and Cage. The cultivation of music as pure sound, rather than logical sonata structures, is behind Debussy, Varèse, and *musique concrète.* The ironic treatment of the solemnities of Western music's most serious tradition is deliberate in the stance of Satie and Cage. Jazz and popular music have also had a profound effect.

Not all of this applies to Ives, but it makes him part of a relatively recent discovery which has brought American arts of all kinds closer to the center—recent in the sense that a wider public is confirming what specialists have known for a long time.

Among composers there is much sympathy for what Ives stood for, and some of his techniques are being developed. Chief among British composers from this point of view is Sir Michael Tippett, who has conducted Ives and whose work has had some American characteristics ever since his early oratorio *A Child of Our Time* with its black spirituals. His recent *Third Symphony* employs quotation and has pronounced blues elements in its vocal solo supported by a kind of big-band jazz harmony. Tippett's later orchestral textures scintillate in a way which is energetically individual, but when the density increases the example of Ives can be felt.

Thea Musgrave based her *Chamber Concerto No. 2* on an interpretation of the Rollo figure and the discussion element in Ives's *Second String Quartet.* Gordon Crosse, in *Some Marches on a Ground,* an orchestral piece based on material from his opera *Vasco,* uses military music in a way which is closer to "Putnam's Camp" than to *Wozzeck.* According to some critics, my own orchestral work *Transformations* owes as much to Ives as to Satie, on whose music it is based. In *Yeibichai,* with its different stylistic levels, Wilfrid Mellers extends some of Ives's concepts, which he has done much to expound in his book *Music in a New Found Land.* More recently, the element of substantial quotation in the work of Robin Holloway has attracted attention.

Some aspects of Ives are paralleled in earlier British music. The hymn-tune textures of Ives's *Second Symphony* are close to those in Vaughan Williams, who reached farther back than Ives into a tradition which included plainsong. Both composers were rooted in popular song. In the *Fantasia on a Theme of Tallis* and *The Unanswered Question* their orchestral spacing is similar, but Vaughan Williams never saw the need to make the effort of accommodation which Ives makes when the wind instruments are imposed on the soft strings and the two levels must coexist.

From the point of view of vision and technique it is more instructive to relate Ives to a great writer and not to a musician at all. Some comparisons between Charles Ives and James Joyce:

1. Both derived from their immediate local culture, often used in disturbingly frank portrayal (*Dubliners; Portrait of the Artist*). They drew on recollections of childhood and youth, sometimes re-created in intense nostalgia but transformed in the artist's later maturity ("Putnam's Camp"; "The Fourth of July").

2. Their earliest works belonged to the intimacy of the salon—Joyce's *Chamber Music* and Ives's sentimental songs and church music. With both figures this early work showed a sensitive response but little indication of the future. Other innovators, like Debussy and Satie, wrote salon music.

3. Ives and Joyce were misunderstood and ostracized. Ives had no sympathetic following—Schoenberg was in luxury by comparison—and Joyce had to live abroad. Both achieved publication only after frustration and delay, Ives issuing works at his own expense and Joyce suffering the banning of *Ulysses*. Their originality perplexed their own generation and they remained controversial.

4. Both, by implication, asserted the right of their own provincial cultures as the material of their art. They raised its level from local to universal, but in the process it became transformed and sometimes distorted. In this respect the larger orchestral works of Ives (*Browning Overture;* second and fourth movements of the *Fourth Symphony*) and parts of *Ulysses* and most of *Finnegans Wake* revel in a sound and fury where not every detail is comprehensible but the creative message is powerfully evident.

5. Quotation is essential to later Joyce and to Ives of all periods. Ives used tunes like literary characters, causing them to crop up in different works and situations. The past is made to belong, through a changed context, in the immediacy of a new present. The belief that life was an entity allowed both Ives and Joyce to work with low comedy and sublime visions, the latter often thrown into stronger perspective through close proximity to the former.

The comparison between the lapsed Irish Catholic, who soon became a European figure, and the New England idealist must not be pressed too far. Joyce retained his Irish inheritance, sharpened by his critical rejection of it and his long residence abroad. Ives, equally affirming life, was rooted in the original New England of an earlier period, and was often bitterly critical of his own society (see "The Majority"), which failed to match up to Emerson and Thoreau.

A discussion of Ives and Joyce may be appropriate because Ives worked like a writer, with ideas, and was inspired by literature. Can the comparison support a comparable international stature for Ives? Until recently it would have seemed presumptuous to make such a claim. But, as I suggested earlier, our musical center of gravity has moved away from the Austro-German traditions which Ives found so alien. Ives has grown in stature with time and with performances. His prophecies have been confirmed by our experience of living, and his apparently parochial involvements act as a symbol of our own efforts to contain a heterogeneous world.

Schoenberg said, "There is a great man . . . "; now we can say, "There is a great composer. . . . "

Some Reflections on Charles E. Ives

HANS G. HELMS

In 1970, when I was producing my two television documentaries about Charles Ives's music and his philosophical and political thought, I interviewed among others the celebrated Ives singer Helen Boatwright. Mrs. Boatwright described some of Ives's vocal music as being like protest songs. She recalled a concert she had recently given at the University of Minnesota and mentioned that the audience "was filled with young people who, one would think, were not music lovers but just coming to hear this man's music. When I sang these protest songs they just thundered with applause. They liked them so much because these things seemed to be speaking their language."

In another interview that I did for the films, the conductor Harold Farberman attempted to formulate more exactly the nature of Ives's protest. "All he contributed to music was this dream. I keep coming back to the word 'dream' because it is so much a part of our lives—like Martin Luther King and what he dreamt for America. Ives dreamt it for America in the early part of this century. The political terms are very strong, especially in his songs. Now we know that Charles Ives was very motivated politically, and that he was very socially minded —a socialist in the sense of wanting everyone to live according to his own needs— almost a communistic concept."

I would certainly not agree fully with Mr. Farberman, and especially not with the last part of his statement, but it does contain a grain of truth. Both interviewees were referring to Ives's continuous interest in the "communistic" (or rather anarchistic) theories of the Concord transcendentalists, especially those of Thoreau. Furthermore, the present world-wide interest in Ives's music, as well as the influence which it has exerted on the musical ideologies of avant-garde composers since Cage, Brown, Boulez, and Stockhausen, can be fully understood only on the basis of the socioeconomic conditions pertaining, on the one hand, to Ives himself and, on the other, to the present-day musical avant-garde. It would seem rather ludicrous to expect a revelation from Hegel's "Weltgeist" describing why else the music of Charles Ives should suddenly—and so belatedly— have become this all-pervading ideological stimulus that it has actually become, if it did not—much more clearly than, for example, the music of the Viennese serialists—directly reflect a general socioeconomic tendency which alone can provide a realistic historical perspective.

Ives's uniqueness lies in the fact that he was able to combine such contrasting positions as (a) "the American dream," i.e., the traditional American ideology which proclaims each man his own master, and (b) an anarchic-socialist theory derived from Thoreau (and ultimately from European thinking), which analyzed man's position within society as being economically and socially interdependent. Finally, Ives was able to express these contrasting and even ambiguous positions with exceptional precision in his music—for instance, in his song *Majority*, written in 1921 as his very personal and violent protest against the election of Warren Harding, who was to become one of the most corrupt presidents of the United States to date. In this song the vocal line (a clearly defined individual construction) is purposefully set against the instrumental clusters of the accompaniment (an equally clear definition of what Ives termed "The Masses," viz. [at the entry of the voice] in measure 8).

Ives's contribution to the perennial argument about the relationship between words and music was crucial and innovative. Ives did not merely regard words as superior—or for that matter inferior—to music (*pace* his German bourgeois contemporary, the composer of *Capriccio*). Words in Ives's music are meant to serve as integrated vehicles of communication between the composer and the performer. For instance, in the third piece ("In the Night") of *A Set of Pieces for Theatre or Chamber Orchestra* (1904–11): "The words under the Solo Horn staff are not to be sung. They are from an old song (suggested in a general way in this part), which was often sung in the travelling 'Minstrel Shows' popular in the '80's and '90's—a form of 'theatricals' that unfortunately has almost disappeared" (to quote from the performance instructions following the score). In the orchestral song *Lincoln, the Great Commoner* (1912), where the words are of the utmost importance, providing the raison d'être of the song, the vocal lines nevertheless are so completely integrated into the orchestral structure that they really function as instruments among instruments.

Innovations of this sort, which provide freedom and discipline for both composer and performer, reflect Ives's understanding of the necessity for enhancing musical and ideological communication with his audience. These innovations are being quasi-rediscovered by avant-garde composers in America and Europe today, as a reaction to the repressive conditions existing specifically in the field of musical production—and in society in general. In Europe, and particularly in West Germany, the Communist composer Hanns Eisler alone exerts a comparable ideological influence.

Of course, there also exist technical reasons why the bulk of Ives's music has only recently entered the general musical consciousness, even among informed performers and listeners. As I tried to demonstrate in my documentaries, one of the reasons was the gap between performance techniques available even to the most advanced contemporary performers in the 1930s and '40s and the performance techniques which are absolutely necessary for a full realization of Ives's intentions. These techniques have really become available to performers through their experience of American and European avant-garde music only since about 1950. This historical discrepancy, incidentally, is still reflected in the often rather corrupt editions of Ives's scores, not a few of which have been altered to suit the convenience of certain conservative performers.

As one of Ives's publishers, Ronald Freed [of Peer-Southern], also pointed out in my film, the renaissance—or rather the naissance—of Ives actually began in continental Europe, specifically in Holland, Sweden, and Germany. It was not until 1961 that Aloys Kontarsky, assisted by his experiences of piano compositions by Boulez, Stockhausen, Pousseur, *et al.*, produced the first recording of the *"Concord" Sonata* in which the diverse statistical—or, as they are nowadays more commonly called, aleatoric—methods employed by the composer became transparent. In other words, the *"Concord" Sonata* was not treated as a nineteenth-century virtuoso piece or as a matter of "manner" (as Ives himself characterized such pieces).

A Great Visionary Musician

ALFRED HOFFMAN

Personally, I had the revelation of Ives's genius when I heard his work *The Unanswered Question* performed as part of a concert of works by the Romanian composer Anatol Vieru in April 1970. Vieru had already spoken to me at length about the profound impression made on him by Ives's *Fourth Symphony,* recorded by Leopold Stokowski. Ives's influence was one of the strongest in molding Vieru's personality, and it was precisely this that the Romanian composer wished to emphasize by including the composition by the American master in a program otherwise made up only of his own music.

I felt that *The Unanswered Question* tackled and synthesized, within a very brief space, the essential problems of human existence and consciousness, with an extremely rare capacity to render in sounds a certain loftiness of philosophic thinking while preserving the specific nature of natural and fluent musical expression. In fact, this seemed to me to be one of the most valuable gifts of Charles Ives's music—always unfolding around a very precise image, to which the complex means of expression are subordinated.

In this way, Ives's extraordinary technical inventiveness never becomes tiresome for the listener, because it goes hand in hand with a very accurate definition of the expressive purpose pursued by the artist. Ives offers the example of a contact with the universe entirely free from prejudices, his striking originality being generated by a mighty, unsophisticated perception of the phenomena of life, not mediated by artificial aesthetic encroachments, as so often happens. That is why he is much closer to the sensibilities of our generation than other well-known reformers of twentieth-century music.

In recent years Ives's music has spread considerably in Romania, thanks partly to the contributions of a number of brilliant American musicians, among them Howard and Helen Boatwright (Mrs. Boatwright introduced us to the fascinating world of Ives's songs) and Alan and Nancy Mandel, as well as Daryl Dayton (who through his enthusiastic lectures offered us a comprehensive view of the great composer's life and works). The writings of Ives himself and of the music critics who discussed his personality have become increasingly well known. Moreover, Ives's music has been included in the repertoire of some of the best Romanian interpreters. The Romanian Radio and Television Orchestra, conducted by Iosif Conta, has offered the public Ives's *Second Symphony;* the Musica Nova group, conducted by Hilda Jerea, and the chamber music group of the Gheorghiu brothers have successfully interpreted the *Piano Trio;* Ives's songs are more and more often included in the recitals of young Romanian singers.

One of Ives's most consistent admirers among contemporary Romanian composers is Liviu Glodeanu. I was particularly interested to know which aspects of the American composer's music impressed him most. He told me that Ives's musical phrases seem to him to unfold out of a special kind of logic, apparently arising out of a romantic feeling which, nevertheless, does not manifest itself in an overflowing, gushing way, being accompanied by a kind of irony which generates a rationalistic tinge, a slightly acid expression (as in the scherzo *Over the Pavements* and the parody moments in *Three Places in New England*). Polytonalism appears to Glodeanu as the most personal facet of Ives's style, being more than a merely incidental solution for bringing into bold relief the various points of an architecture, being a general atmosphere in which the music is produced. It is a kind of polytonalism which—to a greater extent than with Stravinsky, Hindemith, or Honegger, for instance—generates horizontal planes in permanent harmonic tension, which are found in *Chromâtimelôdtune* among others. Finally, further characteristic and exemplary qualities of Ives's music can be identified in the flavor of the sonorities, through the utilization of pure timbres in chamber music ensembles; in addition, there is the rhythm, both as an asymmetrical pulsation of polyrhythms and as an element of coordinating the discourse and building up the form (as in the cycle of pieces *The See'r, A Lecture, The New River, Like a Sick Eagle, Calcium Light Night, Incantation*).

I should like to conclude by referring to the splendid "Epilogue" of Ives's *Essays Before a Sonata,* in which he analyzes the dualism "substance/manner": "The higher and more important of this dualism," writes Ives, "is composed of what may be called reality, quality, spirit, or substance, against the lower value of form, quantity or manner." This is a quotation which I have discussed with some of my colleagues, Romanian musicians, and together we have reached the same conclusion. Whether more abstruse or more direct, more elaborate or more spontaneous, the musical work gains respect and recognition through its conception, through its signification, through what it communicates; and the means of expression, the *manner,* although they are in a tumultuous, breathtaking evolution, have less importance than the indefinable and yet so valuable *substance.*

On Charles Ives

YANNIS IOANNIDIS

Speaking about my personal relationship to the musical phenomenon that is Charles E. Ives, I dare say that I do so also on behalf of many other musicians, some whom I know personally, others whom I have never met, but in any case all of us members of the generation that was educated and formed professionally in music after the end of World War II.

Especially those of us outside the United States got, almost without exception, the same kind of information about Ives, which consisted at the beginning mostly of a very general description of his music and characteristic anecdotes about his life or his way of thinking. Later on we got the wonderful book of the Cowells [*Charles Ives and His Music,* 1955], little by little some recordings, and at last a few copies of his published scores.

For these reasons, it is only in the last few years that we have begun to form a somewhat clearer idea about Ives as a composer and as a thinker and have learned to understand and admire him, to enjoy his music, and also to get the meaning of his example—which can be very useful in moments of confusion, which are not so rare in our days.

But one thing must be cleared up: Ives has always been presented to us with words of extreme admiration; he has always been mentioned as "great" and "incredible" by those who wished to win our interest in him. However, he has been praised only for the most external of his achievements: his "experimental spirit," his "being ahead of his time" or "the first poly-, a-, or microtonalist," and so on; these are the virtues that have always been pointed out.

Now we know that what has real value and importance in his output is not the fact that he was the first in the history of music who used this or that technique, but the fact that his works are products of a purely musical, artistic thinking—products of an absolute necessity to express himself with tones—and that this necessity guided him to the use of all those new technical devices in the most normal and natural way. We are learning now to admire Ives as he really deserves to be admired: for the beauty and meaning of his works. And, there is no doubt, on this subject there is still much to be said.

Charles Ives

BETSY JOLAS

Virtually unknown only twenty years ago, today regularly performed in contemporary-music festivals all over the world, Charles Ives is now viewed as having been in the vanguard of the most advanced American music.

However, have we really accepted him here [in Europe]? Ives certainly fascinates us, but let us admit that he also troubles us more than a little. How, indeed, as Europeans loaded down with tradition, are we to judge such a diverse body of work as his? This splendid sonorous curiosity shop, in which rags and rigorous canons, twelve-tone sets and pop songs, nonretrogradable rhythms, tone clusters, and circus tunes are all mixed up together in the most democratic and thoroughly American way—to what category should we assign it? In what frame of mind should we perceive it? That is what puzzles us!

Is Ives the ingenious innovator celebrated by some, or is he the naïve amateur, the Sunday musician, rejected by others? Might it not be true, instead, that he is both at the same time (as his compatriots have considered him for a long time)?

Why not, in fact, admit it: Ives is unequivocally an amateur. Not, to be sure, in the sense of lacking craft—at Yale he got from the tedious Horatio Parker the most traditional training, with all the requisite harmony, counterpoint, fugue —but rather, in the noblest sense, because he *loved* music, passionately and in a totally disinterested way, even to the point of refusing, contrary to expectations, to make a profession of it.

As everyone knows, he was an insurance man, an especially brilliant one. All his spare time, however, was spent composing music (which no one performed). In other words, and in the best sense of the term, he *was* a Sunday musician—which meant, for Ives, a free musician, free to pursue his sonorous vision wherever he wished, apart from any practical or economic considerations.

Perhaps it is in this decision (which Ives never regretted) that we can find one explanation, at least, for those discoveries which never cease to astonish us. Working essentially in isolation, without contact—or almost so—with the professional musical world of his time, indifferent to current fashions and not seeking performances, Ives was perhaps able, with fewer risks than a career composer, to indulge in "dangerous" experiments, daring to think sometimes even beyond the limits he could actually achieve.

Finally, why not admit that there is now and then a naïve aspect to this music, a profoundly engaging aspect if we realize that it preserves, through the years, something of the innocence of the young Charles Ives at the moment long ago when his father (himself a remarkable musician and one curious about all sonorous phenomena) roused him not only to "music" but to all the sounds of his native New England—church bells, trumpet calls, dances, hymns, camp meetings. . . . All that, Charles Ives never forgot. [Translated from the French by H. Wiley Hitchcock.]

Thoughts on Ives

KARL AAGE RASMUSSEN

When at long last European interest in Ives began to quicken, it was apparently due to the fact that the European avant-garde suddenly could *use* this odd American phenomenon, whom they had formerly neglected completely. The time (late 1950s and early 1960s) needed a hero, and in the arts the heroic deed par excellence was to be the innovator of anything—to challenge the world and musical culture with the untried and the unheard. *Nie erhörte Klänge*—sounds never heard—was the highest praise one could get from the Darmstadt composers, such as Stockhausen and Boulez. Ives was wholly able to satisfy this demand. Suddenly he suited perfectly the very cultural milieu from which, in his productive period, he had been totally isolated. Only then was he canonized—played, recorded, discussed, and analyzed. The formerly all-too-shocking pioneer was suitable, all of a sudden, as ideal and moral armament.

However, I believe that Ives was accepted on rather obscure premises, because of his being an "interesting case" rather than because of real knowledge and empathetic evaluation of his art in its entirety. His originality was praised as an isolated, detached quality, without consideration of its background. But as a matter of fact, the European avant-garde could not conceal that from a European point of view this music in its profound basis was not only *nie erhört* but *unerhört*—above all in its absolute lack of traditional consistency. Ives desists from creating a logical, analytic basis, and this makes him in the long run offensive and unacceptable. His deep-rooted distrust of the cardinal European achievements—synonymity and termination, clarity and artistry—is and will be an undermining of the very base of the traditional European way of thinking about music.

I hope his centennial year will give Ives the opportunity to be heard and comprehended according to his own premises. If so, his influence on the evolution of music will not be limited to its material and technique but will spread to the very way it is heard, thought, evaluated, and used. Ives must not be neutralized as being only something like "the great inventor." His importance should be measured in the light of his being the first composer to dare to make a distinction between *manner* and *substance*. He was doomed to be the first really *lonely* one in our musical history.

Charles Ives in Yugoslavia

ANDREJ RIJAVEC

General. As in most other countries of the world, in Yugoslavia a steady increase in the presence of Charles Ives, this giant of American and world music, is to be noted in the last two decades. This is reflected in the archives of the Copyright Protection Department of the Union of Yugoslav Composers. Ives's music has already become a standard part of the twentieth-century repertoire of Yugoslav radio stations (although live, concert performance of his works seems still to be the domain of visiting American ensembles and soloists).

As regards musical journalism, the first independent article on Ives appeared only in 1961, in the Ljubljana fortnightly for social and cultural questions, *Our Views (Naši razgledi)*; titled "Charles Ives, Pioneer of Modern Music," it was written by Everett Helm.[1] It and other early articles were translations from American authors.[2] In recent years, however, Yugoslavs as well are to be found; let me

1. Everett Helm, "Charles Ives, pionir moderne glasbe," *Naši razgledi*, 10 (1961): 19.
2. E.g., Paul Cooper, "Charles Ives i njegova muzika," *Zvuk*, 7/2, no. 68 (1966): 363–74.

mention "The Musical Transcendentalism of Charles Ives," by Dunja Dujmić,[3] and—the first breakthrough of Ives's musical thought into youth magazines— Milan Stibilj's article, "At the End of a Tragic Day, the Voice of the People Again Arose."[4]

Yet another field of activity that shows an increasing influence of Ives's music and ideas is that of public university lectures, which, among Yugoslav musical centers, are most systematically presented by the department of musicology of the University of Ljubljana. Ives or aspects of Ives's musical language have been the main subjects of lectures, or have at least been touched on, by the following American guests: Nicolas Slonimsky (in 1963), Paul Cooper (1966), Earle Brown (1966), Everett Helm (1967), and H. Wiley Hitchcock (1969).

Specific. From the above, one may infer a (perhaps coincidental) sort of leading role for Ljubljana, the capital of Slovenia, in Yugoslav "Ivesology." This leads to a specific example (which I shall discuss in a moment), which in part is also a result of the activity of a markedly modern and even avant-garde generation of Yugoslav composers, now mostly in their forties, whose formative period, in Ljubljana, dates from some twenty years ago: Darijan Božič, Jakob Jež, Lojze Lebič, Ivo Petrič, Alojz Srebotnjak, Milan Stibilj, and—last but not least—Igor Štuhec. (These were joined later by Vinko Globokar.) These composers and some others (except for Globokar, who lives and works mostly abroad), who were not getting at the Music Academy what they wanted, founded, while they were still students, the so-called Composers' Club (1952), in which they studied and listened to music by the forerunners of today's avant-garde. Ives was not available, for America herself was only then discovering him. However, there is evidence that his name was known to represent someone who, already at the turn of the century, "thought differently."

Each of these Yugoslav composers developed independently, including Štuhec (b. 1932). Being of an anti-Romantic nature, he began with neo-Classicism; then, under the influence of his studies in Vienna with Hanns Jelinek and Friedrich Cerha at the Hochschule für Musik und darstellende Kunst (1964–66), he touched on serialism, only to proceed to more contemporary structural techniques. A visit to one of the concerts of the Viennese ensemble Die Reihe, which at that time had Ives's *The Unanswered Question* on its program, led to his writing a composition which must lead the present conference to inscribe Igor Štuhec's name among the Ivesians. More than fifty years after Ives's important composition, and under its impact, Štuhec composed his *Answered Questions* (1965) as Part IV of the chamber cycle *Silhouettes*.

The philosophical and compositional characteristics of Ives's piece are well known. This is not the case, however, regarding parallel features in Štuhec's. First of all, it would be illusory to search for philosophical parallels, for *Answered Questions* is far removed from any philosophy, let alone transcendentalism.

3. Dunja Dujmić, "The Musical Transcendentalism of Charles Ives," *International Review of the Aesthetics and Sociology of Music*, 2, no. 1 (1971).

4. Milan Stibilj, "Ob koncu tragičnega dneva se povzdigne glas ljudstva," *Pionir*, 28 (1972–73): 8.

Štuhec does not, therefore, pride himself on having answered Ives's "perennial question of existence." On the contrary, Ives's model served only as a formal scheme, an interesting combination of contrasting elements. Thus, in Štuhec's work as in Ives's, the strings (onstage, however) create a static background enriched *con sordini* and *con flagioletti*. With Ives, their music is tonal; with Štuhec, serially organized. Štuhec also calls for trumpet and (instead of flutes—Ives's "fighting answerers") three clarinets (E-flat, B-flat, and bass), plus a trombone as well as a differentiated group of percussion instruments. With Ives, only the trumpet does the "asking," in exchange with the woodwinds ("and other human beings"), but this formal idea represents only the first part of Štuhec's composition; after a culmination in the percussion group, the roles are reversed, and a well-balanced arch form is achieved. Another point: the mocking element, already present in Ives, turns, in Štuhec's *Answered Questions,* into a typically contemporaneous, disobliging dialogue (in the sense of "Why ask at all?"—which might be the only "philosophical" background, if any, of the composition), in compliance wth contemporary, more dissonant idioms.

Personal. It was suggested that one attempt to express "what Ives means to you personally." As a music lover, one is surprised by the multitude of ideas and the variety of expression in Ives's compositions, in which he managed to elevate a vernacular to a cultivated, international level, where local color does not restrict him to regional or national coordinates but represents an enrichment of the world of music, "a pigment of the universal color." As a historian, one is interested in the inner as well as the external impulses that formed Ives's ways of musical thinking, i.e., those dimensions which on the one hand bind Ives with the past and on the other link him with the present—even with the most recent avant-garde ideas—and are a result of his unique personality and prophetic imagination.

Random—and Provocative—Thoughts on Ives

ILHAN USMANBAS

Influence. Only indirect, through Carter and, to a lesser degree, Brant. Indirect, because Ives's music, being too much that of a pioneer, too much that of an independent, and (let's say frankly) sometimes too much that of a regional artist, had to be elaborated in its basic innovations to be ready for universal assimilation. So a Carter's more worked-out metric modulations, a Brant's more audacious and, for me, alive spatial approaches had deeper influence (in 1957–58, during my stay in the United States) than Ives's seemingly experimental beginnings.

My first and most important contact with Ives's music (through recordings, of course) was with the *Second String Quartet,* during my last year as a student at the Ankara State Conservatory, in 1948. The work appeared to me as audacious, but I can't say I was much influenced. The quotations seemed like a game. I was seeking instead the seriousness and dramatic heaviness of, say, Berg's music in his *Violin Concerto.*

I now realize the meaning, after so many successful musical collages (like those of Berio), of the living theater in collage and in the *travesti* figures which animate Ives's music.

I have never been quite able to forsake this feeling of doubt—of insecurity—while listening to Ives. Big holes of time, because of his working habit, make tiny holes in his music, and this may affect its compactness.

Basically he is a great romantic, with that predilection for the grandiose, for the universal, for the natural, of Mahler. This is in conflict with his other self—the experimentalist, the gambler in sound, quite unlike Mahler—his malicious, Mephistophelean side. (Or are his audacities and most of his unconventionalities a revenge on the ignorant present and unhopeful future?)

Prophecy in art. Had it not been used in a pejorative sense by many of Ives's critics, I would like to accept this term. For them, prophecy means unbelieved sayings fully realized in the future, and by others. True, we cannot forget that some of his techniques gained full meaning (only) through Cowell, Cage, Brant, Carter, Partch—all of them Americans, by the way—but is it not the same for all new techniques?

Unfortunately, Ives is becoming a legend, a person much spoken about but not known enough, and, worse than that, an object of tourism. It seems that communities inattentive and careless about their living values try to cover their errors by conferences, symposiums, meetings, festivals, museums, centenaries, postcards, stamps, street names (I deliberately extend the list) for their lost values. This is done, for example, for Bartók by Hungarians, for Enesco by Romanians. I see also in their effort an attempt to create a classic for their own and for universal use. A classic—a taboo. Noble work. But I fear for the legendary artists. Let's let them come back among the living souls of the community, as simple as they were. Let's not dull their works by heavy connotations.

Ives's music cannot have an influence on younger Turkish composers—even assuming that it comes to be known. The output of the two conservatories—the main one in Ankara, the other in Istanbul—is rooted in Paris Conservatory academicism, which, as one may guess easily, excludes any spirit of experimentalism. Moreover, I do not think Ives's grandiloquence in his symphonic works or his wit in the smaller ones can have a lasting effect on us. Nevertheless, the *Tone Roads, Over the Pavements, Hallowe'en*—played and analyzed during my courses —have always made an astonishing impression on my students. (But not more. In fact, a complex attitude is to be seen in Turkey toward the music which comes from America: either it seems too American—only *pièces de genre*—or too experimental, i.e., immature, or, if it is within the general [stylistic] trends, too academic.) Only Ives's two string quartets and *The Unanswered Question* have been publicly played up to now by Turkish musicians. The *"Concord" Sonata* is about to be studied by one of our pianists. That is the present and the near future of Ives in Turkey.

A bas Ives. . . . Ives is dead. These two cries will never occur, I think. Though revolutionary, he never forced his time to hear like him, as did Wagner and Schoenberg. If he is a prophet, he is one without a god.

People adore those who struggle, suffer, and finally win their musical empire. Ives did not suffer and struggle—or, if he did, it was in a very solitary way. He won his Ives & Myrick Co.; music he merely abandoned himself to. How can we make up a musical martyrdom for the large public? Ives defies all attempts. (Or why not through his uncompleted works?)

Two poles of attraction for him were the world of new sonorities and a natural, harmonious simplicity: the new world (the New World) and the eternal world (the World). That was the difficult and precarious balance to create by way of music.

Exclamations while listening to Ives: "How was it possible to do this in 1890?" "Oh! what sonorities! and this already in 1905!" It is a pity that the music world and, in fact, American criticism, instead of trying to erase this date-consciousness, make it worse. Let's not speak of Ives's progressivism. Let's simply learn to listen to him.

True! Berlioz was ahead of his time; so was Webern. But we accept their progressivism as historically true and justified and see through them the continuity of the history of music. Can we say the same for Ives? Is it because, in spite of the Ives-Cowell-Cage chain (the one immediately natural chain one thinks about), American music is still outside the history of music? Or is it because Ives's visions are not in a fully integrated style, not continued, not pursued to their ultimate consequences in all his works? There, perhaps, is the reason for the unavoidable date-consciousness while listening to him.

Random—and, if possible, provocative—thoughts on Ives. An approach to understanding and liking him better. An essay of course unpretentious and certainly far below the standards of today's best musical prose . . . an essay, then, to bring Ives down from the clouds, where everyone likes to place him, to the earth, among us.

Concert Programs of the Festival-Conference

CONCERT 1

Thursday, 17 October
Hunter College Playhouse
695 Park Avenue, New York
8:30 p.m.

MAJOR PIANO WORKS BY IVES

Three Quarter-Tone Pieces for Two Pianos (1923–24)
    1. Largo
    2. Allegro
    3. Chorale
          (George Pappastavrou, Alexander Dashnaw, pianos)

First Piano Sonata (1902–10)
    1. Adagio con moto
    2a. Allegro moderato
    2b. In the Inn (Allegro)
    3. Largo; Allegro; Largo
    4a. [Allegro]
    4b. Allegro
    5. Andante maestoso; Adagio cantabile; Allegro; Andante
          (William Masselos, piano)

INTERMISSION

Second Piano Sonata: "Concord, Mass., 1840–60" (1909–15; rev. ed. 1947)
    1. "Emerson" (Slowly)
    2. "Hawthorne" (Very fast)
    3. "The Alcotts" (Moderately)
    4. "Thoreau" (Starting slowly and quietly)
          (John Kirkpatrick, piano)

CONCERT 2

Friday, 18 October
Hunter College Playhouse
695 Park Avenue, New York
8:30 p.m.

CHORAL AND VOCAL MUSIC BY IVES

The Gregg Smith Singers
with
The Long Island Symphonic Chorale, the Columbia University
Men's Glee Club, the Barnard-Columbia Chorus, and the
Orpheus Chamber Ensemble
Gregg Smith, conductor
Raymond Beegle, piano and organ
(Presented in association with Gomer Rees)

I: SACRED MUSIC

1. *Psalm 100* (1898 or 1899?)
   Combined choirs, organ

2. †*Lord God, Thy sea is mighty* (1893 or 1894?)
   *Crossing the Bar (1891?)
   The Gregg Smith Singers

3. *Psalm 67* (1898; possibly 1894)
   Psalm 54 (1894?)
   Psalm 24 (1897?)
   The Gregg Smith Singers

4. *Psalm 90* (1894–1901?; recomposed 1923–24)
   The Gregg Smith Singers, the Long Island Symphonic Chorale, organ,
   and percussion

5. *Harvest Home Chorales*
   a. *Harvest Home* (1898)
   b. *Lord of the Harvest* (before 1902?)
   c. *Harvest Home* (before 1902?)
   Combined choirs, brass ensemble, and organ

INTERMISSION

258

II: SECULAR MUSIC

6. †[*Serenade*] (1891?)
    The Gregg Smith Singers

7. Solo Songs for Voice and Chamber Orchestra
    The Orpheus Chamber Ensemble and soloists as listed below
    The Last Reader (chamber version 1911; song arrangement 1921)
       Priscilla Magdamo
    Luck and Work (chamber version 1916, from song of 1909[?])
       Lin Garber
    The Pond (chamber version 1906; song arrangement 1921)
       Rosalind Rees
    At Sea (chamber version 1912; song arrangement 1921)
       Patrick Mason
    The See'r (chamber version before 30 May 1913; song arrangement 1913[?])
       Faye Kittelson
    Like a Sick Eagle (chamber version 1906; song arrangement before 1914[?])
       Rosalind Rees
    Tolerance (chamber version 1906; song arrangement 1909)
       Richard Muenz
    The Indians (chamber version 1912; song arrangement 1921)
       Thomas Bogdan
    From the Incantation (chamber version 1909[?]; song arrangement 1921)
       Rosalind Rees

8. Songs for Chorus and Chamber Orchestra
    The Gregg Smith Singers and the Orpheus Chamber Ensemble
    Walt Whitman (orchestral version 1913; song arrangement 1921)
    Serenity (score sketch before May 1911; song adaptation 1919)
    December (1912–13)
    General William Booth Enters Into Heaven (1914; orchestration by John J.
       Becker, 1934)
       Jan Opalach, baritone

9. Songs for Large Chorus and Orchestra
    Combined choirs, Orpheus Chamber Ensemble
    The Circus Band (music 1894, words later; orchestrated 1930s by George F.
       Roberts, with additions by Ives)
    An Election (1920)
    They Are There! (words 1942; music mostly 1917)

---

† Newly edited by John Kirkpatrick.
* First 20th-century performance; edited by John Kirkpatrick.

CONCERT 3

Saturday, 19 October
Whitman Hall
Brooklyn College
8:00 p.m.

A CHARLES IVES KALEIDOSCOPE

The Brooklyn College Symphonic Band
Dorothy Klotzman, conductor
The American Brass Quintet
Bernard Barrow, reader
Jean Hakes, soprano
Michael Rogers, piano
Margaret Linney, reader

Ives on music
Overture and March: "1776" (1903–04)
    The Brooklyn College Symphonic Band

Ives on his book of *114 Songs*
Songs I
   Memories (1897): A. Very Pleasant; B. Rather Sad
   The Things Our Fathers Loved (chamber version 1905[?]; song adaptation
     1917)
   There is a Lane (German version, as *Widmung*, 1897[?]; English adaptation
     1902)
   Mists (second setting 1910)
   The New River (choral version 1911; song arrangement 1913)
     Jean Hakes, soprano; Michael Rogers, piano

Ives on *"The Alcotts"*
"The Alcotts" (transcribed for band by James Thurston)
    The Brooklyn College Symphonic Band

Ives on ear-stretching
Chromâtimelôdtune (1913 and 1919[?])
    The American Brass Quintet

Ives on "a boy's fooling"
Song for Harvest Season (1893)
    Jean Hakes, soprano; The American Brass Quintet

Ives on war
Variations on "America" (1891?) (transcribed for band by William Rhoades)
    The Brooklyn College Symphonic Band

Concert Programs of the Festival-Conference

March: Intercollegiate (1892)

Ives on religious music
"Adeste Fidelis" in an Organ Prelude (1897) (transcribed for band by Keith Brion)
>   The Brooklyn College Symphonic Band

"Ives" by Muriel Rukeyser (1939)

Variations on "Jerusalem the Golden" (1888 or 1889) (transcribed for brass quintet and band by Keith Brion)
>   The American Brass Quintet; The Brooklyn College Symphonic Band

Ives on songs and humor in music
Songs II
>   *The See'r* (chamber version before 30 May 1913; song arrangement 1913[?])
>   *The Sideshow* (lost prototype, for clarinet and piano, 1896[?]; song adaptation 1921)
>   *Down East* (1919)
>   *An Election* (1920)
>   *The One Way* (1923[?])
>   Jean Hakes, soprano; Michael Rogers, piano

Ives on his father and bells
From the Steeples and the Mountains (1901)
>   The American Brass Quintet

Ives's verses for *The Circus Band*
March: The Circus Band (1894; orchestrated about 1934 by George F. Roberts; transcribed for band by Jonathan Elkus)
>   The Brooklyn College Symphonic Band

CONCERT 4

Sunday, 20 October
Battell Chapel
Yale University
5:00 p.m.

BAND MUSIC BY IVES

The Yale University Band
Keith Brion, conductor
James Sinclair, assistant conductor
Jonathan Elkus, guest conductor

March: Omega Lambda Chi (1896)
    Keith Brion, conductor

*Old Home Days — Suite for Band (arranged by Jonathan Elkus)
    1. *Waltz* (1895)
    2. *The Collection* (1920)
    3. *Slow March* (1888)
    4. [*The Opera House*] from *Memories* (1897); with *Old Home Day* refrain
       (1913; revised 1920[?])
    5. *Religion* (1910)

*Finale, Symphony No. 2 (1902) (arranged by Jonathan Elkus)
    Jonathan Elkus, conductor

*Fugue in C Major (1897–98) (arranged by James Sinclair)

*Hymn (1904) (arranged by James Sinclair)

They Are There! A War Song (text 1942; music mostly 1917) (arranged by James
    Sinclair)
    James Sinclair, conductor

March: A Son of a Gambolier (1895) (arranged by Jonathan Elkus)

"Country Band" March (1903) (arranged by James Sinclair)
    Keith Brion, conductor

    * First performance in this arrangement.

CONCERT 5

Sunday, 20 October
Woolsey Hall
Yale University
8:30 p.m.

IVES AND FRIENDS: A 100TH BIRTHDAY CELEBRATION

The Yale Philharmonia
The Yale Symphony Orchestra
The Yale Glee Club
Robert Shaw and John Mauceri, conductors

Participating artists:
William Harwood, conductor
Fenno Heath, conductor
John Kirkpatrick, piano
Charles Krigbaum, organ
Blake Stern, tenor

Charles Ives had definite tastes among other composers' music (for and against). Some of his musical friends are expected to drop in on this 100th Birthday Celebration. Who? Well, Ives considered Bach, Beethoven, and Brahms "among the greatest and strongest in all art," although "not quite as strong and great as Carl Ruggles." The songs of Stephen Foster and the hymns of Lowell Mason were part of Ives's very fiber, and affection for them is reflected in many of his works. Ives apparently knew little of Stravinsky; surely, however, he would be tickled by *Greeting Prelude* (which he would have called a "take-off") and would welcome Stravinsky as an uninvited guest at his birthday celebration.

(Stravinsky) *Greeting Prelude* (1955)

A Contemplation of a Serious Matter (The Unanswered Perennial Question) (1906)
Mr. Mauceri conducting

(Bach) *In dir ist Freude*
Mr. Krigbaum

(Beethoven) *Bagatelle* in A major, Op. 119, no. 10
Mr. Kirkpatrick

(Lowell Mason) *Olivet*
Glee Club with solo trumpet

First Symphony (1895–98)
  Mr. Shaw conducting

(George Ives) two student fugues in A minor and B♮ major for string quartet

(Brahms) *Waltz* in C♯ minor, Op. 39, no. 7
  Mr. Kirkpatrick

(Stephen Foster) *Gentle Annie*
  Mr. Stern and Mr. Kirkpatrick

(Joseph T. Webster) *In the Sweet Bye and Bye*
  Mr. Mauceri and audience

†*Second Orchestral Set* (1911–15)
  Mr. Mauceri conducting

(Carl Ruggles) *Angels*
  Mr. Harwood conducting

*West London (conjectural version for chorus and orchestra with the existing fragment of *Matthew Arnold Overture* as introduction) (1911–21)
  Mr. Shaw conducting

"The Alcotts," *Second Piano Sonata* ("*Concord, Mass., 1840–60*")
  Charles Ives, piano (recorded 1943)

† First performance in this edition.
* First performance.

CONCERT 6

Monday, 21 October
Center Church on the Green
New Haven
5:00 p.m.

SACRED SONGS AND ORGAN MUSIC BY IVES

Helen Boatwright, soprano
Charles Krigbaum, organ
Instrumental and Vocal Ensembles
conducted by Jere Lantz

Fugue in C Minor (1897?)
[Canzonetta] (1893?)
    Mr. Krigbaum

Abide with Me (1891[?]; also a later version)
Down East (1919)
    Mrs. Boatwright, Mr. Krigbaum

Fugue in E♭ Major (1897)
Variations on "America" (1891?)
    Mr. Krigbaum

(John Wyeth [attrib.]) *Nettleton* ("Come, thou fount of every blessing"), with
    Ives's interlude (1892?) between stanzas
        Audience, Mr. Krigbaum

The Collection (1920; possibly adapted from earlier church music)
†*The Last Reader* (1920[?] version; scored from original of 1911)
Forward into Light, aria from *The Celestial Country* (1897–99)
    Mrs. Boatwright, Mr. Lantz

(Lowell Mason) *Bethany* ("Nearer my God to thee"), with Ives's interlude (1892?)
    between stanzas
        Audience, Mr. Krigbaum

"Adeste Fidelis" in an Organ Prelude (1897)
    Mr. Krigbaum

Eventide (1901?)
    Mr. Lantz

    † First performance in this edition.

CONCERT 7

Monday, 21 October
Sprague Hall
Yale University
8:30 p.m.

AN IVES POTPOURRI

Yale Theater Orchestra and Chorus
James Sinclair, conductor
Jere Lantz, chorus director
Lawrence Wolf, piano
The Whiffenpoofs
Phyllis Curtin, soprano

#*The Circus Band* (1894[?]; orchestrated after 1922)

#*Old Home Day* (1913; orchestrated after 1922)

†*Set for Theatre or Chamber Orchestra* (1906–11)
    1. *In the Cage*
    2. *In the Inn*
    3. *In the Night*

*[Set of Incomplete Works and Fragments]
    1. *March in F and C* (1892–94?)
    2. *Polonaise* (1887?)
    3. *Take-off #7: Mike Donlin–Johnny Evers*
    4. *March III* (middle section) (1892–93?)
    5. *Take-off #8: Willy Keeler* (1907)
    6. *March III* (ending) (1892–93?)

†*A Song of Mory's* (1896)

†*The Bells of Yale* (1897–98?)

**The Boys in Blue* (1897 or later?)

INTERMISSION

†*Three-Page Sonata* (1905)

Sunrise (1926)

*Beethoven, *Adagio Cantabile* from *Piano Sonata in F Minor,* Op. 2, no. 1 (arranged by Ives in 1889[?])

#From *Four Ragtime Dances* (1902–4)
    Ragtime Dance #2
    Ragtime Dance #4

Sneak Thief (1914)

#*They Are There!* (1917; text revised 1942)

    * First performance.
    # First performance in this version.
    † First performance in this edition.

———————————————————————

Participants

LOUIS ANDRIESSEN, Dutch composer, studied at the Royal Conservatory in The Hague and later with Luciano Berio. Since 1964 he has lived in Amsterdam and now teaches instrumentation and orchestration at the Hague conservatory. He was one of the founders of the Dutch Charles Ives Society.

WILLIAM AUSTIN, Goldwin Smith Professor of Musicology at Cornell University, is the author of *Music in the 20th Century; Susanna, Jeanie, and the Old Folks at Home: The Songs of Stephen C. Foster from His Time to Ours;* and many articles, among them "Ives and Histories" for the *Kongressbericht, Bonn, 1970.*

GUIDO BAGGIANI, Italian composer and critic, has taught musical composition at the Conservatorio Rossini in Pesaro since 1970. His interest in the combination of live and electronic music led him, in 1972, to establish with three other musicians the Gruppo Team for performance of live/electronic music.

JOHN BECKWITH, Canadian composer and critic, is dean of the faculty of music at the University of Toronto. He was a founding member of the League of Canadian Composers and of the Ten Centuries Concerts, and for years he conducted the important weekly radio program "The World of Music."

REGIS BENOIT, pianist, studied at the Juilliard School of Music and, later, with Nadia Boulanger and Jean-Marie Darré in Paris. He has performed in the major cities of Europe, Africa, and the United States.

J. BERNLEF is a poet and has written prose and plays as well. He has published articles on John Cage and Erik Satie and together with Louis Andriessen wrote *Souvenirs d'enfance,* a collection of piano music and texts. He is secretary of the Dutch Charles Ives Society.

WILLIAM BROOKS is a composer, scholar, and performer who teaches in the music department of the University of California at San Diego. His book-length comparative study of William Billings, Charles Ives, and John Cage will be published by Wesleyan University Press, and he is at work on a revised critical edition of Ives's *Fourth Symphony*.

EARLE BROWN, composer, conductor, and teacher, rose to international prominence in the 1950s as one of the "New York school" of composers. He has taught at the Peabody Conservatory and the California Institute of the Arts and has been a recording engineer and editor for Capitol Records as well as artistic director of the Contemporary Sound Series of Time-Mainstream Records.

NEELY BRUCE is a pianist, composer, conductor, and theorist; he is associate professor of music at Wesleyan University. Previously he taught at the University of Illinois, where he founded the American Music Group, a choral organization devoted to the performance of American music.

MARTINE CADIEU, French novelist and music critic, lives in Paris and is on the staff of the Radiodiffusion-Télévision Française. She has been music critic of the journals *Combat* and *Lettres Françaises* and frequently writes music criticism for *Nuova rivista musicale italiana* and *Opus international*. Among her novels are *La terre est tendre, Soleil d'hiver* (which won an Académie Française prize), and *Mozart*.

GILBERT CHASE, author of *America's Music* and a host of other publications, editor of *The American Composer Speaks* and of the *Yearbook for Inter-American Musical Research,* which he initiated in 1965, has taught at Columbia University, the University of Oklahoma, Brooklyn College, and the State University of New York at Buffalo. He is currently visiting professor in the department of comparative studies at the University of Texas at Austin.

AUSTIN CLARKSON, Canadian musicologist, is chairman of the music department of York University in Toronto. He taught earlier at Yale University, Columbia University, and the University of Saskatchewan. He was founding editor of the journal *Current Musicology* and is presently working on a general study of song.

AARON COPLAND is not only one of America's best-known and widely performed composers but a pianist, conductor, lecturer and writer on music, and teacher. Among his many honors was the presidency of the American Academy of Arts and Letters. He was among the first to perform Ives's music in concert (*Seven Songs,* Yaddo, 1932) and to publish serious criticism of Ives's music ("One Hundred and Fourteen Songs," *Modern Music,* 1934).

ROQUE CORDERO is a Panamanian composer long resident in the United States. His principal connection with Ives has been as an editor of a number of Ives's works for the Peer-Southern Organization.

Participants

ROBERT M. CRUNDEN is professor of history and American studies at the University of Texas at Austin. He is the author of several books on American intellectual and cultural history, including *From Self to Society, 1919–1941,* and is currently at work on a book on American culture during the Progressive Era.

PETER DICKINSON, English composer and pianist, was named in 1974 the first professor of music in the new department of the University of Keele, in Staffordshire, where he has established a Centre for American Music. His interest in Ives's music has been reflected in recitals, BBC talks, lectures, and articles—also by the establishment of an Ives Choir at Keele.

CHARLES DODGE, composer, teaches at Columbia University. Among his honors have been a Guggenheim Fellowship and commissions from the Fromm Music Foundation, the Koussevitzky Foundation, and the National Endowment for the Arts. In recent years he has lectured in Europe and throughout the United States on computer music.

PAUL C. ECHOLS has taught at Brooklyn College, where he was head of the School of General Studies division of the music department, and has written on Ives's music for various journals. His dissertation-in-progress is on gospel hymnody. He is coordinator of editions for the Charles Ives Society.

LEHMAN ENGEL has conducted some 165 Broadway shows and operas and is the author of six books, including *The American Musical Theatre: A Consideration* and *Words with Music.* As conductor of the Madrigal Singers, he was the first to record a choral work by Ives: *Psalm 67,* recorded 22 March 1939.

ALLEN FORTE is professor of the theory of music at Yale University. From 1960 to 1967 he was editor of *The Journal of Music Theory,* and he is the author of *Contemporary Tone Structures, The Compositional Matrix, Tonal Harmony in Concept and Practice,* and *The Structure of Atonal Music,* as well as many articles on musical theory and analysis.

EUGENE GRATOVICH, violinist, has taught at the University of Missouri at Columbia and the University of California at San Diego. His D.M.A. dissertation was a concordance and critical commentary of the violin sonatas of Ives, and he has often presented lecture-recitals on the sonatas, in both the United States and England.

LOU HARRISON, composer, conductor, music editor—also poet, instrument inventor, critic, calligrapher, animal nurse, Esperanto expert, and other things—has lived on the West Coast most of his life. He has long been interested in microtones, nontempered tunings, and Oriental music and instruments. He has done much editorial work on Ives's compositions and in 1946 conducted the first complete performance of an Ives symphony (the *Third*).

HANS G. HELMS works in Cologne as a freelance writer for German and foreign radio networks, newspapers, and journals and as an independent film director for German television networks. Among his numerous TV documentaries are two of 1970 on Ives, the first ever to be made; in the last twenty years he has produced altogether about forty works in various media dealing with Ives.

H. WILEY HITCHCOCK is professor of music at Brooklyn College of the City University of New York and founding director of its Institute for Studies in American Music. He is the author of *Music in the United States: A Historical Introduction* and *Ives* (Oxford Studies of Composers Series), and is editor of the reprint series *Earlier American Music*. He is president of the Charles Ives Society.

ALFRED HOFFMAN, Romanian musicologist and critic, has been principal researcher at the Art History Institute in Bucharest since 1960. He is music critic of the journals *România liberă* and *Contemporanul* and co-author of the prize-winning monograph *Georges Enesco*.

YANNIS IOANNIDIS is a Venezuelan composer and conductor of Greek origin and is professor of composition at Metropolitan University and the National Institute of Culture in Caracas. He is the founder-director of both the Caracas Chamber Orchestra and the chorus of the Venezuelan American Center.

BETSY JOLAS, composer, lives in Paris, where she was born. Her formal education was mainly in the United States; after returning to Paris in 1946, she studied at the Paris Conservatory under Milhaud and Messiaen. Since 1971 she has often taught at the conservatory as a substitute for Messiaen when he is on tour. Among her awards have been those from the American Academy of Arts and Letters and the Koussevitzky Foundation.

JOHN KIRKPATRICK is professor emeritus and curator of the Ives Collection at Yale University. As a pianist, he has long been recognized as a leading exponent of American piano music, and his performance of Ives's *"Concord"* Sonata in 1939, the first complete public playing of it, is legendary. He has edited or realized for publication many of Ives's works (and those of other U.S. composers) and has published two basic sources of documentation on Ives's music and writings: *A Temporary Mimeographed Catalogue of the Music Manuscripts and Related Materials of Charles Edward Ives* and *Charles E. Ives: Memos*.

Participants

JONATHAN KRAMER, composer, has been on the faculties of the University of California and Oberlin Conservatory. He is currently assistant professor of music theory at Yale University. He has published theoretical articles dealing with the aesthetics of musical time, compositional uses of mathematics and the computer, and the pedagogy of new music.

ALAN MANDEL, pianist and musicologist, is professor of music at American University, where he teaches graduate courses in American music and the music of Ives. In addition, he has a rigorous international recital schedule. He has transcribed the unpublished piano works of Ives and has recorded Ives's complete piano works.

NANCY MANDEL, violinist, has been a member of the graduate faculty of George Washington University and has performed extensively in the United States and abroad. She has often performed and lectured on Ives's violin sonatas (often with her husband Alan Mandel).

SALVATORE MARTIRANO, composer, has taught at the University of Illinois since 1963. He has had a Guggenheim Fellowship and an American Academy of Arts and Letters award. For the past decade or so his music has tended to combine styles and media, and he is best known for his music-theater pieces and intermedia events.

JOHN MAUCERI, conductor, was director of the Yale Symphony Orchestra from 1969 to 1974 and has since had conducting assignments for many major orchestras, including those of the Santa Fe and Metropolitan opera companies. He was also musical director of the 1974 revival of Leonard Bernstein's *Candide*. He conducted the premiere of the full-orchestra version of Ives's *Three Places in New England* and has edited for publication the manuscript materials left by Ives for *Universe Symphony*.

ROBERT P. MORGAN is a composer, theorist, pianist, and music critic who has been on the faculty of the College of Music at Temple University since 1963. He is advisory editor of the quarterly *Musical Newsletter* and a regular contributor to *High Fidelity/Musical America*.

GORDON MUMMA, composer and electronic music equipment designer, is on the faculty of music and dramatic arts at the University of California at Santa Cruz. Since 1966 he has been associated with the Merce Cunningham Dance Company and the Sonic Arts Group. He has published numerous articles on contemporary performance arts and electronic technology.

VIVIAN PERLIS is lecturer in American studies at Yale University and research associate in the Yale School of Music. Her book *Charles Ives Remembered* won the Kinkeldey Award of the American Musicological Society for 1974.

She is director of the long-range American Music Oral History Project, which is supported by the National Endowment for the Humanities, and was co-producer of the award-winning Columbia Records album *Charles Ives: The 100th Anniversary*.

KARL AAGE RASMUSSEN is a young Danish composer who teaches music theory and history at the Aarhus Conservatory. His music has been characterized as "part of the vocabulary of a musical language that belongs somewhere between those of Charles Ives and Anton Webern."

ROGER REYNOLDS, composer and author, is professor of music at the University of California at San Diego and director of the Center for Music Experiment there. He has held fellowships from the Guggenheim and Rockefeller foundations and has been active in organizing concerts of contemporary American music in Europe and Asia. In 1975 he published the book *Mind Models: New Forms of Musical Experience*.

ANDREJ RIJAVEC, Yugoslav musicologist, is on the faculty of the University of Ljubljana. He is a member of the editorial boards of several Yugoslav music journals and has written *Music in Slovenia in the Protestant Era, Compositional Technique in the Chamber Works of Slavko Osterc,* and numerous articles over a broad range of subjects.

FRANK R. ROSSITER is associate professor of history at the University of Texas at Dallas and author of *Charles Ives and His America*. His research continues to emphasize the role of music in American culture.

GUNTHER SCHULLER is a composer, conductor, writer on music, musical editor, and administrator. He was named president of the New England Conservatory of Music in 1967 and has taught for many years at the Berkshire Music Center at Tanglewood, of which he became director in 1969. Columbia Records has issued a dozen chamber works by Ives under his direction (of which several are of his editing).

GERARD SCHWARZ, a trumpet player, was a member of the American Brass Quintet from 1965 to 1973; thereafter, he has been co-principal trumpeter of the New York Philharmonic. He has taught at the Aspen School of Music and has been trumpet soloist on many recordings.

JAMES SINCLAIR, conductor, brass player, and scholar, is assistant to the director of bands at Yale University. Active as an editor and arranger of works by Ives, he recently restored Ives's *Three Places in New England* to its original full-orchestra version and completed a new critical edition of Ives's *Second Orchestral Set*. He has been retained by the Charles Ives Society to work on critical editions and re-editions of music by Ives.

Participants

KENNETH SINGLETON is a tubist and a musical editor who took his graduate degrees (M.Mus., M.M.A.) at Yale University. He has been retained by the Charles Ives Society to work on critical editions and re-editions of music by Ives; nine of these may be heard on the Columbia Records album of theater-orchestra pieces, *Old Songs Deranged.*

NICOLAS SLONIMSKY has been active for many years as a conductor, pianist, composer, author, and lexicographer. In 1927 he founded the Boston Chamber Orchestra, with which he performed the premiere of Ives's *Three Places in New England* in the chamber version specially prepared by Ives for the occasion. As an author he is best known for *Music since 1900,* and as a lexicographer for his *Lexicon of Musical Invective* and the fifth and (forthcoming) sixth editions of *Baker's Biographical Dictionary of Musicians.*

CARLETON SPRAGUE SMITH was chief of the music division of the New York Public Library from 1931 to 1959, when he resigned to turn his attention to Latin American music and its promotion in the United States. He has written extensively on American music and edited (with Leroy Robertson) a pioneering anthology of recordings, "Music in America."

GREGG SMITH, conductor, is director of the Gregg Smith Singers, which he founded in 1955. They quckly gained international fame with a wide repertory ranging from Monteverdi and Gesualdo through William Billings and Stephen Foster to contemporary composers. Two of their recordings of music by Ives have been issued by Columbia Records. Mr. Smith has collaborated with John Kirkpatrick on editing a number of Ives's choral works and has taught at Peabody Conservatory, Columbia University, and the Manhattan School of Music.

DANIEL STEPNER, violinist, studied at Northwestern University, Yale University, and the Conservatoire Américain at Fontainebleau. He was a member of the Chicago Little Symphony under Thor Johnson and, since 1970, has been concertmaster of the New Haven Symphony. He is currently teaching at the Longy School of Music in Boston.

ILHAN USMANBAS, Turkish composer, has been a member of the faculty of the Ankara State Conservatory since 1948; he became its director in 1964. Among his honors are a Fromm Music Award, a Koussevitzky Foundation award, and prizes in composition at Poznan and Geneva.

JEFFREY WASSON, a specialist in medieval musicology, is a teaching fellow at Northwestern University. He is an organist and often performs the organ works of Ives.

ARTHUR WEISBERG is a bassoonist and conductor and is particularly identified with contemporary music. In 1960 he organized the Contemporary Chamber Ensemble; in 1975 he was a founding co-director of the New Orchestra. As a teacher, he is best known for courses in performing problems of contemporary music, which he has offered at the Juilliard School, the Yale School of Music, and the State University of New York at Stony Brook.

Index

Index